DEDICATION

To Jim and Geraldine Holloway, my parents, with love and appreciation. Their continuous support, positive encouragement, and the appreciation of the beauty and variations of America that they taught me, provided the basis for my travel adventures and, subsequently, this book. May God richly bless them.

Managing Editor ....Jane Crawford Picknell
Author ....Sharon Holloway
Associate Editor ....Joseph R. Kiefer II
Assistant Editors ....James Kelly
....Liz Redler
....Robin Speake
Editorial Assistant ....Debra Grande
Contributing Writers ....Chris Adams
....Geraldine Baldassarre
....Carrie Beets
....Robert Breitler
....Elizabeth Buell
....Barbara Ferguson
....Nancy Golden
....Maury Hill
....Joseph R. Kiefer II
....Mike and Laura Murphy
....Betty Pennington
....Liz Redler
....Debra Sherwood Rudloff
....Roy Scarbrough
....Sky
....Sherrie O'Sullivan
....Joan Wood
Maps ....David Ruppe
Cover Design ....Laura Kay
Cover Photograph...Mike Longfellow

FOREWORD

San Diego is one of the fastest growing cities in the United States. Reportedly over 9000 people a month move to his lovely, waterfront city with it's fantastic year around climate, and warm friendly ambiance.

The population was Indian, until in 1542 the Portuguese Navigator Juan Rodriquez Cabrillo sailed into San Diego Bay. Later the Francisan Friar, Father Junipero Serro founded the first of 21 missions, scattered through out California, in San Diego. These missions helped to unite California in the years ahead. Being strategically located on the ocean, San Diego became an important port for the export of hides and whale oil to Europe in the 1800s.

Today, San Diego is a thriving, modern city that has retained the history, excitiement and beauty of its mixed heritage There are areas of

Gable & Gray

The Book Publishers

**You are cordially invited
to the**

BEST CHOICES
IN
SAN DIEGO

**For additional copies, write or call:
Gable & Gray, The Book Publishers
1307 West Main Street
Medford, Oregon 97501
In Oregon: 1-800-622-7753
Outside Oregon: 1-800-522-7753**

Published in the U.S.A.

Library of Congress Catalog Card Number: 88-082998
ISBN: 0-944729-06-1   First Edition 1988

obvious Spanish and Portuguese architecture such as Balboa Park. Mexican and Spanish influence is also apparent in other areas such as "Old Town", a charming area of shops and restaurants. Cactus and the majesty of the desert merge with the lush white sand beaches and roll of the majestic Pacific Ocean. San Diego is home to the Navy's 11th Fleet and near Oceanside, Fort Pendleton houses a huge training camp for Marines. Miramar Naval Air Station and a local bar downtown, Kansas City Bar-B-Que, are where *Top Gun*, the movie, was filmed. In fact, "Movie Stars" are becoming a common sight in many areas of this beautiful county. It's the perfect escape from Hollywood, only about a two hour drive north.

Tijuana, Mexico is only about a thirty minute drive south from downtown San Diego and offers tourists and new residents an exciting taste of our border country. Several common projects and interests unite Mexico and San Diego, everything from sailing races to commerce. Tijuana and the Baja tempt us with flavorful Mexican foods and succulent lobster, as well as terrific values in shopping and services.

As I traveled throughout the county I encountered Scandinavian bakeries, incredible Mexican restaurants, Italian and French food that would rival the "Old Country". Shops offered a glimpse of treasures from antiques to one of a kind nautical artifacts. And most importantly, the people of San Diego county are wonderful. Each offers a history, and a perspective, like no one else. Take the time to get to know the owners of the very special places included in "Best Choices of San Diego" as these are the "best" of all the treasured memories you'll keep.

Several very special people contributed to exploration and the subsequent writing of this book. Jack Barnes wrote most of the chapter on Julian in East County. The beautiful countryside, small town charm and incredible apple desserts are renown. Jack found the very best of Julian and with his very special sense of humor, and deep appreciation of the most unique, he describes the best choices with articulate pride. Jack also contributed to the Mission Bay, Pacific Beach, and downtown sections of this book. These were a natural to Jack who loves the ocean and the outdoors. He loves to explore, and has an unquenchable taste for adventure. Since Jack has the unique gift of being able to "fit in anywhere", his descriptions of the finest dining, best sailing, or most glorious "real homemade chocolate shake" will wet your appetite too.

Susan Thompson, a native of La Jolla, California, loves the mountains, skiing, dancing and also has a real appreciation for quality whether in clothes, leather, perfume or adventure. Susan's knowledge of history and local geography as well as her writing skills really were a complement to this book.

Lloyd Smigel, Jon Plaisted, Brigette Pollak, and Dale Gordon also contributed in the effort to complete this project and each contributed

v

substantially to the quality and variety of the Best Choices presented in these pages.

Finally, I want to thank several very close and special friends, whose support and love of this beautiful area were my inspiration in sharing this terrific experience. Gary, Bill and Nancy Miller introduced me to much of the beauty and rich history of San Diego. Their joy and enthusiasm is symbolic of the people I've met all over San Diego. Also, Vicky Lorvick, Sandy and John Finotti, Donna and Ed Motter, and of course my publisher, Bill Faubion, are other people who believed in me, and who subsequently provided much of the positive support in accomplishing this goal.

Most of all, this book is for you. Whether you are spending a few days, or the rest of your life, the rich experiences you'll enjoy here will only be enhanced by the people behind each of the "Best Choices of San Diego." Enjoy!

HOW TO USE THIS BOOK

Best Choices in San Diego is a complete travel guide. You will find information on the best businesses to patronize, as well as parks, museums and maps to help you plan your itinerary. You can also use the book as a shopping guide. Clothing stores, gift shops, candy stores, restaurants, accommodations and many more categories are used to describe the businesses in detail so you can choose those which match your needs and desires.

After introducing you to San Diego County, the book describes the areas of Greater San Diego, North County and South Bay. Each section begins with an introduction highlighting major highways, population, unique appeal and a smattering of history. Additionally, you will find information relating to parks, museums, beaches, historic areas and events.

Next, the "Best Choices" are listed alphabetically by category, then by business name. The book's description of these businesses will give you an idea of the specialties and personalities you can look forward to experiencing. The page on which each of these categories appear within each section is listed in the Table Of Contents. The Index at the back of the book is your easy-to-use guide for finding on what page specific businesses are listed.

As you read about the "Best Choices," you will often find the message "See special invitation in the Appendix" at the end of the copy. Turn to the back of the book to find the invitations listed in the order they are found in the book. The invitations are real! The merchants are inviting you to save at their establishments. Each invitation is for money off or a free gift with purchase. So, use your scissors and cut out you invitations to the "Best Choices" of San Diego.

Remember, not every "Best Choice" was found. If you find a quality business that is not mentioned, please contact Gable & Gray so it can be considered in a future edition. The last page of this book explains how you can get the "Best Choice" book of you choice if Gable & Gray uses your suggestion.

ABOUT THE AUTHOR

Sharon Holloway was born and grew up in a small coastal town in Alabama, near the Gulf of Mexico. She developed a special love of the ocean and a respect for the environment and its beauty. She's an enthusiastic scuba diver and a "amateur" photographer, who can never quite capture the "real beauty" through a lens.

During her college years, her interest in the biological world continued to develop. She loves animals and, while living in Alaska during recent years, studied advanced animal tracking, as well as doing migration research.

Her business career, however, provided the opportunity to travel in eighteen countries, and to work for three major Fortune 100 companies, including a three year assignment in Tehran, Iran.

Because she shares her family's philosophy of sharing with others, she has always dreamed of the opportunity to share her joy of adventure and discovery through writing. Gable and Gray provided that opportunity. Look for her *Best Choices in Hawaii*, soon to be published.

TABLE OF CONTENTS

SAN DIEGO COUNTY

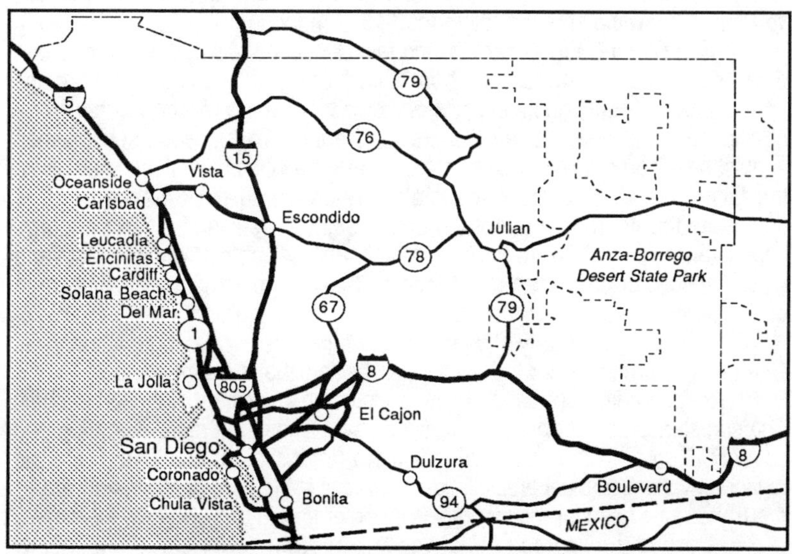

Creating the perfect place to live, work and play would be a tall order. But start with a rich and diverse economy, the kind where the modern office skyscrapers and towering hotel complexes co-exist among art galleries, quaint antique shops, and centuries old Spanish adobes. Combine culturally stimulating urban areas, fertile farmlands and back country wilderness areas. Add a major shipping port to host elegant pleasure crafts, mammoth merchant ships, as well as a modern naval fleet. If you throw in a climate that maintains shirt sleeve temperatures year-round, a stunning coastline and recreational opportunities diverse enough to keep two million people happy, you just might be lucky enough to have created another San Diego County.

San Diego County is many things to each of its 2.2 million residents and the 11 million visitors who spend $2.25 billion. Its 4,261 square miles is more country than what lies in the combined areas of Delaware and Rhode Island. That's room enough for sixteen incorporated cities and many other communities set among wide beaches, frothing seaside headlands, dense forest land, sparkling mountain lakes, parched desert land, and mile after mile of semi-arid chaparral covered hill county.

San Diego County is best understood as having four or five distinct regions: North County, East County Region, Greater San Diego, and South Bay. Generally speaking, North County is made up of smaller towns each with

1

unique and interesting history. Inland, within the hills and valleys between the coast and the Cleveland National Forest, the lifestyle among flower farms, family run ranches and orchards is more relaxed. North County is also where you'll find sprawling suburbs along the I-15 corridor.

San Diego County is one of the few places in the world where one can drive down from a mountain home and enjoy a night of world class entertainment. Although most parts of the county can be reached within a one hour drive, the physical contrasts are staggering. To the west, surf crashes against headland cliffs and sun lovers bask along a long chain of beaches. East the land rises to 6,000 foot mountains covered with thick stands of pine, spruce and fir which rise out of the desert eight miles inland.   To the north, expanses of the vast Camp Pendleton Marine Base contrast with the steel and glass canyons of downtown San Diego or Tijuana's teeming streets just south of the border.

San Diego County's beaches start just below Orange County, at Oceanside, forming a strand of surf and sand that runs right down to the international border. The mild climate adds to the enjoyment of these beaches. The sun shines all but about nine days a year. Temperatures average around seventy degrees with rainfall being a mere ten inches at sea level.   On the higher elevations, annual precipitation increases in the form of snow, enjoyed by thousands who head for the mountains in winter to sled and ski down the slopes.

Despite the sparse natural vegetation at the lower elevations, nearly every community is a lush oasis of streets lined with palms and broad leaf trees. The agricultural resources makes it one of the nations leading growing regions with groves of citrus and nut trees.

San Diego County draws visitors from across the nation and around the world. They come on business, pleasure and often as a combination of both, filling more than 31,538 hotel and motel rooms. Some 300,000 of the 11 million overnight visitors who came in 1986 stayed in campgrounds and nearly 5 million enjoy the region by staying as guest in homes. Conventioners, totaling more than half a million, attended over 1,400 conventions. This has made tourism the third largest sector of the local economy, employing some 86,000 San Diegans in fields directly related to tourism. For visitors and residents alike, the region is friendly and informal. Even in the city itself dress remains casual.

It's little wonder that so many people come here with all of the activities, attractions and cultural events. The activities range from watching the sky bleed several shades of red and orange over the setting sun as whales ply the waters enroute to breeding areas in Baja California, to exhilarating experiences such as hang gliding, hot air ballooning and windsurfing. Golfers have a choice of some seventy courses and nature lovers have hundreds of back country and wet land trails.

There's no shortage of cultural stimulation and nightlife diversions. Musicians bring everything from night club punk to ageless symphonic pieces to the ears of music lovers. There is a wonderful array of galleries and museums. The region's restaurants are a delight of gourmet choices.

A popular day trip for visitors who want to get away form city congestion, but still take in a few attractions, is a trip up I-15 through the North County area of Escondido, then east on State 78 to the San Diego Wild Animal Park, with a stop at the San Pasquel Winery. Continue on State 78 to the town of Ramona and then beyond through a route that winds along rocky ravines past sparkling creeks to the Santa Ysabel Mission. Keep going until you hit the picturesque gold rush town of Julian, which is a favorite stop for an old fashioned soda or apple pie.

For further information on the region, contact the San Diego Visitor Information Center, 2688 East Mission Bay Drive, San Diego, CA 92109, Tel. (619) 276-8200.

SAN DIEGO HISTORY

San Diego is California's Plymouth Rock. San Diego's early history belongs to the first people here. Their story is told in part by ancient rock writings still being studied in the region's back country. By the time the Spanish arrived, San Diego County was populated by a group of Indians the Spanish called San Deiguenos.

It was not long before Spanish padres introduced Christianity. By 1775, the native people had become so angered over the disease that the Spanish introduced to their world that they attacked the San Diego mission, burned it and killed the priest. Eventually, the traditional Indian lifestyle was displaced by a life that revolved around the missions.

The European influence on the region began on September 28, 1542, when Portuguese-born explorer and navigator Juan Rodriquez Cabrillo sailed into the harbor of San Diego. He rowed the boat ashore with a priest and several soldiers and then claimed the new land in the name of Carlos I of Spain. This small party became the first Europeans to set foot on the west coast of what would become the United States. Cabrillo did not stay long, he anchored in the bay for six days, and then continued his voyage. Two months later, Cabrillo died as result of injuries he suffered in a fall during the voyage.

For years Spain showed little interest in settling California, but that attitude change when the English Captain Sir Francis Drake entered a bay in Northern California. Spain then sent ships north to establish a garrison, but decided to do so at Monterey instead of San Diego. When the Russians also began moving down the coast, the decision was made to establish a garrison at San Diego. In 1769 two Spanish ships arrived to establish an outpost, followed by an overland party lead by Father Junipero Serra, who established the first of the California missions in San Diego.

So far removed was this meager settlement, that hardly anyone took notice when Mexico won its independence in 1822. The major changes to come would be the result of Anglo-American settlers. A brief uprising led by John C. Fremont would place San Diego under the flag of the independent California Republic. But when an American war ship sailed into San Diego harbor in 1846, the residents cheerfully raised the American flag over their settlement. Over the weeks and months that followed, American and Mexican flags would be raised and taken down several times, depending on which band of soldiers was capable of entering and taking the town.

The only battle of any great significance occurring in California during the Mexican War was in San Diego County. American General Stephen Kearney marched into the county in December 1847. His scouts discovered the Mexican forces lead by General Andres Pico encamped just east of what is now Escondido. Although his troops were weakened by the long expedition that began in Kansas, he ordered them to launch a surprise attack against the Mexican forces, whose strength he had not determined.

Kearney suffered heavy losses and was forced to retreat. His forces continued to be pursued and harassed by foes until rescued with reinforcements, which ended the fighting. But it was other events that enabled the United States to seize California from Mexico. In February 1848, San Diego and all of California became a territory of the United States.

The economic mainstay of the settlement had been hides. Most of the ships that arrived in the harbor came to trade cash and manufactured goods for the hides. It was a wild and noisy place, especially inside the many raucous saloons. At one point, community leaders were so angered that a law was passed establishing the death penalty for theft of any item valued at more than fifty dollars. One poor fellow went to the gallows for stealing a row boat.

By the time San Diego became incorporated as a city in 1850, whale oil was an important commodity. Migrating gray whales were so numerous that ships entering the harbor were often in danger of capsizing. A land boom occurred in the 1860s when developer Alonzo Horton bought 1,000 acres of bayside property, built a wharf and plotted out 226 city blocks, eventually giving away lots to prospective builders. Up to that point, the town had centered around the original inland settlement along the San Diego River, but Horton realized that the future development would be along the bay front.

More people came to the county about 1870, when gold was discovered at the east county community of Julian. San Diego continued to grow to the point that it had a population of 40,000 in 1887. The boom soon collapsed however, leaving the city with a population of 17,000 in 1890. But over the decades, as San Diego became a center of manufacturing, military and commercial shipping operations, the population doubled nearly every ten years.

GREATER SAN DIEGO AREA

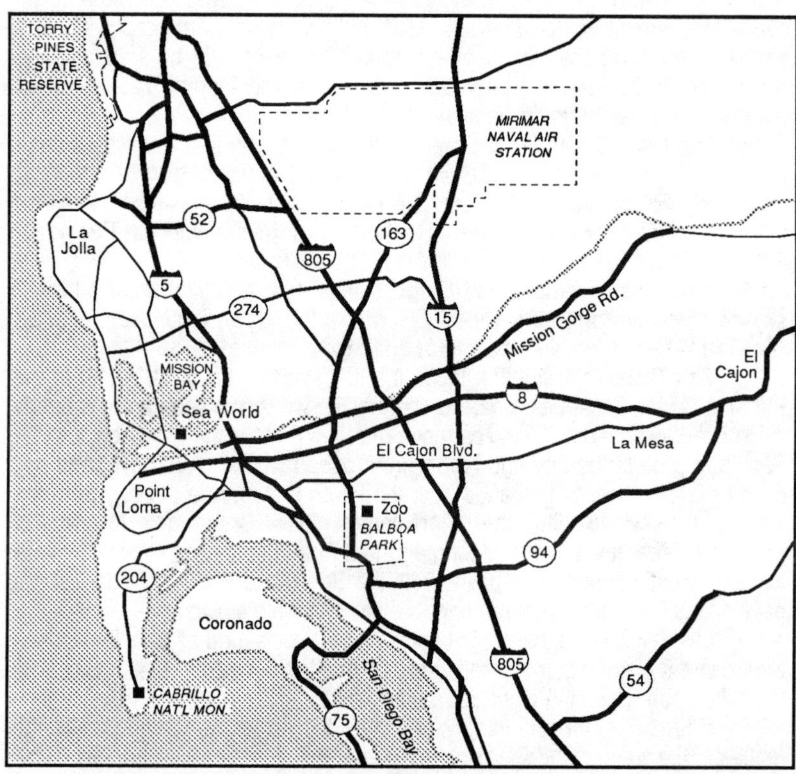

Regular fans of televised sports already know something about San Diego. At the very least they know that it is the home of the San Diego Chargers and the San Diego Padres. Yachting enthusiasts know San Diego as the home port of the *Stars and Stripes*, the famous yacht, skippered by Dennis Conners, that recaptured the America's Cup from the Aussies in 1986.

The tall skyscrapers are evidence of the population and economic growth the city has experienced in the last couple of decades. In fact the city's population has expand threefold since 1950. During that period the city grew from the status of being the thirty-first largest city in the country to its present rank as seventh. By most estimates it appears the growth is likely to continue.

San Diego has become a center for both electronic and Bio-technology firms. There are major research facilities working on the cutting edge of genetics, medicine and oceanography, for example: the Salk Institute and Scripps Institue of Oceanography. 275 electronic firms and 125 Bio-medical companies are at work. In 1984, TRW built a major plant employing 500 people. By 1990 that company expects 2,000 people to be working. The University of California at San Diego is one of the leading recipients for science and research grants in the nation.

San Diego's climate has made it the kind of city that revolves around outdoor pursuits, whether it be strolling through the streets of a shopping district, or windsurfing on the bay. Even in December the average day time temperature is sixty-six degrees. Northern Californians' find the Pacific far more hospitable here than their chilled waters back home.

From the distance, San Diego shines with a newness of mirrored skyscrapers that form its skyline. Elsewhere the urban landscape includes fashionable hillside houses, apartments and condominiums.

San Diego is a city that faces the first Pacific port of call north of the Panama Canal. Except for a narrow channel the well-protected harbor is nearly landlocked. A seven mile long promontory called Point Loma points out into the Pacific to protect the city and harbor from ocean winds. A narrow sand spit called the Silver Strand extends from the south to separate the bay from the ocean. On this strip lies the resort community of Coronado. In terms of geological time, it was not that long ago that Point Loma, and Coronado were islands. But sedimentary deposits from the San Diego River and tidal actions gave rise to the lands that now connect them with the mainland.

Just north of the harbor is Mission Bay, a reclaimed estuary that's been turned into a major water recreation area. Just to the north of Mission Bay are the cliffs upon which the city of La Jolla is built.

With bays and stunning coastlines, it's no wonder that San Diego relates to the water. San Diego enjoys one of the most beautiful harbors in the world. The harbor bustles with activity because it serves as the home port for navy ships, a large sport fishing fleet, thousands of pleasure crafts and an increasing number of commercial cruise ships. The active fishing fleet brings in 300 million pounds of fish a year, including 85 million pounds of tuna worth $135 million to the local economy. San Diego is home port for three luxurious cruise ships, including the one featured on the Love Boat television series. Seven other cruise ships also make regular calls at San Diego. One of the best ways to see the harbor activity is from the water. Close-up views are available through a number of excursion cruise operators.

San Diego is a city filled with entertainment. These delights range from strolling street musicians to huge sellout performances in the San Diego Sports Arena. Nightclubs feature acts to suit any taste, everything from golden oldies to Jazz, Rock and Disco. The San Diego Opera features world class opera stars such as Beverly Sills and Joan Sutherland. The San Diego Symphony hosts many international performers. The Old Globe Theater in Balboa Park is home of the National Shakespeare Festival.

Dining is a pleasure in San Diego. There is hardly an experience comparable to watching the sun dip into the ocean from one of the city's finer restaurants, while enjoying a world class gourmet meal. Although fine restaurants are as lavish as any city restaurant, the experience is more casual and relaxed in San Diego. Diners are frequently dressed more casually than their counterparts in New York.

San Diego's parks set it apart from most cities. Balboa Park is a lush tropical landscape with winding pathways leading to the city's largest concentration of museums and attractions, including the city's world famous zoo. Mission Bay Aquatic Park, is a palm lined bay offering almost any sort of water-related diversions and is home to Sea World, a major marine park and research center.

Recent Gallop Polls have ranked shopping as America's favorite pastime, which explains, in part, why San Diego is one of America's favorite cities. It may be a cliche to say it is a shopper's paradise, but serious shoppers sometimes feel they are in heaven. It's the range of shopping opportunities that pleases so many. You can buy from street vendors, as well as the big shopping centers or exquisite boutiques. You can find nationally marketed fashions, or pick out a one of a kind treasure from a tiny boutique. You can buy something that has the look of next year's up and coming trend, or an artifact of an era long past.

The freeway system in San Diego allows you to reach every section of the city within a fifteen minute drive, even during rush hours. Four major freeways give north/south access through central San Diego and one offers east/west connections. Visitors can buy passes for all buses and trolleys. The Day Tripper Transit Passes are available for one or more days and can be picked up at The Transit Store, 4490 Broadway, San Diego, CA 92101. Tel. (619) 234-1060.

A good first-stop to make is the San Diego Visitors Information Center on Mission Bay. They have a ninety minute tape you can listen to in your car to learn all about the city. You can also pick up the tape entitled, "Sights and Sounds of San Diego" at San Diego Visitor Information Center, 2688 East Mission Bay Drive, San Diego, CA 92109. Tel. (619) 276-8200.

There is so much to see in San Diego, that it's impossible to see everything in one visit. Savvy travelers pre-select those attractions and events they want most to see. Most agree, however, that San Diego is a city that's full of "must-sees."

ATTRACTIONS

For a quick look at the Southern California back country head out past Lakeside to **Wildcat Canyon Road**. The road will lead past the 600 acre **Silverwood Wildlife Sanctuary**, and into the scenic **Barona Ranch Indian Reservation**, where there's a whitewashed reservation church and cows that have a habit of strolling leisurely across the narrow roadway.   The reservation is the homeland of more than 200 Native Americans.

Marshal Scotty's is a small amusement park out in the country east of Lakeside. The twelve acre park has a kind of county fair atmosphere to it and includes a swimming pool and picnic grounds.

You can make quite a splash at the **Sengme Oaks Waterpark and Campground** where there's a river rafting and tire tubing along the San Luis River.   There are also waterslides so take the plunge.   The 800 site campground sits along the banks of the river and offers opportunities for fishing. The park is on the **La Jolla Indian Reservation,** just seven miles west of Lake Henshaw. Closed in winter. Tel. (619) 742-1921.

Fresh mountain air and secluded mountain trails brings visitors to **William Heise County Park**. The park is just six miles south of the picturesque community of Julian and stands at the 4,2000 foot level. Don't miss the view from the lookout point. Both RV and tent camp sites are available. Tel. (619) 694-3049.

Lake Morena offers camping, fishing and water sports amid a beautiful southeast county setting. Within the **Lake Morena County Park**, trails weave in and out of the forestland and lake shore. Camping is also available. Enjoy a hike on the slopes of the 4,000 foot **Morena Butte**. Take I-8 about forty miles east of San Diego to the community of Pine Valley, then south on County S1 to Lake Morena.

Cuyamaca Rancho State Park is 26,000 scenic acres of mountainland forty miles east of San Diego. You can swim or fish in the Sweet Water River and camp out in this natural landscape. Just north of the park is the Cuyamaca Reservoir, which is popular among boaters. There are also campsites for backpackers and equestrians. Te park is south of Julian on State 79. For information and campsite reservation call Tel. (619) 765-0755. For an easy three mile hike, try the Azalea Glenn Trail, which winds through a densely wooded stand of oak and pine, as well as open meadows. The park can be reached by way of I-8 and State 79.   For information contact the park headquarters at Tel. (619) 765-0755.

BEACHES

At **South Mission Beach** you'll see people pulling up in expensive cars and strolling the beach in designer casual wear. There are, however, a few old timers from the 1960s who have yet to acquire the trappings of financial and social success. South Mission Beach draws from the wealthy community of Belmont Park, where money and job titles mean everything. During the 1960s South Mission Beach was the hangout of the college set. Among them were what would become some of the San Diego's most influential residents. Some of them return occasionally for a nostalgic look. A few of the old taverns remain in operation here, the Pennant Bar, for example, retains much of its 60s atmosphere, but the parking lot is now filled with more Porches and Mercedes than battered Volkswagens.

Peoplewatchers like **North Mission Beach**. Irrespective of gender, the well-oiled bodies are young and firm. North Mission is a busy place where beach lovers like to strut their stuff on the boardwalk, or maybe skate or bike. If you want to fit right in, get yourself a can of beer, sit down on the sea wall, and watch the action.

CITY PARKS

When it comes to parks, San Diego does it big. Either one of its two outstanding parks would be enough to make any big city proud, but together they serve to make San Diego stand out as a city that goes out of its way to provide recreational and cultural facilities for its residents and visitors. The two major parks, Balboa and Mission Bay, offer totally different experiences. A third park, Presidio Hill, offers acres of grassy greenery on a site thick with the history of the old Spanish garrison.

Balboa Park started out as a dry chaparral-covered wasteland that has since been turned into a lush subtropical landscape of mesas, canyons, wide boulevards, shaded walkways, broad stretches of greenery, and ornate Spanish rococo buildings that house some of the nation's top museums, the park easily ranks among the top city parks of the world.

Balboa Park's 1,427 acres comes to twice the size of New York's Central Park. The opportunities for relaxation, physical activity and cultural stimulation are vast and may be enjoyed repeatedly. You have simple pleasures such as jogging or cycling, and cultural pursuits including watching a Shakespearean play in the Elizabethan theater, or listening to an organ recital performed on a huge outdoor pipe organ. The zoo, also located in the park, features 3,200 animals and is probably the most extensive collection of rare animals in the world.

The park got off to a pretty slow start after land developer Alonzo Horton and others set aside 1,400 acres for park land in 1868. But keep in mind that San Diego was still a small town of about 900 homes at the time. For the next thirty-five years the park lay unimproved. It was not until 1892 that plans were drawn up for the improvements. An annual tree planting program soon evolved from those plans and in 1902 the community raised $10,000 for planting and grading the southwest corner of the park. In 1910 civic named the park. They settled on naming the facility after Vasco Nunez Balboa, the navigator who discovered the Pacific Ocean.

Horticulturist Kate Sessions established a nursery on the grounds in 1910. Then the park's greatest surges of development occurred as a result of the park becoming the site of two world fairs. The first was the 1915 Panama-California International Exposition, which commemorated the completion of the Panama Canal. In 1936 Balboa Park was host to the California-Pacific International Exposition. Both of these events contributed several of the massive Spanish style buildings in the park.

The array of museums in the park is the largest single concentration of museums outside of Washington D.C. Many of the exhibits rival those of the Smithsonian Institute. These museums feature everything from the works of the old masters to masterpieces of aerospace engineering. Among them are The San Diego Aerospace Museum and International Aerospace Hall of Fame, The Reuben H. Fleet Space Theater, The San Diego Model Railroad Museum, The Museum of Man, The Museum of San Diego History, The Natural History Museum of San Diego, The Photographic Arts Building, the San Diego Hall of Champions and San Diego Hall of Fame and The San Diego Museum of Art. For details see "Museums."

There's usually a nice surprise or two in store for the park's visitors. Often free outdoor concerts, puppet shows, car shows, dog shows, flower and plant shows and many other kinds of exhibits are being conducted in the park. Something seems to be going on almost every weekend in Balboa Park.

Four million visitors a year visit the attractions in the park. Many people enter the park at the Prado, a wide avenue that extends from Laurel and Sixth Street that is lined with the many museums and galleries. The Prado leads across the Cabrillo Bridge, a large concrete structure spanning a 110 foot deep canyon. The bridge offers a view of the city's business district.

The first stop you might want to make is the House of Hospitality on the plaza along El Prado. Here you can get maps and information on the park. The building also contains the offices of the San Diego Opera. It over looks an attractive patio that is a popular venue for weddings.

One of the most popular attractions is The Spanish Village Art Center. This collection of cottages built around a courtyard was one of additions brought by the 1935 exposition. Today it contains the studios of many local artists. Visitors can watch them at work. Works of precious metal, ceramics and lapidary are for sale. A miniature train and a merry-go-round also operate here. The center is open daily and weekends 11:00 a.m. to 4:00 p.m.

Free concerts are frequently performed by musicians on the massive 500 pipe organ at the Spreckels Organ Pavilion. Concerts are given every Sunday. One of the world's largest outdoor organs, the instrument was a gift to the city in 1915 by John D. and Adolph Spreckels.

Stop over at The House of Pacific Relations. Actually, this not one house but a collection of fifteen stucco cottages, each containing an exhibit from a different nation. Inside you'll find displays of native art and crafts. On weekends refreshments are served at each of the houses and frequently, folk musicians perform in the courtyard outside.

Also in the park is the Morley Field Sports Complex. Located just across from the zoo, it features twenty-five tennis courts, an Olympic size pool, softball field, baseball field, and even an eighteen hole Frisbee "golf" course. Morley Field also contains one of the very few banked bicycle tracks in the United States.

Over at the Golden Hill section of the park, there are picnic tables, horeshoe pits, playing fields and a small gym. It is also the site of the Balboa Park Golf Course (619) 232-2470.

One way to see the park is to take a guided walking tour. A firm called OFFSHOOTERS, conducts walking sightseeing tours on Saturdays. Through the tours, visitors become acquainted with the park's architectural and botanical richness. Tours leave at 10:30 a.m. and 12:30 p.m. from the Botanical Building. For further information call (619) 297-0289.

For more information about the park and its facilities call (619) 239-0512.

San Diego is famous for its zoo located in Balboa Park. The zoo is easily the leading single visitor attraction in the city. **San Diego Zoo** attendance is about three million people a year.

Set within a 128 acre tropical garden, it features a huge animal collection and is famous for its many rare and exotic species. There are cuddly koalas from Australia and long billed kiwis from New Zealand, wild horses from Mongolia and the frolicking pygmy chimps from central Africa. The zoo has one of the largest tropical bird and parrot collections in the world.

Walking through the huge zoo has its advantages. You can take your time, linger and just quietly enjoy the surroundings. But an easier and more informative way of seeing the zoo is the forty minute guided bus tour that winds through about three miles of roads, taking passengers up and down the mesas. To catch one of these open double decker buses head for the zoo station; one comes by every few minutes. Another way to see the zoo is the aerial tram way that whisks you on a ride over the animals and botanical gardens.

A special children's zoo gives children an opportunity to pet young animals. Benches and drinking fountains are all scaled down to pint size proportions. A very patient Galapagos tortoise offers rides on his armored back.

Although natural settings for the animals have become the norm in the nation's better zoo, the realistic habitats have always been a hallmark of the San Diego Zoo. Lions roam freely among the natural-looking surroundings, and birds seem to fly freely in a tropical rain forest. You might even see a guinea fowl going about his business looking for insects along the walkway.

San Diego Zoo features animal shows, elephant and camel rides. "People food" is available at the Peacock and Raven Restaurant, and a snack bar is never very far away. Picnic areas are also available.

There's really nothing like this 4,600 acre playground. **Mission Bay Aquatic Park** is the largest man-made facility of its kind in the world, devoted to sunbathing, fishing, waterskiing, swimming, board sailing and general recreation.

Located just north of Point Loma, the dredged out bay offers swimmers and sunbathers twenty-seven miles of custom made sunbleached beaches, an abundance of grassy recreation areas, and a myriad of lagoons and islands to sail around. Looking around the scene you might find families picnicking on the lawn, students flying kites and retirees fishing from lawn chairs for. Bicyclists and joggers make their way along the winding paths and sunbathers lay on the sand. Out on the bay, you'll see sailboarders and paddle boaters plying the waters, as well as sloops and high-throttled hydrofoil boats. The traffic on the water is controlled so that one type of activity does not intrude on another. Water skiers use their own one and half mile course that keeps them away from sailboards.

Getting out on the calm waters of the bay takes many forms. At several locations sailboats and sailboards can be rented and lessons are available. You can also take a high speed ride in a hydro-foil boat.

Nearby there are campgrounds, hotels, an eighteen hole golf course, a children's playground, and several boat launches, as well as picnic areas ideal for family gatherings, kit flying or relaxing. The winding paths make the park popular among bicyclists and joggers.

The park is home to one of the most famous commercial aquatic theme parks, Sea World. Although the setting is entirely man-made, Mission Bay's landscaped lawns and gardens helps visitors feel more in touch with the natural elements that they have come to enjoy. Several swimming and bathing areas have been set aside in the park. They include Bonita Cove, which is opposite Belmont Park off Mission; Crown Point, at the north end of the bay and off I-5;

DeAnza Cove, near the trailer park at the north side of Vacation Island; Leisure Lagoon, just north of the Hilton Inn and off I-5; and Ventura Cove, lying between Bahia and Ventura Point, off Mission Bay Drive.

Mission Bay has a long recorded history. Cabrillo once confused Mission Bay with San Diego Bay. And for years it was known as "False Bay." Throughout the early 1800s the bay was deep enough to allow fairly deep-drafted boats to sail its waters.

For more information contact the Mission Bay Visitor Information Center, 2688 East Mission Bay Drive, San Diego, CA 92109. Tel. (619) 276-8200.

It's no accident that each year millions of San Diego area residents and visitors find their way to **Sea World**. Some, you might say, do it on "porpoise." Others come to watch the killer whale show, the penguins or the sharks. During its twenty years, Sea World has won acclaims as one of the top marine zoological parks in the world.

At Sea World you can watch the acrobatics of a killer whale, pet a friendly dolphin or friendly walrus, and attend a glittering musical variety show. The newest attraction is City Streets, a recreated urban neighborhood that is the backdrop of a musical review where actors and dangers perform in the streets, as well as from rooftops and fire escapes.

For a more "formal affair," there is the Penguin Encounter, with more than 400 arctic birds, many seemingly dressed in black tie, gather on a snow covered ice shelf. Another highlight for many visitors is the dolphin petting pool.

For those prepared to suspend belief, trained seals, otters and sea lions play the parts of a classic mystery set in the haunted "Spooky Kooky Castle." For the more serious, Sea World has thirty educational exhibits. A re-created California tide pool gives visitors an opportunity to learn by experiencing. Guests can pick up and examine many of the creatures, including star fish, sea anemones and lobsters while narrators discuss one of the state's most facinating and rapidly declining eco-systems.

For more information, contact Sea World, 1720 South Shores Road, San Diego, CA 92109. Tel. (619) 222-6363.

Overlooking Old Town is **Presidio Park**, the birth place of San Diego. The site of the old garrison and mission is atop the foothills and offers a spectacular view of the modern city San Diego has become.

Little is left of what was once here. Upon close inspection a few remnants of the Spanish, Mexican and early American occupation can be found, including portions of the walls and residences of the old garrison, an old brass cannon, and the relics contained in the museum.

On the hills overlooking Old Town is the site of Fort Stockton. The small fort was built in 1838, on the spot where Mexican townsfolk had built an earlier fort in defense against an expected Indian attack. When Commander Robert Stockton took command of the region, he ordered a deep trench dug around the fort and that canons be mounted between barrels filled with stone and rubble. The trench is still visible today.

Presidio Park is also the site of the original mission established by Father Junipero Serra in 1769. The mission was, however, later moved to its present location. The park contains the Junipero Serra Museum, which has exhibits and artifacts of the early mission days. The mission style building is home of the San Diego Historical Society. An archeological excavation is open for public inspection.

EVENTS

During just about any week, San Diego County has some city or community celebration or activity going on. Below are just some of the many major events held during each of the four seasons. To get a full schedule of events throughout the county during your visit, contact the San Diego Convention and Visitors Bureau, 1200 Third Avenue, Suite 824, San Diego, CA 92101. Tel. (619) 232-3101.

Christmas On The Prado is the annual Christmas event of Balboa Park. Sponsored by the museums in the park, the celebration includes an outdoor Swedish Christmas fair, carolers, candlelight processions, ethnic food and crafts. Many events are free. Tel. (619) 239-2001.

Christmas is celebrated in Old Town with two popular events in early December. First there is the **Old Town Christmas Parade**, which is followed by the **Old Town Las Posadas**, a culturally rich re-enactment of Mary and Joseph's search for shelter. Tel. (619) 297-1181.

A few days before Christmas San Diegans head out to the harbor to watch the **Christmas Light Boat Parade**. The flotilla of lighted boats begins at Sea Port Village and sails past the Embarcadero. Tel. (619) 222-4081.

Another holiday kickoff is the **Holiday Bowl**, in which the leading collegiate football team of the Western Athletic Conference plays against a nationally ranked opponent. The event is held in Jack Murphy Stadium in Mission Valley. Tel. (619) 283-5808.

The Penguin Day Ski Fest, gives the courageous a chance to brave the waters sans wetsuit to earn a Penguin Patch. This event is held on New Year's Day at De Anza Cove in Mission Bay. Boats and tows available for the skiers. Tel. (619) 276-0830.

For a touch of the Blarny there is the **Saint Patrick's Day Parade** through San Diego during the mid-March Irish holiday. It features floats, Irish dancers, music and more. Tel. (619) 299-7812.

The San Diego Crew Classic is a fine example of not-so-gentle rowing down the stream. Intercollegiate teams from throughout the United States gather in early April to compete in rowing contests on Mission Bay. Tel. (619) 488-1039.

The Kyocera Inamori Golf Classic is an annual Ladies Professional Golf Association tournament held at Bernardo Heights Country Club during the second week in April. Tel. (619) 488-1039.

The Lakeside Western Days and Rodeo, is a community wide celebration in late April featuring a major PRCA rodeo.   Tel. (619) 561-1031

During the last week in April, San Diego's downtown art scene comes alive in the **Downtown Art Walk**. Tel. (619) 232-9915.

Annual Art Alive features Floral interpretations of paintings and sculptures held in the San Diego Museum of Art. Tel. (619) 232-7931.

San Diego State University holds its **Spring Fiesta** during the first week of May to offer a variety of entertainment, art, crafts and games. Tel. (619) 265-6555.

Designers Showcase is an annual event in which a house of historic or architectural significance is selected for renovation by local designers to promote preservation of historic buildings. The site is open throughout May. Tel. (619) 232-6226.

The Fiesta De La Primavera is an annual week long festival celebrating San Diego's historic past. The "Days of the Dons" features strolling mariachis, troubadours and Spanish dancers. Everything takes place in Old Town. Tel. (619) 237-6771.

For one of the largest bike rides in the World, go a little south of the border for the **Tecate-Ensenada Bike Ride**. Some 10,000 riders race or just ride in the seventy-three miles between the towns of Ensenada and Tecate. The race begins in Tecate in mid-May. Tel. (619) 275-1384.

The Marines have their own **Rodeo and Carnival** at Camp Pendleton in late May. The annual rodeo features the personnel and their families. Tel. (619) 725-4905.

As summer opens, so does the famed **National Shakespeare Festival** at Balboa Park's Old Globe Theatre. The professional repertory acting company performs both Shakespearean and contemporary plays. Tel. (619) 239-2255.

At about the second week in August, the U.S. Navy Air Station holds its annual **Miramar Air Show**, featuring the Blue Angels precision flight team, and a variety of stunt and aviation demonstrations. Admission is free. Tel. (619) 537-4082.

During mid to late August San Diego puts on its **America's Finest City Week.** Events include a half marathon run, fireworks after a Padres game, special symphony concerts, and a professional volleyball tournament. Tel. (619) 236-1212.

Imaginatively designed bathtubs sputter, sink and race for prizes at **San Diego's Thundertub Regatta**, held in mid August at Enchanted Cove and Fiesta Island in Mission Bay. Tel. (619) 232-6612.

City Fest: Hillcrest Sign Celebration is an annual exhibition of "outdoor art" and festival held in the middle of August on San Diego's Fifth Avenue. For details call   (619) 299-3330.

Don't worry, you won't need a snorkel to attend the **Annual Underwater Film Festival.** Rest assured films of underwater photography will be shown on land. The major event is held during the second week in September and is hosted by the San Diego Convention and Performing Arts Center. For times and location call (619) 236-6510.

Hyrdoplane Championship races come to Mission Bay in late September for the annual **Miller Highlife Thunderboat Regatta**. Admission is charged. Tel. (619) 232-1289.

The Cabrillo Festival commemorates the discovery of San Diego Bay in 1542. The festival held in late September features a parade and many cultural activities. For details contact the Cabrillo National Monument, (619) 557-5450.

A colorful parade through downtown San Diego, followed by a three hour band review takes place every Columbus Day. Tel. (619) 589-1833.

In late October, The San Diego Museum of Man participates in a Halloween celebration with its Haunted Museum of Man. The museum brings to Balboa Park spooky graveyards, torture chambers and scary scenes. Admission is charged.   Tel. (619) 239-2001.

The Town and Country Hotel hosts an annual **Great American Dixieland Jazz Festival** featuring bands from throughout the United States. Held during the last week of November. Tel. (619) 297-5277.

At the end of November, the **Toyland Parade** signals the Christmas Shopping season in San Diego. The parade is a tradition that's been going on for more than three decades. In addition to the parade the celebration includes food, games and llama rides for children. The event is usually held the last week in November. Tel. (619) 543-0730.

The Festival of the Bells at the Mission San Diego de Alcala, includes the annual "Blessing of the Animals" at the Mission, as well as other events through out the weekend in mid-July, Tel. (619) 283-7319.

GOLF COURSES

There is a good selection of golf courses in and around San Diego and La Jolla.   A few of the many courses of the region are listed below. All are open to the public and are eighteen holes or more.

Balboa Park Municipal Golf Course, Balboa, Park, San Diego CA 92102. 5,900 yards, par 72. Tel. (619) 267-1103

Colina Park Golf Course, 4085 52nd Street, San Diego, CA. 92105. 1,500 yards, par 54. Tel. (619) 582-4704

Mission Bay Golf Course, 2702 Mission Bay Drive, San Diego, CA 92109. 3,175 yards, par 18. Tel. (619) 273-1221

Presidio Hills Pitch and Putt Golf Course, 4136 Wallace Street, San Diego, CA 92110. 1400 yards, par 54. Tel. (619) 295-9476.

Rancho Penasquitos Country Club, 14455 Penasquitos Drive, San Diego, CA 921290. 6,055 yards, par 70. Tel. (619) 279-0700.

Tecolote Canyon Golf Course, 2755 Snead Avenue, San Diego, CA 92111. 3,400 yards, par 58. Tel. (619) 279-1600.

MUSEUMS AND GALLERIES

Unless we're thinking of London, New York, Washington. D.C. or Paris, few city's rival San Diego for museums. San Diego has close to ninety museums, and nine of them are within a few steps of each other in Balboa Park. These museums contain archeological artifacts thousands of years old, works of the Renaissance masters and the high tech products of the space age. You need to know that the major public museums do charge admission, some as much as $4.00. Balboa Park does offer a "Passport" coupon book for $8.00 that's good for $10.50 worth of museum tickets. You can purchase the book at many of the museums.

ART MUSEUMS

The San Diego Museum of Art is one place where the artistic spectrum is so broad that you can see works of the old masters, as well as the masterful works of Dr. Seuss. Established in the 1920s, this museum in the Balboa Park complex comprises 30,000 square feet of exhibits divided into eighteen galleries. The core of the collection consists of the works of Italian Renaissance, Dutch and Spanish Baroque masters. But you will find some fine examples of American art and 20th Century paintings, and sculpture. There are also works of Asian art, not to mention some of the fanciful drawings of Ted Geisel, otherwise known as Dr. Seuss.

Some works that the museum's curators are especially proud of are worth close examination, such as a painting by Juan Sanchez Cotan, *Quince, Cabbage, Melon and Cucumber*. Painted in 1602, the still life is the best known work by the artist who was one of the forerunners of Spanish Baroque Realism. A painting by Luca Signorelli, *The Coronation of the Virgin*, affords visitors an opportunity to examine early Italian Renaissance painting. The museum is open Tuesday through Sunday, 10:00 a.m. to 4:30 p.m. For more information contact, Balboa Park Museums, San Diego, CA 92101. Tel. (619) 232-7931.

For abstract, contemporary and pop art, enjoy the **La Jolla Museum of Contemporary Art**. You will find the works of some of the nation's better known artists, such as Andy Warhol, Ellsworth Kelly and Frank Stella. The museum works hard at acquiring pieces that reflect the ever changing tides of contemporary art. Examples are, southern California artist Billy Al Bengston's *Buster*, which depicts a green sergeant's chevron in the center of what looks like concentric rings of star bursts. John Baldessari's irreverent and iconoclastic *Terms Most Useful in Describing Creative Works of Art* is simply three columns of printed expressions often used by art critics, such as "charm," "give vision" and "out of the ordinary."

The La Jolla Museum of Contemporary Art frequently schedules films and concerts. In the fall it hosts an International Film Festival. The museum hours are Tuesday through Sunday, 10:00 a.m. to 5:00 p.m., Wednesday until 9:00 p.m. The museum is located at 700 Prospect Street, La Jolla, CA. Tel. (619) 454-3541.

The Timken Art Gallery, which is located in Balboa Park, has just fifty-works on exhibit, but experts agree it is a superb collection of 13th through 19th Century European and American paintings and Russian icons. The collection includes paintings by artists most familiar to art lovers such as Rembrandt, Breughel, Rubens and Cezanne. The Timeken also has some extraordinary little-known surprises in the form of Russian icons and the works of American artists John Singleton Copley and Fitz Hugh Lane. The Timekin Gallery can be reached at Balboa Park Museums, San Diego, CA 92101. Tel. (619) 239-0512

Folk art is perhaps the one art form that most clearly binds all peoples together, or so it seems with a visit to the **Mingei International Museum of World Folk Art**. The museum, located in La Jolla's University Towne Centre is comfortable and accessible. A place where the art of many people, from all over the world, is displayed. A sense of connection is conveyed when one sees a life-size clay Indian temple horse, not far from the beautifully crafted carousel horse. Other eye-catching objects include a child's pull toy, a lacquered bowl, a musical instrument, and a clay grain urn. Three to four special exhibitions are presented each year, along with regular programs of folk music, lectures and films. The museum is open Tuesday through Saturday, 11:00 a.m. to 5:00 p.m.; Friday until 9:00 p.m. and Sunday 2:00 p.m. to 5:00 p.m. For more information, contact the Mingei International Museum of World Folk Art, University Towne Centre, 4405 La Jolla Village Drive, La Jolla, CA 92038. Tel. (619) 453-5300.

In Balboa Park, don't miss the **Museum of Photographic Arts**. It is o ne of the world's few museums that is dedicated exclusively to the art of human expression through photography. The museum presents more than eight special exhibitions a year. In addition, workshops and lectures are regularly scheduled. If you go on the first Tuesday of the month, you can get in free. Docent tours are conducted Saturday and Sunday at 1:00 p.m. and 3:00 p.m. and are included in the price of admission. The museum is open 10:00 a.m to 5:00 p.m. daily. For more information contact the Museum of Photographic Arts, Balboa Park, San Diego, CA 92101. Tel. 239-5262.

COMMERCIAL GALLERIES

Apache Trading Post, in San Diego's Old Town, features fine Indian pottery, paintings, jewelry and dolls.

African tribal masks and carvings, as well as pieces from New Guinea are on display at **Ashante African Art**, 1250 Prospect Street, La Jolla, CA 92038. Tel. 454-4026.

The I-A-C Fine Art Gallery in La Jolla offers a dazzling display of contemporary art. For more information contact 955 Prospect Street, La Jolla, CA 92038. Tel. (619) 456-0977.

Art Bazaar at Seaport Village, 805 West Harbor Drive, San Diego, CA 92101. Tel. (619) 239-0855.

Art and Crafts Council of San Diego, Balboa Park Management Center, San Diego, CA 92101. The council sponsors outdoor art shows every weekend at Mission Bay on the lawn at the Hilton Hotel. Tel. (619) 236-5471.

International Gallery, 643 "G" Street, San Diego, CA 92110, features folk art and contemporary arts and gifts from Africa, the Americas and Asia. Tel. (619) 235-8255.

For Western, and contemporary painting, as well as turquoise jewelry and antiques try **Kesler Art Gallery**, 4062 Harney Street, San Diego, CA 92101. Tel. (619) 291-0119.

Split Image Gallery, 4402, Glacier Avenue, San Diego, CA 92120, features original art, fine prints and a variety of unique wheel-thrown pottery that has been handcrafted on the premises. Tel. (619) 281-0967.

MUSEUMS OF HISTORY
CULTURE AND TECHNOLOGY

As of this writing the **Centro Cultural De La Raza** continues to serve as Balboa Park's center for Native American and Chicano art, dance and music. If you're interested, better not wait until your next trip to see it, for as it now stands the facility's days might be numbered. Unfortunately, the center generally receives scant mention in most guides. Now plans call for demolishing the structure, and maybe moving the exhibits elsewhere. The center occupies a converted water tank built for the 1915 Panama-California Exposition. A spectacular and vibrant mural by a group of Chicano artists called Los Toltecas en Aztlan covers the 6,000 foot surface of the tank. In the 1970s, a section of the mural showing the figure of Death staring into a caldron drew some strong objections from segments of the community, particularly from the Naval Hospital that over looks the tank. Officials there didn't appreciate the apparent anti-war sentiment that was being expressed. The offending portion was later painted over and replaced with a portrait of Geronimo, who appears armed with rifle and gazes malevolently toward the hospital. The center is open afternoons, except Mondays and Tuesdays in Balboa Park's Pepper Grove. Tel. (619) 235-6135.

The Firehouse Museum features antique fire-fighting equipment, including historic fire engines, pictures, helmets and memorabilia, all displayed in San Diego's oldest firehouse. Admission is free and the museum is open from 10:00 a.m. to 4:00 p.m. Saturday and Sunday. For information contact Fire House Museum, 1572 Columbia Street, San Diego, CA 92101. Tel. (619) 232-FIRE

La Jolla's Children's Museum, is one place where kids don't have to be told "don't touch." The museum provides a variety of "hands-on" exhibits. It offers young visitors a chance to guide their parents through a television studio, health center art studio, and displays of inventions. The museum is open Wednesday through Sunday 12:00 noon to 5:00 p.m., Saturday 10:00 a.m.-5:00 p.m. Admission is charged, but senior citizens get a discount. For more information contact Children's Museum, Village Square, La Jolla, CA 92037. Tel. (619) 450-0767.

San Diego has one of the richest aviation histories of any city. So it's not surprising that it would have the **Aerospace Museum and International Aerospace Hall of Fame**, both of which are housed in the Aerospace Historical Center in Balboa Park. The Hall of Fame salutes over eighty pioneers of aviation with a wide variety of displays, and memorabilia. The Aerospace Museum displays over fifty airplanes from the early days of daring young men in flying machines to the present. Many of the aircraft are placed in appropriate settings, such as a section of an actual ship's flight deck. The display of historic aircraft rivals the Smithsonian's. Although the Smithsonian has Charles Lindbergh's *Spirit of Saint Louis*, which was built in San Diego, the Aerospace Museum maintains an reproduction of the first plane to cross the Atlantic. The museum is open daily from 10:00 a.m. to 4:30 p.m. Admission is charged. For information: Tel. (619) 234-8291.

A journey to the planets and the stars is always in store for visitors to the **Reuben H. Fleet Space Theater and Science Center**. The facility in Balboa

Park includes a remarkable 3-D planetarium show and a hall containing physical science displays and exhibits where visitors are asked to touch to get a feel for scientific principles. The fifty participatory exhibits are designed to stimulate interest in the laws of physics through visitor participation with the equipment. In addition, there are children's workshops, free films and science demonstrations. The theater/planetarium features a seventy-six foot tilting dome on which are projected astounding displays of light and sound. By wearing special glasses, the audience is treated to the three dimensional sensation of being swept through crowded galaxies. The realism is captured on special wide-frame movie film that's projected through a fish-eye lense. The space center is open 9:45 am. to 9:30 p.m. daily, with shows being presented almost hourly, including evenings. It is located two blocks from the San Diego Zoo on Park Boulevard. For further information contact the Reuben H. Fleet Space Theater and Science Center, P.O. Box 33303, San Diego, CA 92103. Tel. (619) 238-1168.

Another of the excellent Balboa Park Museums is the **Natural History Museum,** which focuses on the birds, animals, insects, reptiles, marine life, plants and geology of San Diego County and related regions. Films are presented every weekend. Hours of operation are 10:00 a.m. to 4:30 p.m. Admission is charged, except for children under six and military personnel in uniform. For more information contact the Natural History Museum, P.O. Box 1390, San Diego, CA 92112. Tel. (619) 232-3821.

Man's diversity, as well as some of his shared cultural heritage, is evident at the **San Diego Museum of Man.** The facility is one of the world's most renown anthropological museums. It emphasizes general human evolution and the anthropology of local Indian and Mayan civilizations. There are demonstrations of Mexican tortilla-making and loom weaving. There's a colorful and varied array of ethnic arts and crafts on display. The museum is open daily from 10:00 a.m. to 4:30 p.m. Admission is modest, and students can get in for mere pocket change. For more information contact The San Diego Museum of Man, 1350 El Prado, Balboa Park, San Diego, CA 92101. Tel. (619) 239-2001.

The Mormon Battalion Visitors Center is a memorial to the 500 volunteer Mormon Soldiers who marched 2,000 miles to San Diego to fight in the Mexican War. The march that took place between 1846 and 1847 is said to be a feat unequaled in American military history. No admission is charged. The center is open from 9:00 a.m. to 9:00 p.m. and is located in Old Town at 2510 Juan Street, San Diego, CA 92110. Tel. (619) 298-3317.

For railroad buffs there's the **Model Railroad Museum** in Balboa Parks Casa de Balboa. You'll see scaled down but realistic versions of Southern California panoramas through which model railroads make their way. A full size signal tower marks the Museum's entry. The mechanism changes its signal arms every five minutes. Inside you'll see four operating layouts   displaying model railroads in three different scale sizes. All are landscaped and modeled after actual historic railroad routes. An HO-scale model of the San Diego and Arizona Eastern Railroad includes a trestle spanning a fifteen foot canyon. Admission is free for children and almost as reasonable for adults. The museum is open from 1:00 p.m. to 5:00 p.m. Fridays, and 11:00 a.m. to 5:00 p.m. Saturdays and Sundays. For information contact the San Diego Model Railroad Museum, Casa de Balboa, 1649 El Prado, San Diego, CA 92101. Tel. (619) 696-0199.

Dedicated sports fans should not miss the **San Diego Hall of Champions**. The museum in Balboa Park includes a theater, museum and store featuring memorabilia commemorating big league San Diego sports personalities from more than forty sports. The theater presents sports and films hourly.   Tel. (619) 234-2544.

The Junipero Serra Museum, in Presidio Park, above Old Town is a classic mission style building with a eighty-two foot bell tower that houses exhibits and artifacts relating to San Diego's Spanish and Mexican Periods. The museum stands on the site of the first San Diego Museum and Spanish Fort. The original tiles in the doorway of the museum were taken from a flume the Spanish padres built to irrigate crops in the nearby valley. The museum operated by the San Diego Historical Society is open from 10:00 a.m. to 4:30 p.m. Tuesday through Saturday and from 12:00 noon to 4:30 Sunday.

The Museum of San Diego History, operated by the San Diego Historical Society brings the decades of 1850 to 1960 alive with displays of historic sights and sounds. The museum exhibits include an extensive collection of photographs, costumes and artifacts. The museum is open daily in Balboa Park on the Prado.   Tel. (619) 232-3821.

Also operated by the Historical Society is the **Villa Montezuma**. Visit the striking 1887 Victorian house built for musician Jesse Sheppard. The villa is open every day but Saturday and Monday. You'll find it at 20th and K Streets.   Tel. (619) 239-2211

The Scripps Aquarium at La Jolla's famous **Scripps Institution of Oceanography** offers an up-close look at a dazzling display of colorful marine life, including a crimson octopus, golden sea horses and striped elephant fish. Without ever getting your feet wet you'll be able to take a walk through a San Diego kelp bed, amble past a submerged pier piling, and examine a coral reef. There's an outdoor tide pool showing creatures found off the San Diego coast. There are also exhibits relating to some of the Scripps Institute's recent findings in its world wide oceanographic research endeavors. Admission is free, but a donation is requested. A good time to go is during the afternoon feeding at 1:30 when the animals are most active. The aquarium is open daily 9:00 a.m. to 5:00 p.m, at 8602 La Jolla Shores Drive, La Jolla, CA 92093. Tel. (619) 452-6933

"Ship Ahoy!" could be the cry for the **Maritime Museum** where you can relive the days of tall ships on a trio of historic ships docked in the San Diego Harbor. The museum's flag ship is the *Star of India*, an elegant sailing vessel that is the oldest merchant ship afloat. She was built in 1863 at the Isle of Man shipyards in the British Isles and survived twenty-one voyages, carrying both cargo and emigrants to the new world. You'll also be able to board the steam-powered *Berkeley,* a San Francisco Bay ferry boat that served commuters from 1989 to 1958, and carried thousands to safety during the 1906 earthquake. Also on display is the 1904 steam yacht, *Medea*, which had been built for a wealthy Scot and saw service in both world wars. You'll find this floating museum on the Embarcadero. It is open daily and evenings from 9:00 a.m. to 8:00 p.m. Admission is charged. For more information contact the Maritime Museum Association of San Diego, 1306 North Harbor Drive, San Diego, CA 92101. Tel. (619) 234-9153.

PERFORMING ARTS

As in the case of theater, other performing arts of San Diego enjoy a loyal following and flourish with an evident cultural appreciation. With so much at home, natives of San Diego have no need to head to the great entertainment and media capital, Los Angeles, to enjoy world class entertainment, whether it be classy night club acts or classical symphonic performances.

To find out what is available call the **Arts and Entertainment Hotline** at (619) 234-Arts, or **The Whim Line** at (619) 295-WHIM, a music line that's updated daily and covers jazz, big band rock, country, and symphonic music. Half-price tickets are available for many performances on the day of the performance at **Arts Tix Ticket Center**, 121 Broadway, San Diego, Tel. (619) 238-3810.

The city is proud of its grand and ornate **Symphony Hall** that has been highly praised for the extraordinary acoustics. For more information, contact the **San Diego Symphony**, 1245 Seventh Avenue, San Diego, CA 92101. Tel. (619) 699-4205.

The **San Diego Opera** features some of the world's most famous talent, earning it a world class reputation in recent years. Such international stars as Luciano Pavarotti, Joan Sutherland and Kiri Te Kanawa have been among the opera's headliners. The opera is in season during the Spring and Fall. Among the more popular series is the **Verdi Festival** held in June. Performances are held at the **Civic Center**. For information, contact the San Diego Opera, P.O. Box 988, San Diego, CA 92112. Tel. (619) 232-7636.

The **La Jolla Chamber Music Society** schedules a variety of musical events through out the year. In the past they have had The Vienna Boys Choir, flutist James Galway and Moscow virtuosi Vladimir Kraineve, as well as quite a few celebrated chamber music recitals. Many of the performances are held in the auditorium of the **La Jolla Museum of Contemporary Art**. For information, contact the La Jolla Chamber Music Society, 7949 Ivanhoe Street, Suite 320, La Jolla, CA 92037. Tel. (619) 459-3724.

The **Organ Pavilion** in Balboa Park usually holds Sunday afternoon organ recitals, using a huge pipe organ built in 1914. Recitals being at 2:00 p.m.

San Diego State University's Open Air Theater schedules a wide variety of performers ranging from classical to rock. Call the box office at (619) 265-6947.

For more than a few laughs, **The Comedy Store** in La Jolla offers nightclub comedy entertainment featuring nationally known comics, as well as an amateur night on Sunday evenings. A cover charge and a two-drink minimum is required and you must be twenty-one. For more information: The Comedy Store, 916 Pearl Street, La Jolla, CA 92037. Tel. (619) 454-4520.

Among the most celebrated of San Diego's theaters is the world renowned **Old Globe Theatre**, home of the West Coast's oldest professional theater company. The Old Globe is among a cluster of three theaters in Balboa Park, known as the **Simon Edison Centre for the Performing Arts**. *Time Magazine* had referred to the facility as "one of the best theater complexes in the U.S." The company performs the timeless classics of Shakespeare and Marlow, but also many contemporary performances. Many of the performances are held in a reproduction outdoor Elizabethan theater, The Old Globe, which holds the summer **National Shakespearean Festival**. Other performances are conducted in the 245-seat Cassius Carter Center Stage, and the outdoor **Lowell Davies Festival Theatre**. Today, the company stages twelve productions a year. For more information about performances, contact Old Globe Theater, P.O. Box 2171 San Diego, CA 92112. Tel. (619) 231-1941.

Only a few years old, the **La Jolla Playhouse**, has all the verve and energy of youth. The theater is dedicated to presenting innovative productions and giving major directors, performers and writers a chance to experiment and take a few chances. Every summer it becomes the place where prominent writers, directors, actors and designers come to share ideas. It has become one of the most technically advanced regional theaters in the country. For information, contact the La Jolla Playhouse, P.O. Box 12039, La Jolla, CA 92038. Tel. (619) 452-6760.

Summer theatrical favorites also include the **Starlight Musicals**, performed in the outdoor **Starlight Bowl** in Balboa Park. Starting in June and running though to early September, the Startlight series performs several popular musicals. Recent productions have included *Best Little Whorehouse in Texas, South Pacific, Annie Get Your Gun*, and *Forty-second Street*. For more information, write Starlight Musicals, P.O. Box 3519, San Diego, CA 92103. Tel. (619) 544-STAR.

If you can't go to Broadway, maybe broadway can come to you. The **San Diego Playgoers Series** sponsors a series of plays performed by Broadway companies that are on the road. For more information, contact The San Diego Playgoers Series, 1399 Ninth Avenue, San Diego, CA 92101. Tel. (619) 231-8995.

The Gaslamp Quarter Theatre, in the Old Gaslamp Quarter of downtown San Diego, is a professional theater company performing in an elegant and intimate playhouse. For information, write Gaslamp Quarter Theatre, 547 Fourth Avenue, San Diego, CA 92101. Tel. (619) 697-8977

Marquis Public Theater, features contemporary and experimental productions on its three stages at 3717 India Street, San Diego, CA 92101. Tel. (619) 295-5654.

In Horton Plaza, the **San Diego Repertory Theater Company** performs on the Lyceum Stage. This well-respected company produces about nine contemporary plays a year, as well as an annual Christmas time production of *Dickens' A Christmas Carol*. For information, contact The San Diego Repertory Theatre, 79 Horton Plaza, San Diego, CA 92101. Tel. (619) 235-8025.

Theatre in Old Town, 4040 Twiggs Street, provides familiar stage comedies such as *Kiss Me Kate*. The U-shaped theater that seats about 200 is known for its reasonably priced seats and convenience to visitors of the nearby historic park. For information: Tel. (619) 298-0082.

Located on Coronado's Silver Strand and overlooking the bay, the **Coronado Playhouse**, features cabaret performances. Contact Coronado Playhouse, 1775 Strand Way, Coronado, CA 92118. Tel. (619) 435-4856.

Fiesta Dinner Theatre, in Spring Valley, features romping musical melodramas for both evening and matinee performances. Ticket prices include dinner. For information, contact the Fiesta Dinner Theatre, 9665 Campo Road, Spring Valley, CA 92077. Tel. (619) 697-8977

The East County Performing Arts Center in El Cajon features both amateur and professional dramatic performances throughout the year. You'll find everything from high school productions to performances by nationally known companies. For information, write East County Performing Arts Center, 210 East Main Street, El Cajon, CA 92020. Tel. (619) 440-0372

Even further east is the **Pine Hills Lodge** in Julian. The dinner theater features contemporary plays such as Neil Simon's *Brighton Beach Memoirs*, as well as special audience participation murder mysteries. For information, contact Pine Hills Lodge, 2960 La Posada Way, Julian, CA 92036. Tel. (619) 765-1100.

Lamb's Players Theatre, in National City, presents eight plays a year ranging from comedies, classics and some world premieres. For information, write Lamb's Players Theatre, P.O. Box 26, National City, CA 92050. Tel. (619) 474-4542.

In North San Diego County, **The Lawrence Welk Village Theatre** presents musical reviews and comedy as part of its dinner theater. What's offered here is a whole lot more than just champagne and bubbles. The theater has done contemporary comedies such as *Last of the Red Hot Lovers* and Woody Allen's *Don't Drink The Water*--all of it very "Wunerfull, Wunnerfull." For information, contract Lawrence Welk Village Theatre, 8860 Lawrence Welk Drive, Escondido, CA 92026. Tel. (619) 749-3446, or 800-932-WELK.

For information about what's happening around town in the arts and entertainment genre, call the **San Diego Arts and Entertainment Hotline** at (619) 234-ARTS.

For ticket information, contact the **Arts Tix Ticket Center**, 121 Broadway, San Diego, or call (619) 238-3810. If you buy your tickets on the day of the performance, you'll be able to get them for half price, otherwise advance tickets are full price.

SAILING IN SAN DIEGO

Even if you don't have saltwater in your veins, you might find the sight of those blue Pacific waters something to set your sails for. So what do you do when you get that primeval yearning for adventure? Your options are nearly inexhaustible, ranging from sailboarding on Mission Bay, to taking a luxury dinner and dance cruise.

For the sight-seer, there are narrated tours operated by Invader Cruises, Harbor Excursion and others. Invader Cruises operates three historic vessels. You'll find an elegant atmosphere, friendly crew, food and drink. Harbor Excursion operates modern and comfortable bay cruise ships offering one and two hours cruises, a dinner and dance cruise, Sunday brunch cruise and a summer evening cocktail cruise. The ticket booth for these cruises is at 1050 North Harbor Drive. Tel. (619) 234-4411.

Invader Cruises operates a 151 foot New England schooner with masts towering 100 feet above the deck. The 1905 vintage vessel broke several sailing records, including one set during the 1932 Transpacific race to Hawaii. The company also operates an authentic stern wheel riverboat and a luxurious 135 fantail motor yacht built in the 1930s. The cruise lasts about three and a half hours and on board facilities include hot food and full bar. Invader Cruises is located at 1066 N. Harbor Drive. Tel 800-445-4FUN nationwide, 800-262-4FUN, California, or (619) 234-TOUR.

For a longer journey, take the Ensenada Express. *The Lucille* shoves off every morning from the B Street Pier, to the Baja. This comfortable boat includes a newly remodeled bar and galley, and has two passenger lounges with movies and stereo. Although all of the cruise lines feature whale watching, this excursion to Mexico offers some of the best opportunities to view the whales during their migration season.

For sailing, on your own, in the protected waters of Mission Bay, several firms rent sailboards, sail boats and Hobie Cats. One of them, CP Sailing Sports, rents Hobie Cats from fourteen to eighteen feet, sailboats ranging from nine to twenty feet, sailboards, and aqua cycles, one size fits all. Sailing lessons are also available.

Other firms offering sailing lessons include the Harbor Island Sailing Club, Annapolis Sailing School and San Diego Yacht Charters and Mission Bay Sports.

San Diego is one of the finest fishing regions on the coast. A number of firms operate charter fishing excursions, as well as boat rentals. San Diego boasts of having one of the world's largest, and most modern sport fishing fleets. It's no wonder, the local waters yield albacore, yellowfin tuna, yellowtail and marlin. Charters can be arranged for almost any size group, or you can join one of the regularly scheduled "open party" excursions that depart for trips ranging from an afternoon, to a week. Among the sport fishing boat operators are Point Loma Sport Fishing, 1403 Scott Street, San Diego, CA 92106. Tel (619) 223-1627. For a a brochure on this and other sport fishing opportunities contact the San Diego Sportfishing Council, 2801 Emerson Street, San Diego, CA 92106.

Boating enthusiasts will find public launches in Mission Bay, as well as San Diego Bay, and on the north coast in Oceanside.

SHOPPING

Fashion Valley is the best known San Diego shopping center. It features six major department stores and 148 specialty shops, restaurants and theaters. The mood in this park-like center is high fashion. Among the nationally known department stores are The Broadway, Neiman-Marcus, Nordstrom and J.C. Penney. The shopping center is at 352 Fashion Valley Road, San Diego, CA 92108. Take Highway 163 to Friars Road. Stores are open Monday through Friday 10:00 a.m. to 9:00 p.m.; Saturday 10:00 a.m. to 6:00 p.m.; Sunday, 12:00 noon to 5:00 p.m. For more information contact Fashion Valley, 352 Fashion Valley Road, San Diego, CA 92108. Tel. (619) 297-3381

Mission Valley Center offers a European atmosphere in a 150 shop center in the Mission Valley section of San Diego. Major department stores include Saks, May Co., Bullock's, and Montgomery Ward. Mission Valley is one of the long standing front runners in regional centers, continuing to expand over the years. Recently it has developed an area of specialty shops. The center is open week days from 9:00 a.m. to 9:00 p.m.; Saturday 10:00 a.m. to 6:00 p.m.; Sunday 12:00 noon to 5:00 p.m. To reach the center take I-8 to Mission Center Road. Contact Mission Valley Center, 1640 Camino Del Rio North, San Diego,CA 92108. Tel. (619) 465-2900.

Downtown San Diego offers **Farmers Bazaar**, where you can get farm-fresh produce at country prices, as well as the creations of local artists and craftsmen. You can shop for antiques, jewelry, house plants and other items. The Bazaar is located in an historic metal warehouse. For information, contact Farmers Bazaar, 205 Seventh Avenue, San Diego, CA 92101. Tel. (619) 233-0281.

Horton Plaza is a seven block downtown shopping complex offering more than 125 special stores, restaurants and boutiques and two performing arts theaters. It includes some of the big department store chains such as Broadway and Nordstrom. But the charm comes from the nearly 100 unique, small shops, restaurants and theaters, not to mention the many cart vendors.

One enters through a courtyard that includes the restored late **Victorian Knights of Pythias Building**, with its fine sculptured details. The Moorish style **Bradley Building** also stands on the main entry court where ramps descend to the **Lyceum Theatre**. Inside, the vibrant colors decorate the arches and pillars supporting three levels of slanting walkways.

Bazaar del Mundo, located in the historic **Old Town State Park,** is a lively market place of nearly twenty international shops and four restaurants. Expect to find creative ethnic crafts, some wearable, some functional, and some purely decorative. Shoppers enjoy strolling through the courtyard, past a cascading fountain, colorful gardens and tropical birds. Each of the four restaurants offer patio and indoor dining. Free outdoor activities and entertainment, such as strolling mariachis and flamenco dancers, are presented throughout the year. Shops are open daily from 10:00 a.m. to 9:00 p.m.

Squibob Square, at Old Town, includes fifteen museum-like shops offering antiques, collectibles, handtooled leather goods, gems and custom goldsmithing. You can dine in the courtyard among frontier style false-front shops. Squibob is open daily 10:00 a.m. to 5:00 p.m. For more information, contact Squibob Square, 2611 San Diego Avenue, San Diego, CA 92110. Tel. (619) 296-1298

Old Town Esplanade, in Old Town, creates the feeling of a Mexican marketplace and features twenty unusual shops, an abundance of green foliage, a delightful aviary and a beautiful tiled fountain.   Tel. (619) 297-7133.

Old Town Galleria, at 2455 Juan Street, is a collection of international boutiques and restaurants amid a hacienda style atmosphere tucked in the hills overlooking the Old Town. Tel. (619) 297-7133.

Spanish Village in Balboa Park, is an arts and crafts center with forty different studios. The village is open 11:00 a.m. to 4:00 p.m. daily. Tel. (619) 233-9050.

Marina Village Shopping Center, 1842 Quivira Road, San Diego, is nestled in the Quivira Basin Marina on Mission Bay, not far from the Hyatt Islandia and Sea World. You'll find five restaurants set along the bay and a variety of interesting shops. Tel. (619) 224-2481.

Seaport Village is a fourteen acre complex on San Diego Bay resembling an old seaside town. Almost every weekend, Seaport Village puts on free entertainment. You can ride a restored 1890s carrousel, which sets the festive mood of the scene! A forty-five foot lighthouse on the south side of the complex overlooks the water. The classic looking structure is modeled after the much photographed Mulkiteo Lighthouse in Everett, Washington.

The village includes eighty-five one of a kind shops, boutiques, galleries and theme cafes, as well as fine dining establishments. The cafes give visitors a chance to eat outdoors and savor a variety of specialty foods. The four major restaurants all overlook the sparkling waters of the bay.

Visitors can walk on the half-mile boardwalk, or go beyond to the **Embarcadero Marina Parks** to the new Marriott Hotel and Marina. Evenings are especially enchanting for walks through the complex where one can watch the bay shimmer in the moonlight. Tel. (619) 235-4014.

Probably no one in San Diego can beat the bargains at **Kobey's Swap Meet**. This swap meet, held in the parking lot of the San Diego Sports Arena, is like 600 garage sales. Some of the millions of items are actually new, but you'll also find collectibles and antiques. The items for sale include clothing, jewelry, electronics, household furnishings, car accessories, tools, plants furniture and T-shirts and much, much more. Swap meets are held Thursday through Sunday from 7:00 a.m. to 3:00 p.m. To get to the swap meet, take Interstate 8 to Sports Arena Boulevard. For more information, Tel. (619) 226-0650.

SPORTS

Although football and baseball overshadow other athletic pursuits, San Diego offers great diversity in sports.

In the fall, football fever is everywhere. The **San Diego Chargers** have what the football aficionados consider one of the most exciting offenses; something that has led them to the playoffs several times in recent years. Games are played at the San Diego Jack Murphy Stadium at Friars Road and Interstate 15. Ticket information is available by contacting San Diego Chargers, P.O. Box 20666, San Diego, CA 92120. Tel. (619) 283-4494. But be prepared because tickets to Charger games are among the most difficult to get. For pre-game entertainment, arrive a couple of hours early to watch the great parking lot tailgate parties.

Among the alternatives to Chargers games are the **San Diego State University Aztecs**, who also play at Jack Murphy Stadium. More than eighty former Aztecs have made the NFL, as have four winning head coaches. For information, contact the **San Diego State University Athletic Department**, San Diego, CA 92182. Tel. (619) 265-5163, or 800-532-3733.

For baseball fans, there are the **San Diego Padres**, who play in Jack Murphy Stadium during spring and summer. If you think baseball falls on the tame side of spectator sports, get a seat off left field where spectators blow horns, wave banners, verbally abuse umpires and visiting team players and have a great time. For more information: San Diego Padres, P.O. Box 2000, San Diego, CA 92120. Tel. (619) 283-4494.

Believe it or not, there is life after football and baseball, and San Diego has plenty off it. Among the non-all American sports is the world's most popular spectator sport: soccer. The **San Diego Sockers** are among the most victorious team in the nation. The Sockers play indoor soccer, making it fast paced and high scoring. The Sockers play in the San Diego Sports Arena November through April. Tel. (619) 280-GOAL.

If you've never seen world class volleyball, you've missed out on a sport that combines the excitement of basketball with the grace of tennis. San Diego is home of the **United States Men's and Women's Volleyball Teams**. The men's team was the 1984 Olympic gold medal winner and the women's captured the 1984 Olympic silver medal. The season runs from February to November. For information on scheduled matches, contact U.S.A. Volleyball Teams, P.O. Box 24219, San Diego, CA 92124. Tel. (619) 692-4162.

DOWNTOWN SAN DIEGO

San Diego today is a vibrant urban center. California's second largest city is full of entertainment, full of sights, shopping and dining pleasures.

Although many parts the nation have experienced a construction slump during much of the 1980s, downtown San Diego has witnessed an unprecedented building boom in recent years, and the end is not in sight. Construction and renovation projects worth billions of dollars are slated in the future.

Locals like to refer to this revitalization as nothing less than a renaissance. *U.S. News and World Report* did a major write up on San Diego in 1982 calling it "Bustling, brawny--downtown chic."

The most visible aspect of the city's downtown redevelopment is the skyline, with its striking new office buildings of mirrored skins reflecting glittering hues of gold, bronze and onyx. Building guidelines have required these projects to include esthetic amenities such as atriums, breezeways and small parks.

Downtown offers a mix of old restored buildings like those of the Gaslamp District, which stand only a short distance from the post-modernistic shopping center, Horton Plaza. City planners are also encouraging development of residential facilities. Several blocks have been designated for residential development. At present downtown residences include the upscale Meridian, Park Row, and Marina Park neighborhoods, and the other accommodations are provided by warehouse lofts and inexpensive resident hotels. Two new condominiums in downtown are turning out to be quite popular. 10,000 people live in downtown residences and that figure is expected to grow by tenfold during the next fifteen years.

Those who have been wealthy enough to afford the downtown condominiums, or resourceful enough to convert warehouse lofts into chic abodes are able to enjoy at their doorstep what many go to a lot of trouble to get to. That includes the music, shopping and street entertainment at Horton Plaza, the refined sounds of Symphony Hall, the drama of The Deane Theatre and Lyceum Stage.

Hotels, both old and traditional or strikingly new, bring in visitors who add just that much more activity to the busy streets. There is the elegantly renovated U.S. Grant Hotel and the towering Marriott. For a bird's eye view of the city, take the glass elevator that runs up the outside of the El Cortez Hotel at Seventh and Ash Streets.

ATTRACTIONS

The Community Concourse covers the entire city block between A and C Streets and included the city's downtown convention and performing arts center, as well as the **City Administration Building**. The **San Diego Symphony** and the **San Diego Opera Company** perform here.

If you read ancient Summarian, **The San Diego Public Library** may be for y ou. Located at the corner of 8th and E Streets, the library includes among its collection 4,000 year old cuneiform tables, as well some the hotest best sellers. The library is one of the most modern and well-stocked municipal libraries in the county.

Also downtown is **Horton Plaza**, the scene for soap box orators, open air art shows, strolling street musicians, and shopping like no other place. The modern twelve acre shopping center is seven city blocks of shopping, dining and entertainment among some of the most striking renovated and modern architecture in the city.

Wyatt Earp ran three gambling halls and refereed local boxing matches in what is now San Diego's restored **Gaslamp Quarter**. This two block strip between Broadway and L Streets at one time contained the stores, homes, gambling rooms and opium dens of the city's Chinatown, and later became a thriving red light district.

Originally this area was the vision of a gentleman named Alonzo Horton. In 1867 he wanted to develop a port district on the land facing the bay. He was able to acquire the land for mere pennies an acre, but soon this new San Diego commerical development became a place where ships' chandlers outfitted tall masted clipper ships, local farmers pick up hardware, and the amorous could find hope for more potent love life by picking up some ground rhinoceros horn from a Chinese herbalist .

Today the images are somewhat different: shoppers inspect the finest goods and fashions, as well as a world class, one of a kind antiques. Cafe patrons become people watchers as they sit under colorful umbrellas next to brick sidewalks. By night, musicians in clubs blow brassy notes from trumpets to the beat of a Dixieland tunes.

Walking tours of the Gaslamp Quarter are offered every Saturday at 10:00 a.m. and 1:00 p.m.. Tours depart from the William Heath Davis House, 410 Island Avenue. For more information contact Gaslamp Quarter Council, 410 Island Avenue, San Diego CA 92101. Tel. (619) 233-5227.

Among the seventeen blocks covering thirty-eight acres, today's visitors find art galleries, fine restaurants, theaters and night spots offering just about every sort of music, from rock to Dixieland.

The handsome Victorian structures comprise a **National Historic District** that dates back to the end of the Civil War. The once ragged buildings have been restored to their Gay 90s splender, housing boutiques, gift shops, ethnic restaurants, offices and artists studios.

Some of the better known restored buildings include **The Broker's Building**, a large three story brick structure now painted white with blue trim. It was headquarters of a wholesale grocery, wine and patent medicine firm. Now the building houses a variety of shops and restaurants.

The **San Diego Hardware,** a renowned hardware business throughout all of California, is pretty much as it was in 1892. Still doing business in hardware, it retains the original wood floors, metal ceilings and storefront windows.

The Pioneer Warehouse was one of the buildings constructed after the district was past its prime. It was simply a furniture storage facility, but now it has been transformed as the Fourth and K Street Mall. You'll find no less than five floors of antiques as well as a restaurant.

Not only is San Diego's **Embarcadero** beautiful, it is a functional working waterfront district. One would have to be numb not to get some sense of excitement from the countless and ever changing activities here. There is sand and grassy parks to relax and lounge on, quaint stores to shop in and fine restaurants to dine in. It is a scene to behold, where great ships arrive and depart, thousands of smaller boats putter about and an occasional supersonic aircraft swooshes through the air.

The invigorating air seems to draw people outdoors. In good weather, which is almost always, there will be joggers, cyclists and strollers in the twenty acre Embarcadero-Marina Park. Some folks come down to the waterfront at day's end just to watch the sunset, said to be one of the best sunset views on the coast.

It is the home of several vintage ships, including the 122 year old *Star of India*, the oldest merchant sailing vessel afloat. The iron hulled ship was built on the Isle of Man and had survived twenty-one around the world voyages. Nearby is the *Berkeley*, a large ferry boat that had carried commuters across the San Francisco Bay. There's also the luxury liner, *Media*, which was built in 1904. All three ships, are open to public tours daily.

The new Cruise Terminal at the Embarcadero serves several luxury cruise ships that sail the South Pacific and the Mexican Riviera. Television's *Love Boat* frequently makes a call here.

Excellent dining facilities are scattered throughout the Embarcadero. Some of the seafood establishments give the choice of buying fresh fish to take home, or dining on well-prepared delicacies. Many visitors like to grab something quick at one of the fast food restaurants and sit on the grass watching all of action in the harbor as sailboats maneuver around each other.

For a look at what dockside life might have been like a hundred years ago, visit Sea Port Village. The complex just south of Market Street at Pacific Highway and Harbor drive is a popular fourteen acre dining and shopping area located on the water. There is also a working Merry-Go-Round!

OLD TOWN

Ordinarily San Diego doesn't conjure up images of the Old West like Tombstone, Dodge City, or El Paso. But there was a time when the streets of old San Diego where as wild and wooly as the streets of Laredo. Walk through the streets of the restored Old Town and you'll pass through the scenes of brawls, beatings, gunfights, public executions, and bear baitings. By any standard definition old San Diego was wild, and it most certainly is part of America's west.

The original townsite was established just below the San Diego River, not along the bay shore where so much of the city's action is today.   The old town began in the 1820s. As was the custom in Spain and Mexico, the early townspeople built their homes and early shops around a plaza to form a social center for the new community.   In the 1830s the settlement was comprised of about forty buildings.

Today Old town is preserved as a California State Park. Some of the old buildings are now open as businesses and restaurants. Old Town endures as a colorful reminder of a mixed heritage San Diego shares with the Old West and Old Mexico. It recreates the setting of early San Diego life during the early Mexican and early American periods. The State of California began operating the site as a state park in 1968.

The Plaza, formerly called Washington Square, was the scene of many loud and raucous gatherings. During the Mexican period many a fiesta and celebration was held here. This is where the American flag was first raised in 1846. Looking north beyond the square, the same direction as the cannon faces, is the hilltop on which the old presidio was built.

Four of the original adobes remain. The Machado/Stewart, adobe with its red tiled roof supported by exposed timbers, was built in1830 by Jose Machado. It was later occupied by Jack Stewart, a ship's pilot who married Machado's daughter. The house was occupied by the descendants of the Stewarts until 1966.

The Casa de Estudillo, with its long flat profile and cupola topped roof, is the most famous of the early buildings. Constructed in 1827 by Captain Jose Maria de Estudillo, commander of the San Diego presidio, the building has long been known as "Romona's Marriage Place" because of descriptions in the Helen Hunt Jackson novel, *Romona*, a popular romance of the 1840s set in California.

The quaint one room wooden schoolhouse built in 1865, the Mason Street School, was the first public school built in San Diego. It still serves as an education facility that is used for history classes. The nearby Whaley House, was San Diego's first luxury two story mansion. Built in 1856, the brick structure was used as the San Diego County Courthouse during the 1860s and 1870s. According to local folk lore, resident ghosts have been alleged to have set off burglar alarms over the years.

Looking somewhat out of place, a New England type frame house is the Casa de Atamirano, at 2626 San Diego Avenue. The structure was prefabricated in Maine and shipped around the Horn in 1851. The building became the first home of the *San Diego Union* newspaper and has been restored as it appeared in 1868 when the first edition of the paper was pulled off the press.

The Mormon Battalion Memorial Visitor Center has exhibits of the march of Mormon settlers from Kansas to San Diego during the Mexican-American War. There are also displays on the United States Constitution and the history of the Mormon Church. The Visitor's Center is at 2510 Juan Street.

Casa de Bandini, the home of the Peruvian born Juan Bandini, became the social center of Old Town after its completion in 1829. Usually involved in some kind of political scheme, Bandini held several government positions under the Mexican rule. He was quick to demonstrate his political acumen with the Americans took over. He invited Commodore Stockton to make his headquarters at La Casa de Bandini! Under subsequent ownership, a second story was added and over the years the building has served as a store, a pickle factory, a hotel and a motel annex before being acquired as part of the Old Town San Diego State Historic Park.

The United States House is closer to American western architecture. A two story wooden prefabricated building assembled about 1850. It has been used as a general store, a butcher shop and match factory.

The huge Seeley Stable is a large barn like structure built in 1867 for the San Diego-Los Angles Stage Line. The stables provided fresh horses to pull stages on the 130 mile trip. Barring accidents or other mishaps, the trip would take less than twenty-four hours. The reconstructed building houses a collection of horse-drawn vehicles and Old West artifacts, including saddles, and branding irons. The collection also features Indian artifacts, some of which are estimated to be three thousand years old. Visitors may view a slide program that outlines the city's early history.

Free tours of the Old Town area are conducted by the State Park Department and the Old Town Historical Society. The ranger lead tours depart from the Park Information Center, 2645 San Diego Avenue, at 2:00 p.m. daily. Historical Society tours, which cover twenty-five historic sites, start off from the Whaley House, 2482 San Diego Avenue at 1:30 p.m. Saturdays.

For a small charge, Old Town Walking Tours conducts thirty to thirty-five minute tours for individuals and groups. You'll find the tour office at 3977 Twiggs Street. Tel. (619) 296-1004.

Old town lies between Juan and Congress Streets. Parking is provided on Congress, as well as on Tiggs Street along Old Town's east side.

ATTRACTION

A graceful bell tower rises out of the lush gardens of California's first Mission. **Mission San Diego De Acala** stands on a knoll overlooking Mission Valley. The plaster and adobe building was built in 1780 to replace the original mission building Father Serra built on Presidio Hill that had been burned in an Indian attack in 1775.

Most striking is the symmetrical arrangement of the campanile, which rises, in three stages, to a simple wooden cross at its peak. The five bells, that hang in separate open bellfries on the tower, add delicacy to the otherwise massive two story facade of the mission.

The path leading to the left of the campanile, leads to a patio landscaped with trees and flower beds. Three small brick crosses stand as a simple memorial to the 450 Indians buried here.

The chapel contains a 150 foot long nave, supported only by the five and a half foot thick walls that stand nearly thirty feet high. The original paintings hanging over the alter werebrought to the mission from Spain. They bear the scorched marks of the fire that destroyed the first mission building on Presidio Hill. The ceiling is supported by heavy, rough hewn timbers running horizontally from wall to wall.

From the beginning it prospered, however it did suffer a setback in 1803 when an earthquake nearly ruined the structure. But by 1813 the mission had been fully restored and enlarged. Following the secularization of the government, the mission fell into disrepair during the 1830s. During the early part of the 20th century, a major restoration effort was launched. Cracks and portions of exposed adobe bricks were purposely left to give it a historic look.

The Father Luis Jayme Museum on the mission grounds contains artifacts of early mission life, including some of the vestments worn by the early padres. This little museum is Southern California's only ecclesiastical art museum.

To get to the mission, take I-8 six miles east of I-5. Take the Friar's Road East Exit, continue on Friar's Road to Rancho Mission Road for a quarter of a mile to San Diego Mission Road. For information, Tel. (619) 281-8449.

ACCOMMODATIONS

THE BEACH COTTAGES
4255 Ocean Boulevard
San Diego, CA 92109
Tel. (619) 483-7440
Seasonal rates are available.

There is a tradition on the beach in San Deigo. For forty years guests who appreciate the calm relaxation of ocean front living, in a casual atmosphere, have been coming to The Beach Cottages on the sands of beautiful Pacific Beach.

The beachfront property on which The Beach Cottages rest has been in the family since 1904. In the ensuing years the Frost family has developed the plot into a very pleasant and tasteful collection of cottages and motel units. Because of the legacy of the land, these cottages are one of only two true ocean front locations in the area. The decor is a pleasing exterior mix of white with green trim that compliments the sands and ocean. Interiors are done in natural knotty pine. The setting is a comfortable one, something like visiting a friend at their home. There is a sense of community among the guests, as people gather to play shuffleboard or cook over an outdoor grill. Full house keeping units are availible. You can go spend a vacation at a beach house without having to pay the high prices of renting a private home.

San Diego is full of wonderful vacation opportunities. This year start your own tradition by spending a relaxing time at The Beach Cottages.

THE BAY CLUB HOTEL AND MARINA
2131 Shelter Island Drive
San Diego, CA 92106
Tel.　(619)　224-8888
　　　　(800)　833-6565　CA
　　　　(800)　672-0800　US
　　　　(800)　345-8834　Western　Canada
Visa, MasterCard and AMEX are accepted.

Set on picturesque and convenient Shelter Island, this new harborside resort hotel has taken a fresh and unique approach to the bed and breakfast concept.

Its contemporary design gives every guest room and suite a private balcony, that overlooks either the Marina or San Diego Harbor. The decor captures the subtle essence of the tropics with its warm earthstone and walls hung with with authentic Samoan tapas. At the same time, rates include complimentary airport limousine service, a full buffet breakfast served in the restaurant or on the terrace, both of which offer dazzling water views. Every room has its own mini-refrigerator and comes equipped with cable TV, oversize pool towels, and an amenities basket filled with personal toiletries and daily vitamins. Afternoon tea is served from 3:00 to 4:00 p.m., and you'll find your bed neatly turned down each night, with a chocolate mint on your pillow to encourage sweet dreams.

Leisure facilities abound here. There is a heated swimming pool and jacuzzi, a delightful informal lounge with a club-like atmosphere, and the Molly Trolley stops frequently to provide inexpensive and whimsical transportation for sightseeing. A caring staff will see to your every need during your stay at this engaging Shelter Island hotel.

THE GROSVENOR INN
DOS AMIGOS RESTAURANT
3145 Sports Area Boulevard
San Diego, CA 92110
Tel.   (619) 225-9999
          (800) 222-2929 CA
          (800) 232-1212 USA
All major credit cards are accepted.

Billed as San Diego's best kept secret, The Grosvenor Inn is an accommodation of intimate elegance. Centrally located near most all of the area's best attractions, this inn, with its adjoining restaurant, the local Mexican favorite, Dos Amigos Cafe and Cantina, makes for a valuable choice for both individuals and large assemblies.

The management and friendly staff at The Grosvenor Inn take pleasure in offering guests "a home away from home." The inn complex consists of a complete selection of on site services including a year around 85° pool, jacuzzi, full banquet facilities, a shopping center, as mentioned a first class restaurant, as well as 205 deluxe guest rooms. The facilities at the Grosvenor Inn "are as affordable as they are desirable." For those travelers who are looking for the ultimate in comfort, Grosvenor provides a Presidential Suite, Jacuzzi Suites and the Grosvenor Garden Suites all with kitchens, wet bars, private balconies, and saunas. Dos Amigos Cafe and Cantina, the home of fresh, informal Mexican street cookings, features American-style breakfast (with Mexican favorites, too), lunch, dinner and Sunday brunch. Dos Amigos offers sizzling Fajitas or a mouthwatering Taco Platter for two, as well as Mexican Stew, shredded beef or chicken Burritos or Enchiladas fixed with several delectable sauces, rice and beans. Try their famous two-glass margaritas or one of the Mexican beers. Happy Hour is Monday through Friday, 5:00 p.m. - 7:00 p.m., with 50 cent taco specials and 1/2 price margaritas. Dance nightly to San Diego's finest in high-tech video and sound system in the cantina.

Come to the Grosvenor Inn where class and luxury are brought to you in a comfortably home-like atmosphere. Conveniently located near the major transportation centers, yet close to the San Diego's recreation spots, Grosvenor Inn is the ideal setting for your next trip to San Diego.

(See special invitation in the Appendix.)

HANALEI HOTEL
2270 Hotel Circle
San Diego, CA 92138
Tel. (619) 297-1101
Visa, MasterCard and AMEX are accepted.

Hanalei is Hawaiian for "Valley of the Flowers." This hotel successfully has created the illusion that the Hawaiian islands have been moved to the mainland. Located on nine and a half acres of towering palms and lush landscaping, the illusion is enhanced by the poolside luaus where traditional Hawaiian feasts are presented weekly during the summer, complete with a Polynesian buffet and authentic Hawaiian entertainment.

Service, luxury and convenience are important at Hanalei. Guests are invited to enjoy the facilities of the nearby Atlas Health Spa, or luxuriate in one of two pools or a therapy pool. Each of the 450 rooms and suites is tastefully decorated and equipped with a color TV, radio, pay TV, and direct dial telephone. Standard amenities include a weekday newspaper delivered to your door, in-room coffee and tea, beauty soap, shampoo and conditioner, sewing kit and shower cap.

The Peacock Restaurant, the Islands Lounge and the Islands Restaurant all combine Oriental and American influences that create dining experiences which are truly Hawaiian. Hanalei is a piece of the South Seas where the East meets the West. You'll want to come back again and again.

HORTON GRAND HOTEL
311 Island Avenue
San Diego, Ca 92101
Tel. (619) 544-1886
Visa, MasterCard and AMEX are accepted.

Oscar Wilde gave Victorian England a chuckle nearly a hundred years ago when he said, "I have the simplest of taste, I am satisfied with only the best." His pungent comment lives on today as the very apt motto for this exclusive hotel, where Managing Director, Billy Riley has lovingly re-created an oasis of elegance in San Diego's historic downtown Gaslamp District.

A masterpiece of Victorian era, the Horton Grand Hotel is the result of a brick by brick restoration of two hotels originally built in the 1880s and now joined by a remarkable two story solarium lobby replete with period wicker furnishings and greenery. Impeccable attention to detail carries through out the hotel. Guest rooms feature canopied queen size beds raised on platforms to "proper Victorian height," armoires instead of closets, gas fireplaces with antique mantles and authentic Victorian wallpaper.

The decor also pays tribute to the Gaslamp's turn of the century Chinatown. The bridal suite is furnished with a traditional Chinese marriage bed, and the Chinese Museum and Tea Room includes antiques from the Chinese Historical Society of San Diego. You will be greeted by valets dressed as 1890s newsboys and check in at an antique oak registration desk served by staff in period dress. The old Palace Bar basks in the glory of celebrities who haunted it in items gone by and offers congenial comfort in its Victorian loveseats centered around the massive fireplace topped by a soaring eight foot gilt mirror.

Escape into a more leisurely past for a weekend of fun and rest, or use the Horton Grand Hotel as a bas for extended sightseeing. The location could not be more convenient, and the atmosphere is an incredible time warp experience in its own right.

HYATT ISLANDIA HOTEL
1441 Quiuira Road
San Diego, CA 92109
Tel. (619) 224-1234
All major credit cards are accepted.

For true elegance in accommodations the Hyatt Islandia offers quality that is associated with the Hyatt name. For the traveler who is accustomed to fine hotels or is simply looking for a place to get away for that special occasion this Hyatt in San Diego provides full services in a location central to many major attractions and recreational facilities.

All rooms give the customer a view of either the bay or ocean. In addition, in keeping with Hyatt standards, rooms are spaciously comfortable. Every guest will find the environs magnificently landscaped with thousands of exotic plants and an over sized swimming pool as a center piece. This setting is a favorite for wedding ceremonies and of course honeymoons. The Hyatt Islandia houses generous banquet and convention facilities. Being within walking distance to the beach, shopping, and several tourist services makes this spot a natural for conventions, family reunions, or the individual.

Newly remodeled in 1986, the Hyatt Islandia offers elegance in a contemporary atmosphere. Make this "Best Choice" a gold star stop on your agenda.

RADISSON HOTEL
1433 Camino Del Rio S
San Diego, CA 92108
Tel. (619) 260-0111
Visa, MasterCard and AMEX are acccepted.

Step up to modern luxury at the Radisson, one of San Diego's newest buildings, and already a landmark. Its location in the heart of San Diego's Mission Valley, puts you in easy reach of almost all of the area attractions and is just minutes from the airport.

Something special is the Plaza Club on the 12th and 14th floors. Guest of the Plaza Club are pampered with their own lounge; with concierge services; library; and complimentary hors d'oeuvres, Continental breakfast and beer and wine. The suites on the 14th floor are spacious with queen size beds, high ceilings, wet bar and private balconies.

The hotel was designed and furnished with comfort in mind. Ample free parking, complimentary shuttle, restaurant, lounge and deli area are typical of the amenities. Excellent business and convention facilities, including an AV theatre, are available.

RAMADA INN OLD TOWN
2435 Jefferson Street
San Diego, CA 92110
Tel. (619) 260-8500
(800) 2-RAMADA
All major credit cards are accepted.

Old Town ranks as San Diego's number one visitor attraction, drawing over four-million people each year. Visitors can rediscover the history and romance of California's birth place as they wander along it's grassy parks and shaded plazas into historic buildings restored to their mid-1800 appearance. When you make a trip to Old Town, be sure to make your lodging as enjoyable as your stay. Ramada Inn Old Town is capable of making your visit a first-class vacation.

The hotel is ideally situated two blocks from historic Old Town, with easy freeway access off I-5 at the Old Town exit. Not only is it close to Old Town, but central to all that's fun to see and do in San Diego. The brand new facility offers standard rooms and luxurious suites all containing a color television set with remote control and individual air conditioning. The inn can accommodate groups as small as ten people or as large as 150 people and offers: 2,781 square feet of meeting and banquet space, four meeting rooms, large patio area for overflow and beautiful hospitality suites. Other features of this hotel include complimentary breakfast, full service restaurant, lounge, room service, laundry facilities and a heated pool and Jacuzzi.

Whenever your next function takes place in San Diego, make the Ramada Inn Old Town your host hotel. For a unique change of pace, enjoy their hospitality and experience San Diego from the place where California began.

SAN DIEGO HILTON HOTEL
1775 East Mission Bay Drive
San Diego, CA 92109
Tel. (619) 276-4010
Visa, MasterCard, AMEX and Discover are accepted.

This conveniently located hotel provides the perfect mix of business and pleasure. Created on eighteen acres of Mission Bay Aquatic Park, this year round resort offers the famous San Diego climate and a delightful bayside location, providing guests with unlimited recreation. Just ten minutes from the international airport and a short drive from San Diego's major points of interest, the Hilton remains a world of its own.

Play on the bay aboard any of the vessels in the resorts fleet, the sternwheeler *Hilton Queen*, the yacht *Lady Hilton*, the deep sea fishing boat *Retriever*, or the flotilla of sailboats, catamarans and wind surfboards that are available for you. Picnic on the bay, strike up a volleyball game on the sand, visit the exclusive Hilton Tennis Club, work out in the Health Club, take a bicycle ride and explore the bay's sandy coves, swim in the pool or relax in the sauna or in one of the jacuzzis. Golf is nearby, as is Sea World.

Sail along Mission Bay on the *Hilton Queen* sternwheeler and enjoy a fabulous view of downtown San Diego from the water while indulging in a luxurious Sunday Brunch. Choose from the lavish salad bar, experience an omelete made to order, or enjoy hot carved prime rib or lamb while experiencing a cruise on an old fashioned paddlewheeler. Able to accommodate up to 200 guests, the *Hilton Queen* is also available for private charter and banquets.

The touches of luxury for which Hilton is famous are everywhere from spacious, well appointed rooms with refrigerators, mini-bars and balconies, to the famous, Four Star restaurant, Tradewinds. Most important, the staff is committed to the concept of excellence and service, a committment which will guarantee your fulfillment.

U.S. GRANT HOTEL
326 Broadway
San Diego, CA 92101-4812
Tel: (619) 232-3121
All major credit cards are accepted.

Among the grand hotels of the world, only a handful are distinguished by an uncommon integrity. A degree of taste, service and personal comfort that fulfills each and every expectation. In San Diego that hotel is the new U.S. Grant, built in honor of the former president by his son Ulysses S. Grant. For decades it has hosted dignitaries, celebrities and others who enjoy the highest qualities of life.

The accommodations feature 280 rooms with include sixty-four suites, devised for privacy and relaxation with understated luxury, and both butler and concierge service available. For business, they offer seventeen meeting rooms consisting of over 28,500 square feet including a 9,000 square foot Grand Ballroom. There are many special services offered, such as full multi-lingual concierge services including car and limousine rental, all dining, entertainment and travel arrangements, secretarial and telex services, guest privileges at Singing Hills Country Club and shopping directly across the street at Horton Plaza Shopping and Entertainment complex.

The lobby plays host not only to guests as they first arrive, but also to the famed Grant Grill Restaurant. This warm, elegant establishment is adorned with English hunt scenes hanging from mahogany walls in the dining area. The menu consists of exquisite gourmet offerings, with each dish being a carefully created balance of color and food placement, specifically designed to make it as pleasing to the eyes as to the taste. Grant Grill and the U.S. Grant Hotel, elegant rememberances of the past that can be relived today. A "Best Choice" in any book. A Mobile Four Star, AAA Four Diamond rated hotel. Member of Preferred Hotels Worldwide and The Krisam Group.

VISCOUNT HOTEL-SAN DIEGO
1960 Harbor Island Drive
San Diego, CA 92101
Tel.   (619) 291-6700
          (800) 255-3050
          (800) 223-5672
Visa, MasterCard, AMEX, Diners Club, Carte Blanche and Discover are accepted.

When in San Diego, a stay at the Viscount Hotel is a must. With seventeen years of experience in catering to your comfort and pleasure and carrying on the tradition of European flair of Trusthouse Forte, the Viscount offers old world charm and extraordinary service.

Ideally located on the water's edge of Harbor Island, the Viscount Hotel offers some of the best views in the city. You may choose from a view of the San Diego Harbor, sunset over the marina or an extraordinary view of the city skyline. Their guests enjoy the quiet beauty of the island while still knowing they are conveniently situated near all business districts and major attractions. In the heart of San Diego, the Viscount is less than five minutes from the San Diego International Airport, only forty minutes from the San Diego Zoo, Sea World, Old Town and a wide variety of recreation and shopping activities. The hotel provides complimentary airport transportation and is the only hotel offering free parking on Harbor Island.

For a romantic evening, begin with cocktails in the lounge and slip away into the waterside dining room for an intimate candlelight dinner overlooking the marina. Whether you're there for lunch, dinner or brunch, the Viscount Chef prepares the best seafood creations and daily specials to meet your every expectation. Your stay at the Viscount Hotel is certain to be a memorable one. Don't let an experience like this pass you by.

ANTIQUE SHOPS

THE CONNOISSEUR
3165 Adams Avenue
San Diego, CA 92116
Tel. (619) 284-1132
Hrs: Mon. - Tue.   10:00 a.m. - 5:00 p.m.
           Thursday   10:00 a.m. - 5:00 p.m.
           Friday   12:00 noon - 5:00 p.m.
Visa and MasterCard are accepted.

Although more than thirty dealers line San Diego's Antique Row on Adams Avenue, one shop clearly stands out from all the rest. In business at the same location for over twenty-one years, The Connoisseur has earned a solid reputation among serious antique buffs both for its honesty and for the quality of its collections. Owners Jackie and Trigg Stewart are long-time collectors who have passed their passion for the best of everything along to their customers.

The Connoisseur specializes in fine eighteenth and 19th century American and English furniture, along with period accessories. They are equally well known for their porcelains, especially blue Staffordshire, Meissen and Chinese export, and an unusually extensive selection of early samplers. You will find value upon value in this treasure house of antiques, early clocks and time pieces, Dedham pottery, Sevres, art glass, firearms, Tiffany items, Patek-Philipe watches, Mettlech, and a superb collection of Georgian Victorian and heirloom silver.

Do plan time for a visit to The Connoisseur and get to know the Stewarts. Their eclectic showroom is irresistible, and the quality and beauty of their wares are unsurpassed on the West Coast.

HOUSE OF HEIRLOOMS
801 University Avenue
San Diego, CA 92103
Tel. (619) 298-0502
Hrs: Mon. - Sat. 9:30 a.m. - 5:30 p.m.
Visa and MasterCard are accepted.

How many people can say they were born in the very spot where they work? Ruth Schulman can, because the House of Heirlooms is located in what used to be the surgical wing of the first hospital in San Diego. Many years ago that building was moved to its present location and eventually became home to the House of Heirlooms.

Ruth learned to appreciate antiques from her mother. She and her husband Victor, already a successful businessman, opened the business fifteen years ago. Their goal was to provide authentic, top notch English Victorian antiques and collectibles to San Diego. The House of Heirlooms carries furnitures, clocks, china, silver, lamps and linens from England and Scotland. The Schulmans travel to Europe twice a year to personally choose the items that will be displayed in their store. They also carry a good variety of American furniture and decorative items. Personal shopping is one of the special services provided to clients. If there is a particular item you are looking for, it's added to the Schulman's shopping list

The House of Heirlooms offers free delivery in the San diego area. The House of Heirlooms is a pleasant change from many antique stores, because the interior is light and airy. Lots of space gives customers a chance to truly admire each item.

OLDE CRACKER FACTORY
448 West Market Street at Columbia
San Diego, CA 92101
Tel. (619) 232-7961
Hrs: Tue. - Sun.   11:00 a.m. - 5:00
Visa and MasterCard are accepted.

The Olde Cracker Factory is Southern California's original Antiques Shopping Center. The old brick structure first housed the Bishop's Cracker Factory, famous in downtown San Diego for its candies, crackers and hand-dipped chocolates from 1911 to 1935.

This lovely old building has been beautifully restored, and its three floors transformed into a fascinating Victorian Village housing individual antique dealers. Inside, one will find a year-round Christmas Shop, Georgia's Doll Shoppe, the Willow Tree's paper dolls, Maximilian Art and Design picture framing and an irresistible Oriental Treasure Box. Elegant antique furnishings abound in shops such as Bert's, The Goode Collection and the extensive Heritage Art Center. For crystal, china, silver and all the other collectible memorabilia are shops operated by such professionals as Elva Newcomb and Ben Kantor, as well as Olson's Potpourri and Dulcie Gubin's Antiques. Plus, the enormous display presented by Third Floor Antiques is practically overwhelming.

The Coffee Shoppe, in its antique setting, is a lovely spot on the first floor for lunch and a rest between shopping sprees; and then perhaps a visit to Seaport Village, just a block away.

The Olde Cracker Factory has long been a favorite for tourists and locals alike, and promises to become even more interesting as future plans emerge as realities.

APPAREL

CHIC ACCESSORIES
333 Fashion Valley
San Diego, CA 92108
Tel. (619) 291-3311
Hrs: Mon. - Fri.   10:00 a.m. - 9:00 p.m.
       Saturday   10:00 a.m. - 6:00 p.m.
       Sunday   12:00noon - 5:00 p.m.
Visa, MasterCard, AMEX, Carte Blanche and Diners Club are accepted.

So often, accessories are handled by clothing stores as an afterthought, a sort of necessary add-on to fill out the lines of apparel. At

Chic Accessories, they are far from a filler, they are everything. As fashion conscious women know, accessories can make or break an outfit. Chic Accessories is a family business, started in downtown San Diego over thirty years ago, and moved to the Fashion Valley Mall when it opened some twelve years later. A second store opened in La Jolla in the University Towne Center.

Chic Accessories feature one of the largest selections of cubic zirconium jewelry available, and is justly proud of its wide array of European and domestically produced fashion jewelry. There are 14k gold chains and charms to add that perfect touch of richness to any costume, and which make great gifts that say, "I care." Visitors to San Diego will particularly appreciate the variety of souvenir charms. Chic also carries unique handbags and handsome fashion belts to add versatility and style to any wardrobe. You'll also find scarves and gloves.

When you visit Chic Accessories, be sure to add your name to their extensive mailing list so that no matter where you are you always have the store at your fingertips.

(See special invitation in the Appendix.)

JOEL'S
1640 Camino Del Rio North
Mission Valley Center
San Diego, CA 92108
Tel. (619)293-3977
Hrs: Mon. - Fri.   10:00 a.m. - 9:00 p.m.
        Saturday   10:00 a.m. - 6:00 p.m.
        Sunday   12:00 noon - 5:00 p.m.
Visa, MasterCard, AMEX and Joel's Charge Card are accepted.
Also,
Fashion Valley Mall
Tel. (619) 692-9644

Back in 1953 when the first Joel's store opened, the idea was to provide the best quality clothing for women. Shoppers at Joel's would be treated like guests in Joel's own home. The idea seemed to work; by 1955 there were eight Joel's stores, by 1970 there were fourteen and today there are thirty Joel's stores in Southern California. Good service is always in demand and good customer service is a must at Joel's.

As in the beginning, every Joel's store carries a huge selection of career women's quality clothing at affordable prices. From evening wear to sports wear and everything in between, Joel's has what it takes to create your own special look. Joel's carries distinctive name brands of apparel such as Michael

Blair, Wild Rose, Phoebe, Francine Browner, Melrose, Climax, Visions, Cache, and Nilani. Accessorize with wild abandon. A large selection of scarves, belts and watches lets you put your personal stamp on each outfit. Hats by Bet Mar, Soni and Georgi finish the look.

The staff is career oriented, knowledgeable and professional making the service they give you the best. You'll know you've been pampered when you receive a thank you note after every purchase.

LONDONTOWNE
4417 La Jolla Village Drive
University Towne Centre, Suite Q3
San Diego, CA 92122
Tel.   (619) 452-6477
Hrs: Mon. - Fri.   10:00 a.m. - 9:00 p.m.
          Saturday   10:00 a.m. - 6:00 p.m.
          Sunday   12:00 noon - 5:00 p.m.
Visa, MasterCard and AMEX are accepted.
Also,
200 E Via Rancho Parkway, Suite 217
North County Fair
Escondido, CA 92025

Building one's wardrobe is an art. Owner Jackie Dergazarian has brought to the States the artistic and fashion skills she learned while in the clothing business in London, England. Londontowne has now become a classic feminine, traditional clothing store with an emphasis on personalized style.

One can expect to find classic separates by famous makers such as Cricketeer, Geiger, Corbin, and Albert Nipon. Sweaters are by Anni Barrie and Robert Scott. Ginnie Johansen accessories are featured.   A private collection with the Londontowne label is also available. Jackie takes care to emphasize the beautiful texture and color of all natural fiber such as wool, silk, cashmere, cotton and linen. Jackie's staff is warm, helpful and attentive to individualized wardrobe planning.   Alterations, shipping, accessory demonstrations and seminars about wardrobe planning are all services of Londontowne.

Enjoy Londontowne's comfortable ambiance and sincerely helpful staff while you take delight in the beautiful traditional English/American fashions.

(See special invitation in the Appendix.)

NOW SHOWING MATERNITY
1400 Camino de la Reina
San Diego, CA 92108
Tel.   (619) 299-0804
Hrs: Mon. - Sat.   10:00 a.m. - 6:00 p.m.
         Sunday   1:00 p.m. - 4:00 p.m.
Visa and MasterCard are accepted.

Just because you're pregnant doesn't mean you have to stop being sexy, contemporary, and fashion conscious. Owner Nancy Guttman fills that void in the maternity wear market. When you leave "Now Showing," you'll look and feel great. Nancy offers a wide range of exclusive merchandise in sizes four to sixteen that include upscale fashions in day wear, evening wear, swimsuits, and anything else you need.

From the moment you enter "Now Showing" you'll feel pampered. The carpets are plush, the dressing rooms are spacious, and a rattan lounge has been created for friends or children. There's even an adorable stuffed toy section. Most of all, the staff is ready to assist you in any way they can to make you comfortable and happy while you examine the exciting array of fine clothes displayed for you.

"Now Showing" has everything a woman may need. Whether you're sophisticated, casual, professional, sporty, intellectual, down home, or up town, "Now Showing" has the fashions to fit your image beautifully. A preview catalog is available of the current collection. The designs are excellent, the prices are modest.

PRICE BREAKERS APPAREL MART
824 Camino Del Rio North, Suit 201 B
San Diego, CA 92108
Tel. (619) 295-5559
Hrs: Mon. - Fri.   10:00 a.m. - 9:00 p.m.
         Saturday   10:00 a.m. - 8:30 p.m.
         Sunday   11:00 a.m. - 6:00 p.m.
Closed Easter, Christmas and Thanksgiving.
Visa and MasterCard are accepted.

Danny and Ronnie Maman are two brothers who emigrated from Israel. Both were fascinated by American business and saw a need for a famous label discount store. Their operation is simple. They buy large quantities from suppliers, mostly overruns, then, offer the famous labels at bargain prices. The Maman effort has done well. Starting with a small store eight years ago, the Mamans now proudly oversee six large stores throughout San Diego.

The stores are organized into a sportswear section, and a designer district section which carries high fashion and evening wear at discount prices. Racks of clothes and accessory cases fill the interior of Price Breakers. The decor isn't fancy but the bargains are terrific. The store is a haven for the discriminating buyer who wants designer labels at affordable prices.

Danny Maman says, "There's no place like this place anyplace! A bargain house like this you find once in a lifetime, sometimes never!"

(See special invitation in the Appendix.)

WORKOUT WEAR UNLIMITED
3545 Midway Drive Suite F
San Diego, CA 92110
Tel. (619) 224-2277
Hrs: Monday   10:00 a.m. - 8:00 p.m.
           Tue. - Thu.   10:00 a.m. - 9:00 p.m.
           Fri. - Sat.   10:00 a.m. - 6:30 p.m.
Visa, MasterCard, AMEX and Discover are accepted.

If you're looking for the best in fitness apparel, consider a stop at Workout Wear. They specialize in running and aerobic gear and carry such brand names as Flexitard, Dance France, Brookes, Danskin and many others.

According to the folks at Workout Wear, there are three stages in the evolution of a fitness wardrobe. Beginners often don "sweats" in an attempt to be inconspicuous about what they have to lose. However, the minute they notice a difference in their shape, it's off with the sweats and on to stage two, characterized by more style and color, as the newly initiated fitness buff combines tights with leotards and baggy T-shirts. Finally, when they've reached their ideal shape, stage three sets in. In a word, this stage is "sexy." This is the time for skimpy leotards, high-cut running shorts and belts to cinch up that tiny waist.

Workout wear carries something for every stage and all the accessories you'll need, such as weights, headbands and books.

ARTS AND CRAFTS

ARTS AND CRAFTS CENTER OF MISSION HILLS
928 Ft. Stockton Street
San Diego, CA 92103
Tel. (619) 297-ARTS
Hrs: Mon. - Fri.   9:00 a.m. - 9:00 p.m.
Credit cards are not accepted.

Like its beauty, the value of art lies in sharing it. Because neither a masterpiece nor a child's first small drawing can be appreciated unless it is seen, Carol Mayfield and Katie Zolezzi opened the Arts and Crafts Center to bring together anyone and everyone interested in art in any form. It is a school and workshop, an environment where artists can share what they do with the community and with each other, where the more experienced can help those who are just beginning, and everyone can find someone to appreciate the latest creation.

There are three classroom-workshops and a display gallery in the light and airy building, with different things going on in each of them at any given time. There seems to be no limit to the media available with which to work. The association of people working together in different forms is both instructive and stimulating to others. There are children working with clay, paper and basket reeds, and learning to sew; young people are crafting stained glass and practicing calligraphy, while others are learning oil painting, watercolor, and how to make mobiles. The classes are small, but not so small the synergy of a working group is lost; no fewer than eight and no more than ten in a class.

If this center sounds like a place for children, it is; but it's also an art environment for teenagers, and adults as well as a school where teachers can come to learn more about teaching art in their own classrooms. In fact, it's where anyone can go who has something to share as well as something to learn.

ART GALLERIES

BEASLEY GALLERY
2802 Juan Street
San Diego, CA 92110
Tel. (619) 295-0075
Hrs: Mon. - Sat.   10:00 a.m. - 5:30 p.m.
Visa, MasterCard, AMEX, Diners Club and Carte Blanche are accepted.

For the up and coming artist and long time professional alike, the Beasley Gallery is the place to see and be seen. This gallery is light, inviting, and not crowded. Murray Tarleton, who owns the gallery, believes in personal, friendly service. He also has a handpicked staff of highly qualified professionals who do consulting for corporate art as well as private.

The gallery specializes in the best regional artists in the country and is a very popular gallery. The theme of the art is mostly contemporary and abstract. Total service to the customer is give from preservation of art to custom framing and lighting. A few of the noted artists represented by Beasley Galleries include Richard Baron, Lloyd Blakley, Jeannette Debonne, Anne Ebree, Fritizi Morrison, Geer Morton, Dyan McClimon and Clint Stoddard. You will enjoy visiting the Beasley Gallery where you will see represented the finest contemporary works on the West Coast.

THE CONNOISSEUR
3165 Adams Avenue
San Diego, CA 92116
Tel. (619) 284-1132
Hrs: Mon. - Tue.   10:00 a.m. - 5:00 p.m.
             Thursday   10:00 a.m. - 5:00 p.m.
             Friday   12:00 noon - 5:00 p.m.
Visa, MasterCard and AMEX are accepted.

Although more than thirty dealers line San Diego's Antique Row on Adams Avenue, one shop clearly stands out from all the rest. In business at the same location for over twenty-one years, The Connoisseur has earned a solid reputation among serious antique buffs both for its honesty and for the quality of its collections. Owners Jackie and Trigg Stewart are long-time collectors who have passed their passion for the best of everything along to their customers.

The Connoisseur specializes in fine eighteenth and nineteenth century English and American furniture, along with period accessories. They are equally well-known for their porcelains, especially blue Staffordshire, Meissen and Chinese export, and an unusually extensive selection of early American samplers. You will find value upon value in this treasure house of collectibles-- early clocks and time pieces, Dedham pottery, Sevres, art glass, firearms, Tiffany, Patek-Philipe, Mettlech, and a superb collection of Georgian silver.

Do plan time for a visit to The Connoisseur and get to know the Stewarts. Their eclectic showroom is irresistible, and the quality and beauty of their wares are unsurpassed on the West Coast.

STRICTLY GRAPHICS
4465 La Jolla Village Drive
University Towne Center
San Diego, CA 92122
Tel. (619) 450-1821
Hrs: Mon. - Fri.   10:00 a.m. - 9:00 p.m.
        Saturday   10:00 a.m. - 6:00 p.m.
        Sunday   12:00 noon - 5:00 p.m.
Visa, MasterCard, AMEX and Discover are accepted.

Strictly Graphics combines the best of graphic art with the finest of contemporary framing. Their unique blend of limited edition and graphic art attracts viewers from all over Southern California. Come in and meet Jim and Celeste Piper, owners of Strictly Graphics, and their manager Lisa Leonard. These friendly and knowledgeable people will help you select the perfect piece of art for your home or business needs. The gallery features contemporary art as well as impressionist, Southwestern and Oriental art. Their beautiful selection of limited edition art includes artists such as Pegge Hopper, Sawada, Gorman, Carol Grigg and Bob Boreman.
Strictly Graphics also offers a corporate decorating service and has provided many San Diego businesses with the finest art available at a competitive cost.
Customer service and satisfaction is the name of the game for Strictly Graphics; they are determined to provide the very highest quality product available. All work is fully guaranteed. Special services offered include custom framing, matting and design. You'll find their expertise helpful in all these areas. So come in and visit. Jim, Celeste and Lisa look forward to meeting you!

TARBOX GALLERY
1202 Kettner Boulevard
San Diego, CA 92101
Tel. (619) 234-5020
Hrs: Tue. - Fri.   11:00 a.m. - 9:00 p.m.
        Saturday   5:00 p.m. - 10:00 p.m.
Closed Sundays and Mondays.
Visa and MasterCard are accepted.

Visiting is a pleasant experience at the Tarbox Gallery. Owner/Director Ruth Tarbox has chosen an inviting combination of greys and raspberry colors setting off the paintings and sculptures in a homelike atmosphere. The gallery, which has been established for seventeen years, first in La Jolla and, for the last three years downtown, is well-known for its wide ranging selection of carefully chosen art. There are national artists in all media and new artists, rated as good early investments, are premiered regularly in bi-monthly shows.   The gallery offers one of the finest selections of room sized sculptures in the city. Service is friendly and knowledgeable. The location is the restored historic McClintock Plaza Building where two of San Diego's finest restaurants face the gallery in the tiered atrium.

Projectors are always ready to show the slides of additional art carried by the gallery. Semi-classical music from compact discs is a soft background for your viewing.

Framing designs are offered for customers wishing something new. The actual work is done by a custom frameshop. Expert shipping service is available for any of your art choices. You will find that the Tarbox Gallery offers an enjoyable interlude in your day or evening.

THE WOODEN BIRD GALLERY
Mission Center Mall/ Camino del Rio
San Diego, CA 92108
Tel. (619) 450-0677
Hrs: Mon. - Fri.   10:00 a.m. - 9:00 p.m.
       Saturday   10:00 a.m. - 6:00 p.m.
       Sunday   12:00 noon - 5:00 p.m.
Visa, MasterCard, AMEX, Discover and The Wooden Bird Credit Cards are accepted.
Also,
I-5/University Towne Centre
4545 La Jolla Drive
La Jolla, CA 92122

At first glance, it's hard to believe the joyous celebration of American wildlife and western art in The Wooden Bird Galleries sprang from the leisure time interest of an intrepid antique collector.

Ray E. Johnson, using an antique lathe as a prototype, came up with a modern equivalent and began producing incredibly smoothly carved decoys in 1975. Soon he opened a showroom next to the factory, then a retail store in St. Paul, Minnesota. The company added more locations, kept growing, and now there are Wooden Bird Galleries California as well as in the Midwest. The Wooden Bird's woodcarving selection has grown to nearly thirty varieties, including waterfowl and gamebirds.

Along the way, The Wooden Bird Galleries started showing and selling limited edition prints and lithographs by many of America's noted wildlife and western artists. Art now is the focal point of the galleries. Artists include Olaf Wieghorst, Michael Atkinson, Bev Doolittle, Robert Bateman, Ozz Franca,

Derk Hansen, Terry Redlin, Keneth Riley, Les Didier, Ted Blaylock and Jerry Raedeke. And they have become the San Diego source for original weavings by Mexico's Zapotec Indians, symbolic stone fetiches carved by Zuni Indians and truly unique Southwestern gift items.

And to think the whole thing started back in St. Bonifacius, Minnesota, population 700.

AUTO RENTAL

SOUTHWEST CAR RENTAL
1111 Fashion Valley Road
San Diego, CA 92108
Tel.   (619) 291-RENT
          (800) 551-7251
Hrs: Mon. - Fri.   8:00 a.m. - 6:00 p.m.
          Sat. - Sun.   8:00 a.m. - 5:00 p.m.
Visa, MasterCard, AMEX, Carte Blanche, Diners Club and Discover are accepted.

What causes an auto rental and leasing company to stand out among all the others, including the national "No. 1" and "No. 2"? Simple: personalized service, extra service, friendly service and a choice of vehicles unheard of and unavailable at the larger national outfits. In fact, their slogan is "The luxury of choice - for less."

Although Southwest has been around for almost thirty years, it's biggest change and growth have taken place during the past two. In 1986 the company was carved into three entities, Southwest Leasing, Southwest Motor Car and Southwest Car Rental, to provide the best in service and equipment to three distinct clientele. Under the management of Karen Christman-Hutter the fleet of rental vehicles has grown from forty to over 200. There are commercial and corporate accounts in both rentals and long-term leasing, sales, and consumer rentals, and a long list of special services such as airport service, vehicle delivery and pickup, and special touches such as cellular phones in some of the cars. The most distinguishing feature of the company is the variety of vehicles available for rent or lease, from budget cars to the classiest, and from standard to the unusual. If you're in the mood to cruise in a Porsche or Ferrari, or want to arrive in style in a Rolls or Mercedes, Southwest has them.

A wide choice of vehicles, fair prices, personal service and a commitment to all aspects of quality have made Southwest prominent in the automotive rental and leasing business.

(See special invitation in the Appendix.)

BAKERY

THE DESSERT CART
4414 Baynard Street
San Diego, CA 92109
Tel. (619) 483-2990
Hrs: Mon. - Sat.   9:00 a.m. - 5:00 p.m.

The Dessert Cart is the answer to any cake lover's prayer. It's an irresistible kind of store that draws you back again and again.

It started when Eileen Droege wanted to bring a "real New York cheesecake" to San Diego. She's accomplished that and a lot more. Now there are eleven different flavors to choose from including the original New York, Amaretto, Mocha Kahlua, Lemonade, Orange Delight, Raspberry Daquiri, Strawberry Romanoff, Black Forest, White Chocolate Marble, Chocolate Chip and Coconut Creme. These cheesecakes are massive, feeding up to twenty people each. The Dessert Cart also makes "petite" cheesecakes that serve twelve people. Eileen wasn't satisfied with just making cheesecakes, however, and has expanded her line to include a variety of other cakes, pies and baked goods.

Brownies from the Dessert Cart are gaining quite a reputation. They consist of a layer of chocolate cake and nuts, a layer of chocolate chips, a layer of caramel and a final layer of chocolate icing. The stuff legends are made of.

The Dessert Cart is located in a quaint chalet style building, caters to individuals and restaurants, and is a "Best Choice" for anyone with a sweet tooth.

BED AND BREAKFAST INNS

BALBOA PARK INN
3402 Park Boulevard
San Diego, CA 92103
Tel. (619) 298-0823
Visa, MasterCard, AMEX and Diners Club are accepted.

You can swing into the room named for Tarzan's ancestral estate, or be carried up the staircase to a bedroom fit for Scarlett O'Hara. Either way, you'll be enjoying the Balboa Park Inn.

Each room is decorated in its own contemporary motif. Tarzan's Greystoke has a touch of the jungle, specifically designed for visiting curators of the nearby San Diego Zoo. And Tara has a feel of the old south, Scarlett O'Hara and Clark Gable. Built in 1915 for the World's Fair, the Spanish colonial style Inn features twenty-five rooms and suites clustered around a courtyard. The smiles and the personal service that you get from the staff help to make every stay here special. It's the kind of place that makes you wish that home was like this. Lily Tomlin checked in one day and stayed for six weeks. Among the optional services are breakfast in bed, picnics to go , and romantic candlelight dinners. All suites include sitting area, queen size bed, refrigerator and premium cable TV. Special features include fireplaces, private decks, patios, wet bars and in-bath jacuzzi tubs.

The inn is located in a quiet residential neighborhood on the north edge of Balboa Park. It's just a short walk to fine museums, shops, restaurants and the Old Globe Theater. At the Balboa Inn, even a swinger can get carried away.

BRITT HOUSE
406 Maple Street
San Diego, CA 92103
Tel. (619) 234-2926
Hrs: Check in time   4:00 p.m. - 8:00 p.m.
Visa, MasterCard and AMEX are accepted.

A favorite gettaway for Hollywood types seeking a weekend escape, the Britt House offers its guests private accommodations with the charm of a 100 year old Queen Ann Victorian mansion on a quarter block of formal gardens.

Each of the rooms is different, but in every one of them you'll find complimentary cookies, oranges, and fresh flowers. Bathrobes are provided. Each room has its own stuffed animals or dolls to help keep you company in the dark. Each of the nine rooms have an air of posh amid polished wood and glass. Everywhere there are windows: bay windows, floor-to-ceiling windows, stained glass windows.

One of the outstanding features of the Britt House is the food, for which owner/innkeeper Dawn Martin is rightfully proud. Tea is served every afternoon with fresh baked goodies, all from scratch. Breakfast is a real treat, especially with the freshly-baked yeast bread. Expect a few distractions from the delightful smells coming from the kitchen. For bed and breakfast accommodations, Britt House is a "Best Choice" in charm and comfort.

EDGEMONT INN
1955 Edgemont Street
San Diego, CA 92102
Tel.   (619)   238-1677
        (800)   822-1955 Southern CA

In the year 1900, the Edgemont Inn was first built by a Senorita from Mexico, little did she realize at the time what a beautiful bed and breakfast inn it would eventually become. The original structure had a distinct Spanish air about it, but in 1932, after renovation by a talented French architect, it took on a new flavor, one of comfort and elegance. Today, the Edgemont Inn is owned by Rosemary Johnson, who is proud to welcome guests to share the amenities of her home.

Edgemont Inn has four guest rooms decorated in their own special mood. The Ribbons and Roses room features white wicker and chintz, all pink, yellow and blue and a double bed that's very fluffy. The Western room is warm and comfortable with a touch of the old west. It features a wooden double bed, panelled walls and a ceiling fan. The Country room is a cheery chamber filled with dolls and teddy bears. It has a balcony and California king/twin beds. Finally, there's the Bridal Suite. It's an extra large room with a private bath and a king brass bed. From this room, share a sunset or enjoy the moonlight from your own balcony.

Awake to the sound of birds chirping and the delicious scents arising from the fresh brewed coffee and baking bread. Breakfast is served when you are ready, and is sure to satisfy any appetite. It includes Belgian waffles, fruits, breads, omletes, breakfast meats and much more. Ahhh, if only the Senorita could have seen this. She would have been proud of the Edgemont Inn. Come, share it's heritage and enjoy.

HERITAGE PARK BED AND BREAKFAST INN
2470 Heritage Park Row
San Diego, CA 92110
Tel. (619) 295-7088

When you want to keep a reputation for being the most romantic place in town, you've got to go out of your way, even if it means rounding up a dozen rubber duckies for a couple to enjoy in their bath.

And that's just what the staff at the Heritage Park Bed and Breakfast Inn had to do one evening. Of course, there have been many more conventional requests, like calling in a chamber music quartet for a couple to listen to over their dinner. It wasn't enough for owner Lori Chandler to furnish and refurbish a nine room Victorian house set on a 7.8 acre park in Old Town, fill it with charming antiques, and hang out the "Vacancy" sign. She wanted to make romance the place's specialty. The huge wraparound porch is a favorite place for weddings. The Heritage Park Bed and Breakfast Inn is where illusions become reality, a place that dreams are made of. The inn is dolled up with antiques and lace. In the early evenings, guests are served Hors d'oeuvres and beverages in the parlor, where they can later sit down to watch a vintage movie.

As part of the pampering process, guests get to choose when they want their breakfast served, and may have it in their rooms or out on the veranda. It is a full breakfast, featuring an award-winning Strawberry Jam Loaf. So for a "Best Choice" in breakfast, beds, service and romance, The Heritage Park is a real standout.

KEATING HOUSE INN
2331 Second Avenue
San Diego, CA 92101
Tel. (619) 239-8585
Hrs: Check in time   2:00 p.m. - 5:00 p.m.

On a hillside overlooking the San Diego Bay is a Victorian house many would love to call home. Many do become guests of the innkeepers, George Pearn and Jason Price, for whom this has been home for fifteen years.

It was just three years ago that Pearn and Price and their friendly family of Irish setters began welcoming guests to stay in the beautiful Queen Anne building. Built in the 1880s, the house has a gabled roof featuring an octagonal turret with a conical peak. Four guest rooms share two baths in this home decorated with plants and country antiques. You can relax in the lush gardens or in the sun-shaded patios. The Inn is just three blocks from Balboa Park with its museums and its many shops and restaurants.

The rates are very reasonable, but you still get touches such as fresh flowers, complimentary wine and a continental breakfast of juices, fruit and fresh-baked bread. The back parlor has a grand piano and guests often play the piano and socialize there. With all this, it's easy to see why guests begin feeling at home at Keating House Inn.

BOATS

CALIFORNIA YACHT SALES
2040 Harbor Island Drive Suite 111
San Diego, CA 92101
Tel. (619) 295-9669
Hrs: Mon. - Sun.   9:00 a.m. - 5:00 p.m.

Very few of us haven't dreamed of owning our own boat and escaping the pressures of daily life on an ocean going whim. Well, for those of you who wish to make that dream a reality, California Yacht Sales has the integrity, knowledge, and personal care to make your purchase an intelligent, comfortable decision.

When dealing with the staff at California Yachts Sales, it is refreshing to find a sales philosophy that emphasizes a quality transaction, rather than the commission broker who is mainly interested in just closing the sale. Proprietor Suzi Green, as well as the rest of the staff, has a long history of nautical experience, including 18,000 miles of blue water sailing. Among the personal touches that are part of a sale are the inclusion of couples in the planning of a purchase so that the interior, as well as the exterior are comfortable and agreeable to both parties. California Yacht Sales will take care of any contingencies necessary to the completion of your yachting purchase. This includes finding moorage for your craft and residence contracts with the state if required.

California Yacht Sales is a well established and well respected brokerage in the community with a working relationship with many other brokers. This assures the network needed to find just the boat you request. Isn't about time you look into "the best in floating condominiums" at California Yacht Sales.

KETTENBURG MARINE
2810 Carleton Street
San Diego, CA 92106
Tel.   (619)   224-8211
          (800)   321-1307   CA
          (800)   231-7335   U.S.
Hrs: Mon. - Fri.   7:30 a.m. - 6:00 p.m.
          Saturday   8:00 a.m. - 5:00 p.m.
          Sunday   8:30 a.m. - 3:00 p.m.
Visa, MasterCard and AMEX are accepted.
Also,
3010 Carleton Street
San Diego, CA 92106

When one owns a boat, you can bet that a good marine shop is at the top of their list of those places that they visit often. A person who takes boating seriously is always looking for ways to improve their knowledge of sailing as well as the condition of their craft. If you're looking for a good marine shop, visit Kettenburg Marine. They're the professionals who can navigate you through any of your boating needs.

Kettenburg Marine is owned by a family who knows more than the ropes. J.J. Fetter Isler, the daughter, was named 1986 Rolex Yachtswoman of the Year. What's more, son-in-law Peter Isler is the Navigator of the highly acclaimed vessel, *Stars & Stripes*. With this background, you can easily ascertain why the services and quality of merchandise at this marine shop are the best on the West Coast. Offering a large selection of marine hardware, Kettenburg has whatever you might be seeking. For marine electronics, their selection is overwhelming and has to be seen to be believed. Engines and accessories of all shapes, sizes and make can also be found at Kettenburg.

For repair services, you need not worry. This facility accommodates a travel lift, two marine railways and a 150 ton synchro-lift which allows the company to service recreational and commercial boats from 20 to 115 feet. Kettenburg Marine is also the largest Yacht oriented facility in Southern California. This is a boat lover's paradise. So with this in mind, make a sharp tack over to Kettenburg Marine for anything pertaining to boating services.

BOAT CRUISES

ENSENADA EXPRESS

1150 North Harbor Drive B Street Pier
San Diego, CA 92101
Tel.   (619) 232-2109
        (800) 422-5008 CA
        (800) 926-4815 US
Hrs: Mon. - Sun.   8:00 a.m. - 5:00 p.m.
Visa, MasterCard and AMEX are accepted
Reservations are requested.

Ensenada Express is an absolutely wonderful idea, combining a visit to Ensenada with a cruise down the coast of Baja California, all in one day. Not only does it make a great day, but it allows you to avoid the heavy traffic and long lines at U.S. and Mexican customs and immigration at the border. While the less imaginative wait, the slick one hundred foot motor cruiser of Ensenada Express is cruising out of San Diego Harbor and along the Pacific shore.

At 9:00 the vessel departs Pier B of the San Diego Cruise Ship Terminal and slowly ventures out of the harbor; an enjoyable beginning for the day. You'll sail past Coronado Bridge, the city skyline, and pass by elements of one of the two largest naval fleets in the world, then out into the coastal waters and South for a three hour cruise at twenty-two knots to arrive at Ensenada just after noon. The cruise itself is worth the fare; the vessel is comfortable and attractive, and if you wish you can enjoy breakfast on board, served hot and fresh from the galley. On the return trip after an afternoon spent sightseeing and shopping, dinner entrees are available on board, and a full service bar is open. For the adventurous, a part of the afternoon can be spent cruising to *La_Bufadora*, The Blowhole, still leaving time for shopping and wandering in Ensenada. If you wish, an overnight journey can be arranged, traveling to Ensenada one day and returning the next.   Overnight accommodations can be arranged. Reservations are requested.

In addition to the regular cruises, Wedding Cruise Parties can be arranged, the price not only includes the champagne, flowers and cake, but the ceremony too, performed on board by the ship's captain. The vessel is also available for charters.

(See special invitation in the Appendix.)

RED WITCH
1380 Harbor Island Drive
San Diego, CA 92101
Tel. (619) 542-0646
Visa, MasterCard and AMEX are accepted.

Are you looking for something special to do? Perhaps something exciting and adventurous? Well, have you got a surprise coming. It's called the Red Witch and it's ready to take you upon one of San Diego's most fabulous bay cruises.

The Red Witch is a gaff rigged schooner of classic design, her lines and proportions are based on working schooners which operated along the New England Seaboard and the American West Coast between the Civil War and the 1930s. Constructed in 1986 by master shipwright Nathaniel Zirlott, she consists of the finest materials, such as massive, double sawn frames of cypress and planking of choice Hondras mahogany. The Red Witch is seventy-two feet long overall and can accommodate as many as forty-nine people! If this isn't enough for you, they have the ability to provide additional vessels to augment their capacity.

The Red Witch makes regular bay cruises; two on Thursday and Friday and three on Saturday and Sunday. All bay cruises include snacks and soft drinks. There are special options which include live music or a beautiful wedding package. Sign up for a cruise and have the adventure of a lifetime.

(See special invitation in the Appendix.)

SAN DIEGO YACHT CHARTERS
1880 Haror Island Drive
San Diego, CA 92101
Tel.   (619)   297-4555
        (800)   444-4333
Hrs: Mon. - Fri.   9:00 a.m. - 5:00 p.m.
Visa and MasterCard are accepted.

Should you spend very much of your time near the water in San Diego, you will eventually be bitten by the sailing bug. Always tugging at your sense of adventure are the thousands of sailboats in this fair city of palm trees and warm breezes. Well, with some instruction from San Diego Yacht Charters you can go from a novice dreamer to being able to charter your own boat.

One of the best features of learning to sail at San Diego Yacht Charters is that you are able to stay aboard the vessel overnight and, by doing so, save the cost of a hotel room. No, you would not be sacrificing any of the amenities you would find in a hotel. Why? Because all instructional yachts include CNG stove, cassette stereo, cockpit cushions and full galley equipment, plus a highly trained professional captain. Once you have had the pleasure of completing the necessary instruction, you are then qualified to charter and captain you own boat from San Diego Yacht Charters.

While the instructional boats are all thirty-foot Catalina's, bareboat charter vessels are available from thirty to forty-five feet, depending upon your verifiable experience. All boats come equipped with the best electronics, safety equipment and ground tackle. So don't just sit around dreaming of your adventure, make it happen. At San Diego Yacht Charters you can turn your grandest fantasy into reality.

(See special invitation in the Appendix.)

SEAFORTH-MISSION BAY BOAT RENTAL
1641 Quiuira Road
San Deigo, CA 92109
Tel. (619) 223-1681
Hrs: Summer   Mon. - Sun.   7:00 a.m. - 7:00 p.m.
            Winter   Mon. - Sun.   8:00 a.m. - 5:00 p.m.
Visa, MasterCard and AMEX are accepted.

It's hard to believe that so many different choices could be availible to the ocean going water sport enthusiast in one place. If Seaforth Boat Rentals in San Diego does not have a water craft to fit your fancy, bets are that you won't find it elsewhere.

Jerry Kurtz and his family have been developing their business for the last ten years into a very complete, well maintained, and personally run facility. You like sailing? Try this list on for size: Hobie 12, Lido 14, Omega 14, Newport 16, Victory 21, and Hobie 16. All these boats rent by the hour. If you are looking for more worthy ships then a Santana 21 or Catalina 30 are available. For those of you in the crowd who prefer the wind whipping through your hair at a more exciting clip, five different varieties of speed boats are up for rent. Try skiing in the bay. Ski boats are set up to go. Of course lessons are availible for all of the above mentioned activities. Tamer craft can be rented also in the form of peddleboats, or canoes. If you haven't tried it yet,come on down and get into that popular new sport sailboarding. All kinds of fishing options exist, including sport fishing charters.

Plan ahead and reserve your day for fun in the sun at Seaforth Boat Rentals where you make the choice and they provide with a welcome as sunny as the day. Also a sister operation of Seaforth is at Chula Vista Marina in Chula Vista. Stop by or call (619) 585-SAIL.

BOOK STORES

GROUNDS FOR MURDER

2707 Congress Street
San Diego, CA 92110
Tel. (619) 294-9497
Hrs: Tue. - Sun.   11:00 a.m. - 6:00 p.m.
Visa and MasterCard are accepted.

If it's cloak and dagger you thirst for, then look no more! Grounds For Murder is a bookstore specializing in nothing but mysteries.

Founded six years ago by transplanted Midwesterner Phyllis Brown, Grounds For Murder is stuffed to overflowing with new and old whodunnits, detective stories, tales of adventure, romantic mysteries, suspense and espionage. There are also children's mysteries, stories of true crime, as well as reference books about mysteries and mystery writers.

Looking for the obscure? Grounds For Murder offers a search service and will mail order books anywhere that has a postal service. There is also a used book section and a selection of gifts, games and periodicals.

Grounds For Murder frequently hosts author autograph receptions. You might meet your favorite sleuth there. Housed on the second floor of the "Old Town Mercado" with its Spanish stucco and tile roof motif, Grounds For Murder is a welcome haven for mystery aficionados to browse.

MIDWAY BOOKS

3944 West Point Loma Boulevard Suite E
San Diego, CA 92110
Tel. (619) 222-1174
Hrs: Mon. - Fri.   10:00 a.m. - 7:00 p.m.
       Saturday   10:00 a.m. - 6:00 p.m.
       Sunday   12:00 noon - 5:00 p.m.
Visa, MasterCard and AMEX are accepted.

In the maze of self-help programs available today, Midway Books has carved out a corner concentrating on the metaphysical with a particular emphasis on handwriting analysis. Owner Beverly Keys has twenty years experience in the field.

Motivated by a desire to offer a means for people to better their lives, Beverly opened her store six years ago. She has since developed a certain amount of notoriety for her skills and now does individual counseling by appointment. Also through the bookstore a variety of classes and seminars are offered.   Among the services offered are self-help for cancer sufferers.

Recently Ms. Keys was interviewed and put to the test on her handwriting analyzing skills by the local newspaper. After being given a few anonymous samples of local celebrities, she proceeded to give an analysis of each that was appropriate to each writers position in life.

However, Beverly's emphasis is not so much in identifying people as in using the handwriting analysis to identify character traits and implement changes where desired through a change in writing style. Midway Books has a variety of motivational helps in stock. Surely this would be an interesting stop along your way.

(See special invitation in the Appendix.)

UPSTART CROW
Seaport Village
835C West Harbor Drive
San Diego, CA 92101
Tel. (619) 232-4855
Hrs: Sun. - Thu.   9:00 a.m. - 10:00 p.m.
           Fri. - Sat.   9:00 a.m. - 11:00 p.m.
Visa, MasterCard, AMEX and checks are accepted.

If unusual book stores turn you on, you have an extravagant treat waiting for you. Upstart Crow offers comforts far beyond the ordinary-- not only a very fine collection of books, but also an, "Intellectual espresso bar," that serves gourmet coffee and delicious pastries, with comfortable spaces for conversation.

You can sit awhile, sip awhile, and browse to your heart's content. What more could a book lover ask for? For many years a vital part of San Diego's literary scene, Upstart Crow is a full service bookstore that specializes in fiction, poetry, drama and children's books. It also carries an extensive line of fine stationery and a unique collection of one of a kind craft items. Staff members enjoy talking about books and are extremely knowledgeable and very helpful.

New owners Marie Heacock, Ivor Sack and David Pain have continued the traditions of excellence and hospitality that built the store's outstanding reputation. In addition to the customary live entertainment several nights a week, they plan readings by local authors and poets, as well as forums to discuss books and topics of current interest. Truly, there's no better place in San Diego to find good conversation, good coffee and good books.

BRASS SHOP

BRASS TOWN
4004 Taylor Street
San Diego, CA 92110
Tel. (619) 296-4307
Hrs: Mon. - Sat.   10:00 a.m. - 6:00 p.m.
         Sunday   12:00 noon - 5:00 p.m.
Visa and MasterCard are accepted.
Also,
144 W. Washington Avenue
Escondido, CA 92025
Tel. (619) 747-0305

Located in the historical old town section of San Diego, Brass Town has been the most respected dealer of fine quality brass and fireplace accessories since 1952.

More brass than you have ever seen in one place is featured at Brass Town. There are picture frames, beautiful fireplace screens, numerous fireplace tool sets, chimes, candle holders, sculpture pieces of horses and seagulls, bathroom accessories, bookends, vases, wood buckets, the list goes on and on. Handmade bellows of ash, oak and other woods are also featured. The knowledgable staff will design custom fireplace enclosures. They also have wood burning stoves and gas barbeques.

You are sure to enjoy browsing in this "Best Choice" for anything you could possibly need in brass or fireplace accessories.

CAMPING RESORT

CAMPLAND ON THE BAY
2211 Pacific Beach Drive
San Diego, CA 92109
Tel. (619) 274-6260
Visa and MasterCard are accepted.

For a vacation of a lifetime, stay awhile at the famous Campland on the Bay in San Diego! This is far more than just a place to camp, it is *your* Destination Resort on Mission Bay. Once here, you don't have to leave as everything is provided for your camping pleasure; boat rentals, laundry, a grocery store, restaurant and playground.

Campland on the Bay is an incredibly picturesque site surrounded by the blue waters of Mission Bay. Campland on the Bay welcomes children and pets.

One of the main camping attractions for families is Section "P", special campsites for people who love the water and want their own private beach. Campland has seven hundred campsites and private banquet facilities that will accommodate up to a thousand people. On the bay, private boat slips are available as well. You may wish to wind surf, use paddle boats, canoes, ride inner tubes, or go fishing with full bait and tackle provided, all of this is available at your finger tips in this vacation paradise.

Top tourist attractions such as Sea World, the fabulous San Diego Zoo, Wild Animal Park and other favorites are only minutes away. During the summer season a water taxi is available to take guests to Sea World. Campers receive discounts on tickets year-round. If this isn't enough, you have many choices of bike rentals, scooter rentals and others as well. There are many beautiful gift boutiques for your shopping pleasure. The food at the Cafe on the Bay is delicious. One of many favorites campers enjoy is the Coconut Battered Shrimp. There are at least three nightly specials.

This campground by the bay is so popular, they recommend that you reserve your place in the sun up to a year in advance, and it is well worth the wait. A campsite near the beautiful bay is waiting for you at the fantastic Campland on the Bay.

(See special invitation in the Appendix.)

COFFEEHOUSES

JAVA
837 G Street Corner of 9th and 6th Streets
San Diego, CA, 92101
Tel.   (619) 235-4012
Hrs: Sun. - Thu.   11:00 a.m. - 1:00 a.m.
             Fri. - Sat.   11:00 a.m. - 2:00 a.m.
No credit cards are accepted.

The best of art and the best of coffee make for good conversation. Centered in the heart of San Diego's downtown art community, Java strives to be a pulse point for the neighborhood.

People come to Java to view the latest in contemporary California art and to share with friends thoughts and feelings of what it's all about. Java was conceived as a contemporary experience of Edward Hopper's painting "Nighthawks" by owner Douglas Simay. The coffee quality is as high as the art work and table conversations. Manager Stanley Fried oversees the selection and preparation of each bag and cup of java. Each cup is ground just prior to brewing and served with individual flair. European trained pastry chef, Karen Krasne, creates the finest in pastries. Douglas Simay says, "We support the community. We are very supportive of the work they do. This is a community service and we care about the people who make up the urban community."

Nothing is taken for granted at Java, from the coffee to the pastries to the art work and most of all to the conversations.   Java is the place to find a good brew of art, coffee and conversation.

PANNIKIN COFFEE & TEA
675 G Street
San Diego, CA 92101
Tel. (619) 232-2897
Hrs: Mon. - Sat.   9:00 a.m. - 6:00 p.m.
          Sunday   10:00 a.m. - 5:00 p.m.
Visa and MasterCard are accepted.

The first thing you'll notice a block away from Pannikin is the tantalizing aroma of roasting coffee which draws you inexorably to the store. Once there, you'll find an astonishing assortment of thrifty coffees from around the world. Some, like Sumatra, are familiar to coffee drinkers, others are so exotic as to be unheard of, but certainly worth trying. How about "Panamanian Volcan Chiriqui" for starters?

The tea is also intriguing, whether you like fragrant Earl Gray or a curious blend of your favorite Tisane, you'll find it here. A wonderful assortment of coffee makers and tea steepers are available for making the style you prefer, from Melior to Melitta, and espresso to cappuccino. Pannikin stores (there are more than one in San Diego) are more than purveyors of beans, leaves and machines. They vary in size and completeness, but in many you can enjoy a breakfast of eggs and pastry or a lunch of soup, salad and cheese board, along with a sweet and your favorite coffee or tea. The walls are hung with framed coffee bags from foreign places and old metal barn signs. Antique glass display counters hold a large assortment of goods from hand painted serving spoons to brass coasters.

Wonderful coffee and tea, good food, many machines and an assortment of interesting gifts and goods combine to make Pannikin well worth a visit.

QUEL FROMAGE?
523 University Avenue
San Diego, CA 92103
Tel. (619) 295-1600
Hrs: Sun. - Thu.   8:00 a.m. - 11:00 p.m.
          Fri. - Sat.   8:00 a.m. - 12:00 midnight

Are you craving a terrific cup of fresh ground coffee made with purified water and served with real half and half? There's only one place to get it in San Diego's uptown area, and that's at Quel Fromage. Nine years ago, Gene Coster and Richard Clifford saw the need for a good coffee shop in the area and did something about it by opening this delightful business.

Their espresso bar is a rescue project from the old WM. Penn Hotel in downtown San Diego, and adds a special ambiance to this oasis for the coffee lover. Coffee sacks of burlap adorn the walls, and there is a small upstairs balcony that creates it's own special mood. But atmoshpere apart, the delicious aromas of the many different types of coffees and tasty foods beckons the attention. Several chocolate desserts, eight kinds of truffles, cheesecake and ice cream, as well as bagels and quiche of the day are only a few of the delicacies you can enjoy with your cappuccino, espresso or any of the special blends of coffees.

Quel Fromage also hosts an art show every month to give the up-and-coming artists an opportunity to be shown. This diverse coffee shop is also one of the best places to find out what's going on around the community. Notices of meetings, seminars and gatherings are all posted on a handy bulletin board. Quel Fromage is a true boon to this area of San Diego. Stop by for a cup of coffee, a gourmet delicacy and some fine conversation.

SAME OLD GRIND
3007 Clairemont Drive #E
San Diego, CA 92117
Tel. (619) 276-7500
Hrs: Mon. - Sat.   10:00 a.m. - 6:00 p.m.
          Sunday   12:00 noon - 5:00 p.m.

While walking around in the Village, if suddenly you find   your feet carrying you after the aroma of rich, freshly brewed   coffee...don't fight the urge. Follow the siren perfume to its end, to the Same Old Grind. You'll enter a shop that possesses a warmth of wood that will welcome you like a wonderful living room. Owner Pat Phelps will offer you a sample of fresh roasted coffee to reward your odyssey.

Coffee! Coffee! Coffee everywhere! Pat maintains a full variety of freshly roasted coffee beans to satisfy every taste and every pocketbook. Also available are her own blended, flavored dessert coffees, at least ten different flavors at any one time. You can even purchase unique gift boxes to be mailed anywhere within the continental United States. One of your gift selections might include exciting chocolate covered espresso beans.

Although Pat is proud to present the most competitive prices in town for the quality offered, you can still go crazy over some very special coffees, such as Jamaica Blue Mountain or Pure Kona. Coffee and tea accessories also are available from basic to high-tech.   Toshiba and Krups brewers and grinders are here, English bone china tea pots, and even a variety of animal puppet pot holders.   Your complete coffee and tea needs can be met at the Same Old Grind. Follow your nose.

(See special invitation in the Appendix.)

DOLL SHOP

YE OLDE DOLL SHOPPE
2465 Hertiage Park Row
San Diego, CA 92110
Tel. (619) 291-1979
Hrs: Mon. - Sun.   10:30 a.m. - 5:30 p.m.
Visa and MasterCard are accepted.

A drive up to the restored yellow and brown Victorian that houses Ye Olde Doll Shoppe immediately sets the stage for what you will find inside. There are three separate rooms filled with fabulous dolls and collectibles from around the world.

Alice in Wonderland shrank to a small size after drinking the magic potion and you may think you have too as you enter through the front door into this kingdom of small folk. Indeed the first items to greet the visitor is a showcase of wonderous miniatures. Arlys Rapp loves the beautiful and exquisite and has filled this shoppe with nothing but the best. A variety of the best and the small is there. Keep wandering and you will find a whole room that contains one intricate and fully appointed dollhouse. This little house is completely furnished for the discriminating doll. Stained glass lamps hang over desks. Mirrors are placed to provide convenient primping. Invite your friends over to play a little chamber music in the parlor on the provided instruments. If you'd rather have a paper doll to call your own, why not go with a celebrity the likes of Clark Gable or Vivian Leigh. There are books of paper dolls at Ye Olde Doll Shoppe. Almost everyone who thinks of collectable dolls usually thinks of porcelain at some point. Ye Old Doll Shoppe has over twenty two doll makers represented with one the world's largest collections of Porcelain.

Many other wonderful collectibles are contained in this magical shop. The list goes on with hand painted eggs, music boxes, beautiful thimbles, jewelry boxes, bisque figurines, and more. So make your way to Heritage Park near Old Town, up to the old Victorian and venture into wonderland at Ye Olde Doll Shoppe.

FISHING SUPPLIES

HOOK LINE AND SINKER
1224 Scott Street
San Diego, CA 92106
Tel. (619) 224-1336

San Diego is the home to some of the world's best deep-sea fishing. It's also the home of one of the best bait and tackle shops any angler could ever hope to find. Namely, Hook Line and Sinker.

Located at the entrance to Shelter Island, Hook Line and Sinker is a fourteen year old business with a proven track record for providing correct bait for the people who love to fish. The success of their products and service speaks for itself when you look at the hundreds of trophy pictures hanging on the walls. Whether you are a novice or an experienced angler, you will appreciate the help from the courteous and professional staff. Manager Daniel Hart is a former captain of a sportfishing boat and has a well earned reputation for knowing where the fish are and what to bait to use.

If you would like to do a little fishing in Mexico, Hook Line and Sinker can take care of all the necessary boat permits and licenses. They also handle the permits for California. Hook Line and Sinker is a specialty shop in the finest tradition of the word. Anything related to deep-sea fishing can be found. For a good bet towards insuring a successful fishing trip, cast on over to Hook Line and Sinker.

(See special invitation in the Appendix.)

SEAFORTH SPORTFISHING
1717 Quivira Road
San Diego, CA 97109
Tel.   (619) 224-3383
Hrs: Mon. - Sun.   6:00 a.m. - 6:00 p.m.

Have you got the urge to try sport fishing in the warm sun of the tropics? You might be surprised to find that ideal trip closer to home. Sport fishing in the semi-tropical climate of San Diego can be a dream come true.

Seaforth Sportfishing Corporation has the experience and know-how to bring you back to port with the catch of the day that includes a tan with your fish. In operation since 1959, Seaforth has the distinction of being one of the two oldest sportfishing operations in San Diego. It is experience that counts in this business, because that's what catches fish. Catch them they do, by the boat load. Summer fishing is best in the kelp beds. Day long runs for Albacore tuna will really get you a fish that fights for his right to the ocean. Winter fishing, minus the suntan, is best for Rock Cod. Everything you might need is available on board, either for sale or rent. A fleet of seven boats with capacities from 50 to 150 are available for individuals or private charter. For you whale fans Seaforth runs whale watching trips spring and fall.

Write to Seaforth today and they will send brochures to help you plan a sportfishing trip into your vacation. You might be surprised at how close to home paradise really is.

FLAGS

ALL THE KING'S FLAGS
2707 Congress Street
San Diego, CA 92110
Tel.   (619) 295-9392
        (800) 428-5400 CA
        (800) 223-FLAG   US
Hrs: Mon. - Fri.   9:00 a.m. - 6:00 p.m.
        Saturday   9:00 a.m. - 5:00 p.m.
Visa, MasterCard and AMEX are accepted.

If you are in the market for a flag, chances are you will find it at All the King's Flags in Old Town, San Diego. There are flags from over 160 countries in stock at any given time, and of course, every state in the Union is represented (territories, too). Flags range in size from 4" x 6" miniatures for the desk top all the way up to 30' x 50' - a great way to really let the neighbors know where your heart lies!

All The King's Flags first began in Arizona over twenty years ago, founded by Warren King, the current owner. His love of deep-sea fishing made him a regular visitor to San Diego. Finally, he devised a plan to help support his habit. He hired his son, Kerry, to open another flag store in San Diego, which he still manages. But that was four years, many fish and many flags ago.

Today, the staff at All The King's Flags is happy to demonstrate their knowledge and enthusiasm by telling you everything you've every wanted to know about flags, and more! It's easy to order by phone, and your flag can be mailed anywhere in the U.S.A., freight free. HAPPY FLAG WAVING!

FURNITURE

SCANDIA INTERIORS
3191 Sports Arena Boulevard
San Diego, CA 92110
Tel. (619) 225-9471
Hrs: Mon. - Sat.   10:00 a.m. - 6:00 p.m.
          Sunday   12:00 noon - 5:00 p.m.
Visa, MasterCard and AMEX are accepted.

Buying furniture, accessories for the home, special gifts, or just browsing for future purchases requires a setting that helps one visualize their actual purpose or use, whether decorative or practical. Scandia is such a place. In this large store with its pale gray carpeting and huge windows, furniture is displayed in a manner that provides the buyer with an idea of how to arrange it or use it in their home.

The finest quality European names in furniture made of teak, rosewood and leather, handmade rugs and a wide selection of useful and innovative cooking utensils are featured. These, as well as the finest Scandinavian crystal, china, linens and decorative pieces such as Orrefors, Dansk, Arabia, Rosenthal and Thomas Arcta will tempt anyone looking for ways to enhance the home.

Special services for individual decorating needs, advice, or special orders to provide exactly the right piece for you from anywhere in the world are offered. All you have to do is ask. Delivery, shipping and a minimum of a two year warranty are standard at Scandia, and a twenty-four to forty-eight hour home trial enables buyers to be certain that a piece of investment quality furniture is just right, taking the risk out of such a purchase. Even with all these services, you can rest assured the prices are always fair at Scandia.

GAMES

GAME TOWNE
3954 Harney Street in Old Town
San Diego, CA 92110
Tel. (619) 291-1666
Hrs: Mon. - Sat.   10:00 a.m. - 6:00 p.m.
December   Mon. - Sat.   10:00 a.m - 8:00 p.m.
All major credit cards are accepted.

Desperation is often the key to success. Such was the case when, eight years ago, Clark Knapp went in search of his favorite games. After a series of frustrating attempts, Clark threw in the towel and started his own store, Game Towne. Never again would he be disappointed when the urge to play a new game overcame him. Nor, he vowed, would anyone else. He made it his goal to satisfy game addicts everywhere.

And he has! Game Towne has absolutely everything in the way of games and puzzles and all the accessories. Recent favorites include "Pictionary" and all the new murder mystery and war games. To top it off, Game Towne offers discount prices on main line merchandise. There is even a catalog for mail order customers.

Game Towne recently moved to a new building, a beautiful Spanish stucco covered with flowering Bougainvillea. Now there is room for the new book section, computer games and software, antique game display and, of course, thousands of games.

As if that's not enough, Game Towne sponsors San Diego's annual Game-Fest, held each August. It's ten days of gaming mania, including over fifty game tournaments, costume competition, scores of game demonstrations, and over $1,500 in prizes!

GIFT SHOPS

THE CALICO COMPANY
1774 A Garnet Avenue
San Diego, CA 92109
Tel. (619) 274-2202
Hrs: Mon. - Fri.   10:00 a.m. - 7:00 p.m.
        Saturday   10:00 a.m. - 6:00 p.m.
        Sunday   11:00 a.m. - 4:00 p.m.
Visa, MasterCard and AMEX are accepted.
Also,
445 Encinitas Boulevard
Encinitas, CA 92024
Tel. (619) 274-2002

If it's made with love, you'll find it at The Calico Company. Specializing in country home decor and gifts, The Calico Company is the place to go for a one of a kind gift, even if its a gift to yourself.

That might be a fine antique, a bite of fudge, kitchen wear, linens, potpourri, a picture, a wreath and even a rocking horse. There are handmade dolls, baskets and folk rugs. Try on an apron for size or a ribbon for your hair. The personnel is knowledgeable, warm and helpful. They'll even take care of shipping that special goodie for you. People leave the shop with a feeling of happiness. If you drop in during Christmas season, you'll see that they have gone all out to deck the halls.

If you love country living, you'll find something special at The Calico Company.

CASA DE LA DAISY
2522 Congress Street
San Diego, CA 92110
Tel. (619) 291-9295
Hrs: Mon. - Sun.   10:00 a.m. - 5:00 p.m.
Visa and MasterCard are accepted.

Each of the rooms of this great one hundred year old red frame house are filled with dozens of contemporary artifacts appropriate to it. Owner Laverne Halterman has amassed a wonderful selection of special items for gifts or personal use, all hand made, and all products of local artisans.

The "look" of the items in Casa De la Daisy is out of the ordinary because they are not purchased from the usual trade shows. When you go into the dining room, you'll find collectible dinnerware, an assortment of items for the table and wall hangings appropriate to dining rooms. In the bedroom, are the hundreds of items which would go well in bedrooms anywhere in the country. Then, of course, there are the things which are universally enjoyed, from stuffed animals to life sized dolls, stained glass pieces and—believe it or not—designer brooms.

Casa de la Daisy is located in "Old town," and it seems a part of the past, down to the picnic table in the shade, for resting upon after wandering the streets of this great district. It's just another small service offered by this delightful store. They'll also wrap and ship your purchases anywhere in the U.S. So stroll along the shady path from San Diego Avenue—you'll find Casa de la Daisy a nice diversion and a splendid place to shop.

RUDOLPH SCHILLER'S BOOK AND MERCANTILE
2627 San Diego Avenue
San Diego, CA 92110
Tel. (619) 298-0108
Hrs: Sun. - Thu.   9:00 a.m. - 6:00 p.m.
           Fri. - Sat.   9:00 a.m. - 9:00 p.m.
No credit cards are accepted.

Step into Rudolph Schiller's and enter a different world, filled warmth and charm. Named for the first photographer in Old Town, whose house stood on the very same site in 1869, Rudolph Schiller's is filled with the smells and smiles of a bygone era.

Antique posters, gourmet foods, wonderful Dover books, seeds, old wooden barrels filled with delights, such as horehound and sassafras candy, Indian wall hangings, dulcimer and music box tapes await you. It is fun to explore and discover, as they strive to be unique.

John Locke, the proprietor at Rudolph Schiller's invites you to stop by "and set a spell after a leisure stroll through Old Town State Historic Park." You'll experience old-fashioned hospitality, the sights, smells and slowed down pace of the most delightful and unusual shops to be found.

SHARP CABRILLO GIFT CORNER
3475 Kenyon Street
San Diego, CA 92110
Tel. (619) 221-3544
Hrs: Mon. - Thu.   9:00 a.m. - 5:00 p.m.
                                   6:00 p.m. - 8:00 p.m.
            Friday   9:00 a.m. - 5:00 p.m.
            Saturday   11:00 a.m. - 2:00 p.m.
Visa and MasterCard are accepted on purchases of $10 or more.

This outstanding gift shop is staffed by volunteers from the community who give generously of their time and energy. It is located to the right of the main lobby entrance to the Sharp Cabrillo Hospital, just off Midway Drive in the heart of San Diego.

The Gift Corner is just as inviting as any "for profit" retail store anywhere in the community. An excellent selection of moderately priced, unique and tempting merchandise attracts a following of those who know the best places to shop for any occasion. You will find books, music boxes, jewelry and handmade items contributed by local artisans. Raggedy Ann and Andy dolls and stuffed animals by Avanti, for adults all make for delightful and unusual gifts.

Proceeds from sales of the Gift Corner are returned to the hospital and the community through the purchases and donations of major pieces of equipment, makes your purchases doubly rewarding.

(See special invitation in the Appendix.)

GOLF COURSES

MISSION BAY GOLF COURSE
2702 N Mission Bay Drive
San Deigo, CA 92109
Tel: (619) 273-1221
Hrs: Summer until 10:00 p.m.
            Winter until 9:00 p.m.
            Restaurant   Sun. - Sat.   7:00 a.m. - 9:00 p.m.
            Lounge   Open until   2:00 a.m.
Visa and MasterCard accepted

Billed as an executive golf course, Mission Bay Golf Course is a more than challenging par 3 course. While most of the holes average about 150 yards there are 4 par 4's that stretch out 300 yards. A comfortable course with a range of services, Mission Bay Golf Course provides a fine recreational stop for all the golfers in the family.

The environs of this course are pleasant with plenty of water complete with ducks. The landscaping is well appointed, the lush fairways are lined with mature eucaliptus and conifer trees. And for the evening, lights are installed to make playing after dusk possible. A fully featured pro shop rivals any in the area for selection and taste. Warm up on the driving range or practice putting on a beautiful green in the middle of a waterfall fed pond. For the 19th hole visit the Sandtrap restaurant and lounge. Meals are very good and the servings are plentiful. Daily specials are available at both lunch and dinner with the regular menu that includes at least four varieties of fresh fish. Fresh baked pies are a specialty of the house.

Bring the whole family, if they are not up to a regulation game of golf, Mission Bay has a great miniature golf course as well. Now there is no excuse for not stopping at Mission Bay Golf Course!

MISSION TRAILS GOLF COURSE
7380 Golf Crest Place
San Diego, CA 92119
Tel. (619) 460-5400
Hrs: Course open daylight hours.
       Snack Bar   6:00 a.m. - 2:00 p.m.
       Lounge   10:00 a.m. - 7:30 p.m.

Few pleasures in life are as serene as teeing up while the morning sun glistens on the lush grass of a dew sparkled fairway. Whether you are traveling in the San Deigo area or live there, Mission Trails Golf Course is a place to remember for finely groomed grounds in a casual atmosphere without prohibitive prices.

This quiet course is removed from the noise of the city in the sunbelt of San Deigo where it's dry and warm nearly all year long. From the clubhouse set among trees on a hillside you have a view of this fine facility and the surrounding rugged mountains of the desert country. A par seventy, eighteen hole course, Mission Trails offers a good variety of holes with interesting terrain and well placed hazards. A real challenge to your skill might be hole seventeen which is one of the most difficult par threes in San Diego. All of the services you'd expect from a quality club are available including a beautiful driving range, putting greens, a new fleet of golf carts, four qualified golf pros, club rentals if you couldn't fit yours in the trunk, and a well-stocked pro shop.

Those who know about this place use it often, so it is advised to call for tee times a week in advance if possible. Peak play greens fees for eighteen holes is a very reasonable thirteen dollars (at the time of this publication.) Make this "Best Choice" a stop for you and tee up to that welcome fairway.

JEWELRY

CARTER'S DIAMONDS
861 6th Avenue, Suite 329
San Diego, CA 92101
Tel. (619) 236-9812
Hrs: Mon. - Fri.   10:30 a.m. - 6:30 p.m.
         Saturday   11:00 a.m. - 3:30 p.m.
Visa, MasterCard and AMEX are accepted.

Carter's Diamonds is a family business and by golly you'll be treated like a member when you shop at their store! With an emphasis on honesty and fair value, customers will be warmly welcomed and graciously served. Carter's Diamonds features "The best quality available at the lowest prices" and the proprietors are determined to live up to their slogan.

Candy, nuts and roses greet customers from atop glass cases, making visitors feel more like guests than clients. It won't be long before you are on a first name basis with the folks at this old fashioned store, deliberating over sparkling gems and lovely custom jewelry designs. Grandfather Carter began the business with a pawn shop, and the next generation's love of the finer pieces led to the evolution of the store. The only things that haven't changed over the years are old traditional values. Exquisite diamonds are featured at "rock bottom" wholesale prices as well as an excellent selection of gold jewelry, custom rings, wedding rings and much more, all at a fraction of the usual cost. You will also find a qualified appraiser on site.

You could go to Cartier's and pay the price of the spendy name. Or you could go to Carter's, where you'll find the same quality gems without the high price tag. You'll find something else at Carter's Diamonds. Customer satisfaction at no extra charge.

(See special invitation in the Appendix.)

DIAMOND DESIGNS
Mission Valley Center
San Diego, CA 92121
Tel.   (619) 297-3934
Hrs: Mon. - Fri.   10:00 a.m. - 9:00 p.m.
          Saturday   10:00 a.m. - 6:00 p.m.
          Sunday   12:00 noon - 5:00 p.m.
La Jolla store open until 9:00 p.m. and closed Sundays.
Visa, MasterCard and AMEX are accepted.
Also,

Grossmont Center   La Jolla Village Dr./Regent Road
La Mesa, CA   La Jolla, CA

Clairemont Mesa Boulevard   Terra Nova Plaza
Corner of Convoy   I-805 at H Street
San Diego, CA   Chula Vista, CA

Highway 78 at Nordahl Rd.
San Marcos, CA

In Southern California, the place to find some of the world's most exciting fine jewelry and timepieces, at competitive prices, is at one of Diamond Design's six convenient locations.

Diamond Designs carries tasteful, fine jewelry, priced as low as twenty-five dollars, and up to fifty thousand dollars. You'll enjoy their enormous selection of outstanding pieces when you are in the mood for a diamond and gold fantasy. You'll also find a wide array of gold bracelets, necklaces, pearls, beads, fine watches, silver and platinum. Expert repair, custom design and remounting is done on the premises.

Integrity and service complement the quality merchandise featured at Diamond Designs. Each store's friendly, knowledgeable staff knows the importance of giving the kind of service and attention that will keep a customer returning time after time.

Give a diamond from Diamond Desgins; then watch the sparks fly!

(See special invitation in the Appendix.)

KITCHEN WARES

COOK'S CORNER
6404 Nancy Ridge Drive
San Diego, CA 92122
Tel. (619) 452-7300
Hrs: Mon. - Fri.   10:00 a.m. - 9:00 p.m.
      Saturday   10:00 a.m. - 6:00 p.m.
      Sunday   12:00 noon - 5:00 p.m.
Also,

Plaza Camino Real   Fashion Valley
2525 El Camino Real #231   290 Fashion Valley #535
Carlsbad, CA 92008   San Diego, CA 92108
Tel. (619) 434-1797   Tel. (619) 574-6980

North County Fair
200 E Via Rancho Parkway
Escondido, CA 92925
Tel. (619) 747-8907

You'll never be a customer at Cook's Corner, you'll always be a guest. That's the promise that welcomes you into these contemporary mall shops, but it's the merchandise that will keep you there, unwilling to leave until you've explored every nook and cranny.

The wonderful aroma of gourmet coffee is the first lure. Over thirty varieties are ground fresh daily, and you can special order others, as well. You'll also find a wide selection of coffee making equipment and accessories. Then, settle in for a serious hunt through the 2,000 other kitchen items that offer endless fascination for any dedicated cook. You'll find coeur a la creme molds, krumkake cones, checkerboard cake pan sets, French bread pans, tortilla basket makers, deep dish pizza pans, pasta machines with drying racks and ravioli attachments. And more, much more.

These clean, bright uncluttered shops also stock gourmet foods, table accessories, and cookbooks. And always ready with the extra touch, the Cook's Corner catalog is laced with enticing recipes. Whether you are shopping for your own kitchen or looking for unusual gifts, these readily accessible shops are just the ticket.

(See special invitation in the Appendix.)

LEATHER SHOP

LEATHER GALLERY
1640 Camino Del Rio North
San Diego, CA 92108
Tel. (619) 297-5533
Hrs: Mon. - Fri.   10:00 a.m. - 9:00 p.m.
          Saturday   10:00 a.m. - 6:00 p.m.
          Sunday   12:00 noon - 5:00 p.m.
Closed major holidays.
Visa, MasterCard and AMEX are accepted.

Unique leather clothing is becoming a major force in fashion. In San Diego, the place to find these luxury garments is Leather Gallery, in the Mission Valley Mall. Owner Gregario Deitz began his career in the clothing industry twelve years ago in South America. Five years ago, he and his wife, Annette, opened Leather Gallery, where their goal is to offer basic leathers at affordable prices, without forgetting good fit and good fashion.

Leather Gallery likes to stay on the leading edge of leather fashion and the Deitz's are not afraid to take a risk in bringing something new and exciting to San Diego patrons. They rarely repeat items and prefer to carry one of a kinds. You will find basic leather apparel such as skirts, jackets, and pants. They also carry many high fashion leathers, belts, dresses, sweaters with leather detail and men's fashions, many of which are imported from Spain. Gregario and Annette are very proud of the unique Fashion Forward pieces featured at Leather Gallery.

All alterations at Leather Gallery are free and if an item purchased there needs repair in the future, it can be returned and repaired at no charge. Keep an eye open for many wonderful accessories, always chosen to complement the fashions there. For the finest and most exciting looks in leather, take a trip to the Leather Gallery.

FALLING STAR LEATHER
4099 Mason Street
San Diego, CA 92110
Tel. (619) 295-6570
Hrs: Tue. - Sun.   11:00 a.m. - 6:00 p.m.
Visa, MasterCard and Discover are accepted.

If you're looking for a saddle that will last a hundred years, a hand tooled belt or a fine leather jacket, Falling Star Leather is the unique and ideal place to go. Owned and operated by two skilled artisans, Joseph Powers, who designs and carves leather and his wife, who patterns and sews it, the bywords at Falling Star are "Quality" and "Endurance."

Inside, a grand old wooden structure, once a stable, there is a small display area filled floor to ceiling with handmade leather products. You'll find simple accessories and more complex pieces, men's shirts, ladies' blouses, backpacks and leather luggage. The care and attention to detail of tooling, planning and design are immediately evident. Endurance and quality are found in everything from the selection of leather to the seams and stitching in garments and leather art.

Because of the special care given each piece, if you want something special made, don't be in a rush. It may take from a few weeks to as much as a year, as in the case of a custom made, hand tooled saddle, to have your order completed. Of course, there are many items on display, ready to be taken with you. It feels good visiting Falling Star Leather, just to smell, touch and watch the fine leather goods being made.

MUSEUM

THE GASLAMP QUARTER
410 Island Avenue
San Diego, CA 92101
Tel. (619) 233-5227
Hrs: Walking Tours
        Saturday   10:00 a.m. and 1:00 p.m.
        William Heath Davis House Museum
        Mon. -Fri.   11:00 a.m. - 2:00 p.m.
        Saturday   10:00 a.m. - 2:00 p.m.
Donations are requested.

The Gaslamp Quarter presents a truly unique opportunity for those who enjoy and cherish the heart of a city. It's not very often that such a place can be located on a map. San Diego's nationally recognized Gaslamp Quarter is just such a district, a place that can be seen and experienced as the historic heart of downtown.

Within this city with its feet planted firmly in this century, and looking forward to the next, is a sixteen and a half block area that looks back to San Diego's history and the century past. Led by knowledgeable volunteers, regularly scheduled walking tours of this district start at Gaslamp Quarter offices in the William Heath Davis House. They give a fascinating perspective of the Quarter and its era, embodied in its carefully restored elegant Victorian buildings and in stories of the colorful characters that shaped the west.

While you delight in this wonderful glimpse of the past, you can also enjoy the present. Specialty shops, galleries, cultural activities and some of the best restaurants in San Diego bring visitors back time and again to savor the old and the new. Whether it's your first visit to the area, or if you live there, a visit the Gaslamp Quarter is a must.

MUSIC RECORDING EQUIPMENT

SONGMASTERS
4150 Mission Boulevard Suite 216
San Diego, CA 92109
Tel. (619) 581-3406
Hrs: Mon. - Sun.   10:00 a.m. - 8:00 p.m.
Visa and MasterCard are accepted.

Remember watching *American Bandstand* where they always had the 'lipsync' competition? There was Freddy or Sue mouthing the words of an Everly Brothers tune or Patti Page. Well now days you don't have to mouth the words of your favorite tunes; you can sing the lead yourself with accompaniment tapes, video or audio.

SongMasters in San Diego is a store recently opened to meet the needs of this exploding trend in entertainment. With their state-of-the-art equipment and over 4,000 titles to choose from, you can become the star of your own show. SongMasters features Karaoke recording equipment. From this company the customer has the choice of a variety of machines to fit their performance requirements. Now when the gang gets together for an evening you can not only sing along with Mitch, you can be Mitch. Guaranteed to be a whole lot of fun for the crew, these machines also work as recording studios, making it possible to produce your own performance tape. Vocalists who perform for groups will appreciate the convenience of a Karaoke system from SongMasters. To back all this equipment is that extensive library of tapes. Who's your favorite, Frank Sinatra, Barbara Streisand, Billy Joel, or Linda Ronstadt? They have them all from musicals to seasonal music, country to contemporary rock.

While you're traveling, stop on in and take a tape home for some goodtimes for all. Remember it's SongMasters, " Where you can be the star."

(See special invitation in the Appendix.)

PARTY SUPPLIES

THE MERRYMAKER
4230 Adams Avenue
San Diego, CA 92116
Tel. (619) 283-0303
Hrs: Tue. - Sat.   10:30 a.m. - 6:30 p.m.

Most people enjoy going to parties, but feelings are mixed about giving them. Wouldn't it be wonderful to have the fun of giving a party without all the work?   Finding the favors, decorations for different themes, arranging catering, special entertainment, and even arranging for photographers can be done for you by someone else: The Merrymaker.

Mrs. S. K. Sidhu and her daughter, Ruby, are specialists in the field of party giving. They have created their business because it's something they love to do, and because they know how to entertain for special occasions. The art was learned from their own background of society in India, Europe and the United States. They bring an inventive and spontaneous warmth to any event for children or adults by their own talents and good taste. You as the host or hostess get all of the complements.

When you go into The Merrymaker you'll see the shop was designed just for the purpose of providing party necessities. You'll find a large selection of party decorations, favors, tableware, paper cups, balloons, pinatas, gift wrap, small gifts and candy. But first the invitations. Now, who would you like to invite?

PHOTOGRAPHY SUPPLIES

NELSON PHOTO SUPPLIES
1909 India Street Corner of Fir
San Diego, CA 92101
Tel. (619) 234-6621
Hrs: Mon. - Fri.   8:30 a.m. - 5:30 p.m.
       Saturday   8:30 a.m. - 5:00 p.m.
Visa, MasterCard and Discover are accepted.

With little doubt, Nelson Photo is the leading photographic store in San Diego, and has an outstanding reputation throughout Southern California. It's the result of almost forty years of hard work and skillful development. In the early years, Nelson's was strictly an industrial photographic supplier, which means that the demands for quality in products and service were exacting.

It's no wonder, that the retail department, started in 1957, began as the best possible.

The growth of the retail department required a complete new building to better serve the public and display everything from a complete line of cameras to darkroom equipment, telescopes, lenses, film, chemicals and every accessory imaginable. This is a substantial, diverse and integrated company in the world of visual and photographic arts.

Despite its size, Nelson Photo Supply remains a family managed company. Whether you're a beginner or a pro, you can find everything you need at this great store, including good advice from those who know the business.

(See special invitation in the Appendix.)

PRODUCE AND GIFTS

FARMER'S BAZAAR
205 Seventh Street
San Diego, CA 92101
Tel. (619) 233-0281
Hrs: Tue. - Sat.   9:00 a.m. - 5:30 p.m.
          Sunday   9:00 a.m. - 5:00 p.m.

Just a stone's throw from major tourist attractions such as Seapoint Village is a turn of the century world where farmers and craftsmen come to sell their wares: Farmers Bazaar. Housed in a huge 100 year old redwood truss building is a place where you can delight in a potpourri of tastes, smells, and sights.

Stroll among the market stalls that display gifts and curios, fruits and vegetables from the far corners of the earth, and savor the taste of fresh fruit. The produce dresses up the area with a massive display of colors and scents. In addition to the usual goods found in most produce markets, the Farmers Bazaar carries some of the more exotic items, such as mangoes, papayas, tamarinds, nopales, yucca and malanga root. There are five mini-restaurants providing a wide variety of American and ethnic food that you can eat there, or take home or to the beach. The meat and fish market provide the raw materials for a first class barbecue.

In the hayloft upstairs you will find Mexican and Oriental imports including fashion jewelry, western fashions and many toys and man-made crafts. The spice shop stocks a large variety of bulk herbs and spices. To spice up your visit to San Diego, head for the Farmers Bazaar.

RENTAL MANAGEMENT

PENNY REALTY VACATION RENTALS
3803 Mission Boulevard
San Diego, CA 92109
Tel. (619) 272-3900

Planning a vacation to the San Diego area? You should get in touch with the professional staff at Penny Realty. With over 150 listings and twenty years experience, they are well qualified to provide you with a beach rental to make your vacation more pleasurable.

All of Penny Realty's properties are either on the water or within one block of the beach or bay. Each rental is fully equipped with housekeeping facilities. Rentals range from casual to elegant, large or small. After contacting the helpful staff and describing your preferences, they will send you photo brochures of those units available on a daily basis (two night minimum), weekly or monthly basis. Summer rentals are weekly from Saturday to Saturday.

San Diego has many recreational opportunities and points of interest, all of which are within a short drive. Why not make your vacation in San Diego a special occasion with a stay at a private beach house through Penny Realty. Once you get there, you'll like it so much you'll probably want to stay, in which case the Sales staff will gladly guide you to that perfect home or investment property.

RESORTS

THE BAHIA RESORT HOTEL
998 West Mission Bay Drive
San Diego, CA 92109
Tel.   (619) 488-0551
       (800) 542-6010 CA
       (800) 821-3619 US
Visa, MasterCard, AMEX, Diners Club, Carte Blanche and Discover are accepted.

The Bahia Resort Hotel is situated on a fourteen acre peninsula surrounded by warm, sandy beaches on sparkling Mission Bay, and just a short walk to the enticing waves of the Pacific Ocean. 325 guest rooms offer a variety of options, including high rise studios and bayfront "cottage style" rooms and suites. Studios and some suites include kitchens.

Recreational facilities include an outdoor heated pool, whirlpool spa, lighted tennis courts, watersport rentals, and moonlight cruises on Mission Bay aboard the *Bahia Belle*. The Bahia offers casual dining in the coffee shop, either indoors or on the patio, and elegant Continental cuisine in the Mercedes Room overlooking Mission Bay. There is live entertainment nightly in the Mercedes Lounge and Piano Bar. The resort is just minutes from Sea World, the zoo, airport, downtown, shopping and Tijuana.

When visiting California's finest seaport, stay at the Bahia Resort Hotel. Few other places blend round-the-clock activity with relaxation as well as the Bahia.

THE CATAMARAN RESORT HOTEL
3999 Mission Boulevard
San Diego, CA 92109
Tel.   (619) 488-1081
       (800) 542-6010 CA
       (800) 821-3619 US
Visa, MasterCard, AMEX, Diners Club, Carte Blanche and Discover are accepted.

Come see our new look! Located on the shores of Mission Bay, and just a short walk to the ocean, the Catamaran Resort Hotel recently emerged from a $21 million renovation with new and expanded facilities and services.

Included are two new guest room buildings and refurbished existing guest rooms, over 21,000 square feet of meeting space, a new pool and whirlpool spa, and bayside restaurant and lounge with live entertainment nightly. The hotel continues to provide watersport rentals and moonlight cruises of Mission Bay aboard the Bahia Belle.

The Resort's original Polynesian theme is accented with collections of museum-quality art, a stunning twenty foot waterfall in the lobby and lush, rare tropical foliage throughout the property.

The Catamaran Resort Hotel is proud to present new guest facilities while preserving its quality of service in a relaxed, comfortable atmosphere. Consider the Catamaran when business or pleasure brings you to San Diego.

DE ANZA HARBOR RESORT
2727 De Anza Road
San Diego, CA 92109
Tel. (619) 273-3211
Hrs: Mon. - Sat.   8:00 a.m. - 6:00 p.m.
             Sunday   9:00 a.m. - 6:00 p.m.
No telephone reservations are accepted on Sunday.
Visa and MasterCard are accepted.

Your vacation is one of the most valuable times of the year. For days, weeks or months you and your family or friends have eagerly awaited, planned and saved. So make it one of the most exciting, fun filled and memorable of all of your vacations. Bring your family, trailer and boat to De Anza Harbor Resort. There, right on San Diego's fantastic Mission Bay, you'll have the time of your life enjoying 4,600 acres of fun under the sun.

De Anza is an 820 space, modern mobile home and trailer park with over 250 spaces for travel trailers, motor homes, campers, and tent trailers. Full hook-ups are provided for your every need. There are facilities available for boat, car and trailer. De Anza Harbor Resort is located on it's own private cove near all the major attractions this area of California has to offer. However, there's plenty to do at the park itself: boating, swimming, shuffleboard, picnics, dancing, golf and many more entertaining features abound at this resort.

This is the finest, most contemporary, well kept park that you'll find anywhere. Every convenience is provided to make your stay here truly delightful. As advanced reservations are usually a must, let them hear from you soon.

(See special invitation in the Appendix.)

THE GOLDEN DOOR
3085 Reynard Way
San Diego, CA 92103
Tel. (6l9) 295-3144

Recognizing that true human potential is not possible unless there is total harmony between the psyche as well as the physical aspects of life, The Golden Door created a regimen and ambiance which assists in merging these elements. Located on 177 acres of countryside in Southern California, in an area once sacred to the Indians, the visitor to The Golden Door is at once removed from those outside influences of stress and anxiety. As the worries of the outside world slip away, your body begins to crave an outlet for the newfound energy it has discovered. A typical day may start with a crisp sunrise hike in the surrounding hillside, pre-exercise warms ups, or breakfast in bed. Activities are geared toward your level of fitness and personal instructions are given to assist you in measuring and building your physical strengths.

Weight training, pool exercises, water volleyball, tennis, dancing, or Hatha Yoga are also on the list of activities available during the day. The Dragon Tree Gym is equipped with state of the art Hogan Camstar Equipment and houses a spacious bathhouse, steam room, sauna and Japanese tub. To reward and relieve those weary muscles, therapeutic messages, herbal wraps, whirlpool soaks, manicure, pedicures and facials are offered by a caring and fastidious staff.

The Golden Door is recognized as a pioneer in introducing gourmet flair and taste to low-calorie, high nutrition natural foods. Each dish prepared by the chef is a work of art and assails the visual senses as well as the palate. Most foods are grown in The Golden Door organic vegetable gardens and orchards and are picked fresh just prior to preparation. Low calorie hors d'oeuvres and non-alcoholic beverages are served before dinner.

Your private accommodations feature an individual Tokonoma or a decorative shrine, with fresh flower arrangement on a raised platform, a private garden and a moon viewing deck. A wardrobe includes warm up pants, shorts, white kimono, gloves, scarves, and a terrycloth robe; an indication that you are in the caring and personalized hands of experts.

When not pursuing a path of vigorous physical activity, relax and enjoy the esoteric tranquility in one of four beautiful landscaped gardens. The Golden Door has been rated as the best of the world's greatest spas by Lord Lichfield, great nephew to Queen Mother of Great Britain. When it comes to giving yourself the best, make it The Golden Door. The Golden Door "can lead you along the path to a healthier, happier life, but only you can walk the path."

RANCHO LA PUERTA
3085 Reynard Way
San Diego, CA 92103
Tel.   (619)   294-8504
         (800) 422-7565   CA
         (800) 443-7565   US

Originally founded in 1940, Rancho La Puerta is recognized as being the oldest residential health spa in the Northern Hemisphere. Before being healthy was considered "in", Edmond and Deborah Szekely were effectively combining physical exercise with a holistic life style. Located three miles south of the international border in Tecate, Baja California, Mexico, Rancho La Puerta is nestled against a backdrop of mountains and rolling countryside. During your stay at Rancho La Puerta, the chocking vestiges of city life and its stresses are stripped away leaving only tranquility and a zest for life.

Your accommodations consist of private cottages, built in the traditional Mexican style and with locally fired bricks and painted tiles. Each room is accented with native arts and crafts, colorful furnishings and many have cozy fireplaces. Public buildings boast superbly crafted stained glass windows in contemporary Mexican designs, high vaulted ceilings, Mexican Colonial furnishings, balconies or terraces decked with a colorful array of plantings.

From dawn to dusk, your day is filled to the brim with a variety of physical activities or stupendous sights to view. Select from six lighted tennis courts, six aerobic gyms, one weight training gym, four swimming pools, five whirlpool therapy pools, three saunas a volleyball court, secluded men's and women's centers for massage, herbal wraps, and facials. Individual guidance counselors are available to design an exercise package within your specific limitations and goals. To relax, sample the splendor of flowering cacti, desert flowers and indigenous wildlife in the surrounding terrain by taking a walk along the miles and miles of hiking trails, bask by the pool side, or be lullabied to sleep in the gentle swaying of a hammock.

A culinary treat awaits you during mealtimes. Produce grown from Rancho La Puerta's organic gardens and orchards provide a repast which is low in calories, high in nutrition and a treat for the palate. Nightly entertainment consists of guest speakers on symposiums from how to manage stress in your life, diet and nutrition, to exercise or craft classes and films.

Whether needing to get away from it all, learning how to play or rejuvenating the body and spirit, Rancho La Puerta provides the perfect atmosphere. Your entire being is made whole through a program of vigorous exercise, ultimate relaxation, controlled diet and specialized care from a staff of dedicated and loving individuals. Rancho La Puerta, "where the fitness revolution began."

SAN DIEGO PRINCESS, A PRINCESS CRUISES RESORT
1404 W Vacation Road
San Diego, CA 92109
Tel.   (619) 274-4630
        (800) 344-2626 Reservations only
Visa, MasterCard, AMEX, Diners Club, Carte Blanche and Discover are accepted.

Welcome to a real fantasy island! The San Diego Princess is breathtaking. There is no other place like it. Forty-three acres of beauty and elegance. If you are looking for fun, sun and glorious white sand beaches, this is it.

Millions of flowers mixed with a blend of Polynesia and the Far East lend to this enchanting hideaway. Oriental foot bridges reflect over the waters in meandering lagoons. An immense variety of exotic plants and flowers add their beauty to the peaceful environment.

The San Diego Princess has 450 cottages for their guests and each has its own view of the exquisite surroundings. The cottages are ideal for families and are spacious with floor to ceiling windows with plenty of room to relax and enjoy the accommodations. Many rooms have complete kitchens. Every imaginable type of recreation is available such as sailing, tennis, swimming and biking. Over 24,233 square feet of meeting space is available for conferences, conventions and banquets. On location audio/visual and equipment rental is available for convention and conference purposes.

You have the choice of five magnificent outdoor pools as well as the calm salt water surrounding the island's white sand beaches. Over seventy golf courses are within a fifteen to thirty minute drive. The restaurants available in this island paradise are fabulous. Try the Dockside Broiler, the finest of Continental cuisine plus dancing and live entertainment will be sure to please. More casual dining is provided by the bright and cheery Village Cafe. For excellent Polynesian dining, the Polynesian Princess Restaurant is the very best. In this unique environment you can play for days and never do the same thing twice. For a vacation treat of a lifetime, come to the real fantasy island at the San Diego Princess.

RESTAURANTS

BACI'S RESTAURANT
1955 Morena Boulevard
San Diego, CA 92110
Tel.   (619) 275-2094
Hrs: Mon. - Sun.   11:00 a.m. - 10:00 p.m.

Baci's is not very prepossessing from the outside, just a plain, small building on a busy street. However, once you enter you'll find yourself in another world. For starters, the Italian staff wears coats and tails! The light from overhead gas chandeliers is intimate, the feeling enhanced by a dark beamed ceiling and stained glass windows. Still life paintings, sculpture, and wall plants in handpainted ceramic containers and soft, pleasant music provide a lovely background for the elegantly appointed tables where fine crystal is augmented by complete serving sets of multicolored Italian pottery.
Baci's specializes in homemade pasta, milk-fed veal, fresh seafood and succulent steaks. Recommended dishes include veal Toscana, scampi and oyster Genovesa. Desserts feature all kinds of delicious torts and, of course, zabalone. This elegant restaurant has been producing some of San Diego's most authentic Italian cuisine for over eight years and is certainly worth a visit.

(See special invitation in the Appendix.)

THE BAKERY RESTAURANT
619 Fashion Valley Shopping Center
San Diego, CA 92108
Tel. (619) 296-2198
Hrs: Mon. - Fri.   10:00 a.m. - 9:00 p.m.
            Saturday   9:00 a.m. - 6:00 p.m.
            Sunday   11:00 a.m. - 5:00 p.m.
Visa, MasterCard and AMEX are accepted.
Also,
421 West B Street
San Diego, CA 92101
Tel. (619) 232-3085

Turkey items are so popular at both outlets of The Bakery Restaurant that they use nearly one ton of turkey breasts per month. Turkey isn't their only forte. Specializing in quality, homemade, "authentic" food, owners Beverly Nelson-Zike and Jim Zike recommend the teriyaki chicken, and an interesting mystery dish called "The Mess" - described as "a staff special with an egg on top."

The Fashion Valley's decor is enhanced with an open air balcony available for casual dining. The downtown restaurant is located in a building that is almost one-hundred years old and features brick walls and high ceilings in its spacious decor. The architect who assisted them with the redesign has won eleven national awards for his renovations.

For casual, comfortable and healthy eating at reasonable prices, try either of The Bakery Restaurants. The service is excellent, the staff is friendly, the coffee is good and the menu offers something for everyone.

BALI HAI RESTAURANT
2240 Shelter Island Drive
San Diego, CA 92106
Tel. (619) 222-1181
Hrs: Mon. - Fri.   11:15 a.m. - 11:00 p.m.
            Saturday   5:00 p.m. - 12:30 a.m.
            Sunday   10:00 a.m. - 10:30 p.m.
All major credit cards are accepted.

Bali Hai is calling any time, any where. Maybe you remember the song from South Pacific. "Here I am, your special island," is the call of the singer. The lure of the tropics is recreated at Bali Hai restaurant on your special island, Shelter Island in San Deigo.

"Hawaii on the mainland" is their motto. Surrounded by authentic trappings of every major Polynesian culture, the diner can travel out over the Pacific by a short walk through the door. Start your evening with one of the famous refreshing cocktails. The Aloha Kiss will set the mood with its accompanying orchid lei. Menu offerings are touted as one of the most authentic and extensive in the world. How do ribs smothered in sauces of island fruit sound to your tropical taste buds? One house speciality is Chicken of the Gods. During lunch a luau buffet is served with a spread of Polynesian pleasures. Bali Hai is equipped to handle any size dining needs you may require from an intimate couple to a banquet for a hundred. It's also a great place for parties and wedding receptions.

Diners from the world over steer their course to Bali Hai. Bali Hai is calling you, "Come to me, come to me."

CALIFORNIA CUISINE
1027 University Avenue
San Diego, CA 92103
Tel.   (619) 543-0790
Hrs: Tue. - Fri.   11:00 a.m. - 10:00 p.m.
            Sat. - Sun.   5:00 a.m. - 10:00 p.m.
Visa, MasterCard and AMEX are accepted.

They say things happen first in California, then they spread to rest of the nation. San Diego's California Cuisine is just the place to find out what's soon to be on its way.

Like so much in California, the menu at this restaurant is always changing, so you are not likely to see any single item become a key specialty. You can, however, count on it to be fresh, savory, and several cuts above the ordinary. The restaurant has become famous for its warm chicken salad and pasta la tortola. Diners have also raved about a strange sounding combination of tossed noddles with tender chunks of duck, lobster, sliced pears and chopped pistachios. The eggplant bisque is another favorite. For a seafood favorite you might also try the charbroiled Hawaiian mahi mahi served on steamed cabbage.

The dining room is comfortable and the outdoor patio is a peaceful and charming place. But it's the people, both fellow diners and staff, that create the pleasant atmosphere of casual elegance. If you find that the food is too good to walk away from, think about taking advantage of California Cuisine's fine catering service. For a "Best Choice" in California cookery, don't pass up California Cuisine.

CARLOS MURPHY'S
3890 Twiggs Street
San Diego, CA 92110
Tel. (619) 260-0305
Hrs: Mon. - Sun.   11:00 a.m. - 1:00 a.m.
All major credit cards are accepted.
Also,

4303 La Jolla Village Drive
San Diego, CA 92122
Tel. (619) 457-4170

1904 Quivira Road
San Diego, CA 92109
Tel. (619) 223-8061

5500 Grossmont Center Drive
La Mesa, CA 92041
Tel. (619) 698-9757

2525 El Camino Real
Carlsbad, CA 92008
Tel. (619) 434-1758

420 E. Via Rancho Parkway
Escondido, CA 92025
Tel.   (619)489-5932

Families love Carlos Murphy's. From the free hors d'oeuvres during Happy Hours to the clowns making balloon characters for the kids, everyone has a good time here. Carlos Murphy's has combined good food and good times like nobody else can. Located in a hacienda style building surrounded by huge oak trees, it's the perfect setting for getting out with the family. There's even a perfectly maintained covered wagon from the early settlement days out front for the kids to inspect. All your favorite mexican dishes are on the menu including tacos, enchiladas, and ribs. Also featured are steaks, stir fries and seafood.

Monday nights are big at Carlos Murphy's when the big screen lights up with Monday Night Football and your favorite hors d'oeuvres such as buffalo wings, nachos, salsa and chips, onion rings, vegetables and hot dogs. When not watching the game check out the outrageous collection of crazy artifacts and antiques collected from all over the country.

The patio is lined with shrubs and plants for a pleasant outdoor eating experience. The dining room is great for families. Carlos Murphy's can also arrange for banquets of up to 150 persons.   Where else can the entire family get the foods they love while being so thoroughly entertained?

CELADON, 3628 Fifth Avenue, San Diego, CA 92101. Tel. (619) 295-8800. For a delicious and taste tingling experience, Celadon is a must for Thai cuisine aficionados.

THE CHEESE SHOP
401 G Street corner of 4th and G
San Diego, CA 92101
Tel. (619) 232-2303
Hrs: Mon. - Fri.   7:30 a.m. - 5:30 p.m.
        Saturday   9:30 a.m. - 5:30 p.m.
Closed Sundays.
Visa and MasterCard are accepted.

If a Turkey, Jack and Avocado sandwich on fresh sourdough, with a side of homemade potato salad and a fresh out of the oven, gooey chocolate chip cookie makes, your mouth water, visit the Cheese Shop. This wonderful shop is a great place to enjoy a favorite sandwich or order a picnic to take to the beach on a sunny San Diego day.

At the Cheese Shop, cheese is the featured product, but meats, pates, homemade breads and pastries do not take a back seat. The regular flow of customers to San Diego's favorite sandwich shop enjoy the personalized service of Dave and Phil Schutz who split the duties of preparing and serving the superb food. Fresh salads are all made from scratch from the finest and freshest ingredients.

The Schutz family has been a fixture in San Diego since 1972, preparing and serving a variety of good foods to enjoy on the spot or take out. Catering, special occasion gift baskets and custom made cakes and pastries bring people back over and over again for the variety and quality of the foods offered. The historical surroundings are great too. Where else can you eat or shop in the carriage works building that formerly housed San Diego's streetcars?

CHEZ BEAT AND ROLF
1762 Garnet Avenue
San Diego, CA 92109
Tel. (619) 483-2600
Hrs: Tue. - Sun.   7:30 a.m. - 10:00 p.m.
Visa and MasterCard are accepted.

Award winning Chez Beat and Rolf is an experience not to be missed. Taste bud tingling aromas greet you from the bakery located near the front of the restaurant, and from there it just gets better and better. Owners Beat Wick and Rolf Steiner started Chez Beat and Rolf with the idea of sharing gourmet health foods, creating new ideas in cuisine, and following current taste trends. The results are spectacular.

Some pastry specialties include apricot teacake, champagne truffle, Bailey's cheesecake, and a vast array of small pastries suitable for gift baskets. The most recommended appetizer is snails bourguigonne in puff pastry. Lunch can include chicken curry salad with apricots. The dinner menu is rich with exciting selections like veal zurichoise - thinly slice veal sauteed with mushroom cream sauce and spatzli, or homemade pasta with shrimp sauteed in cream sauce, to name a couple.

The Swiss team of Beat and Rolf is a dynamic one. While Beat performs in the open kitchen, Rolf greets the customers and takes care of the business side of the restaurant. They have combined their best talents for the pleasure of all who visit Chez Beat and Rolf.

EL INDIO SHOP
3695 India Street
San Diego, CA 92103
Tel. (619) 299-0333
Hrs: Mon. - Sat. 8:00 a.m. - 8:00 p.m.

On any given day at lunch time, there is nearly as much excitement and exertion at El Indio as there is at Jack Murphy Stadium during a hot-matched football game. This is truly one of the most popular eateries in San Diego. Heaping amounts of delicious and inexpensive food have kept the patrons returning to El Indio on a customary basis since 1940.

It started out as a tiny tortilla shop with Ralph Pesqueria Sr. and three women pounding out approximately thirty dozen tortillas a day. Now it has a staff of one-hundred employees and enough capacity to turn out over 500 dozen tortillas an hour! Even though the hot corn tortilla is their speciality, their menu selection in quite broad. Chimichangas, quesadillas, tostadas of every type, nachos, tamales, enchiladas, tacos, rice and beans, fruit burritos and another speciality, taquitos, are all served within minutes of your order.

All the meals are authentically Mexican in taste and all come laid out in plastic take-out plates, the kind that look like giant Styrofoam oysters. El Indio accepts telephone orders, and your food will be waiting upon arrival. This is without a doubt one of San Diego's finest take-out restaurants. It might be a little crowded at lunch, but with food this good it's well worth the wait.

Coming soon: the Grand Opening of their newest restaurant, located at 4120 Mission Boulevard in Pacific Beach.

FILIPPI'S PIZZA GROTTO
1747 India Street
San Diego, CA 92101
Tel. (619)232-1346
Hrs: Mon. - Sun.   11:00 a.m. - 12:00 midnight
Visa, MasterCard and AMEX are accepted.
Also,

82 Broadway Chula Vista, CA	5353 Kearny Villa Road San Diego, CA
962 Garnet Pacific Beach, CA	8035 Broadway Lemon Grove, CA
114 West Grand Escondido, CA	3673 Merrill Avenue Riverside, CA
948 North Marshall El Cajon, CA	4530 Camino De La Plaza San Ysidro, CA
9969 Mira Mesa Blvd. San Diego, CA	10330 Friars Road San Diego, CA

Filipi's Pizza Grotto is a third generation Italian eatery that has become a San Diego tradition. The was chain started in San Diego by Mama and Papa DePhilippis as a grocery store that expanded into selling pizzas and sandwiches. The original location still provides gourmet ingredients such as imported cheese, pasta, cured meats, olive oils, as well as tasty Italian cuisine.

Combining an Italian Delicatessen and specialty store with a pizza parlor has worked well for Filipi's and his is often called the best Italian food in town.   Be sure to try a Pizza with "the Works," a true Italian pizza or for dessert the wonderful cannoli. Beer, wine and cocktails will complement any meal you select.

You'll enjoy the noisy, yet relaxed atmosphere and the friendly crew who make sure you feel at home. Filipi's is also a great place to hold your next family gathering or celebration. They can accommodate up to 50 people for special parties. The Filipi family is devoted to the restaurant business and there are eleven different stores each owned by a member of the family.

FIREHOUSE BEACH CAFE
722 Grand Avenue
San Diego, CA 92109
Tel. (619) 272-0200
Visa, MasterCard and AMEX are accepted.

Days in San Diego can get pretty warm, in fact, downright hot. To cool down, you need some shade, a nice breeze, a chilled beverage and an enchanting view of the ocean. Okay, now that you've got the prerequisites for getting out of the heat, the question is where to go? The answer is simple: The Firehouse Beach Cafe.

Located only a few feet from the Pacific Ocean, this restaurant offers rooftop dining that features inspiring views and provides a refreshing refuge from the hot sun. While the temperature a few miles east will be in the mid nineties, the rooftop of The Firehouse will be in the mid seventies. Now that you're comfortably cool you can start thinking about food. One of the most important aspects about dining here is that the beautifully prepared and generously served meals are all totally natural. Foods made with preservatives are not even allowed on The Firehouse's menu.

Before you order, above all, be sure your appetite is large, especially if you order one of the omelets or deli sandwiches. To help wash down these delicious meals, try some of their fresh-squeezed juices. And for dessert, you can't miss their delightful cheesecake. What a way to cool down! dining at The Firehouse Beach Cafe is like taking an exhilarating dip in a clear mountain stream.

THE FRENCH CAFE
9823 Carroll Canyon Road
San Diego, CA 92131
Tel. (619) 566-4000
Hrs: Mon. - Sun.   6:30 a.m. - 9:30 p.m.
Brunch   Sunday   10:30 a.m. - 2:00 p.m.
The bar is open until 2:00 a.m.
Visa, MasterCard and AMEX are accepted.
Fifteen minutes from downtown and La Jolla.

Discovering a wonderful French restaurant in unlikely surroundings is a joy. Sampling the sublime delicacies from the kitchen of The French Cafe is heaven. Tucked away in, of all places, the Eucalyptus Square Shopping Center just off I-5, the French Gourmet is a delight. Simple, yet sophisticated lunch and dinner menus offer a little of everything for the discriminating palate. The French Cafe is not a formal dining experience, but rather a country cafe. Its charming ambiance includes the warm and romantic touch of a local guitarist on Mondays and weekend evenings. All is supervised by the very French, friendly and knowledgeable Eric Vandenhaute.

The hot lunch main courses are poached salmon, marinated lamb in thyme, rosemary, olive oil, grilled and served with Bearniase sauce and the sauteed chicken liver in peppercorn sauce. Dinners are the crowning glory of the French Cafe. Start off with a delicate appetizer of Asparagus in Puff Pastry, served with a creamy cilantro sauce. Or perhaps you will prefer Coquilles Saint Jacques Normandie, scallops sauted and baked and served with champagne sauce. Chef Christian Arnaud is especially proud of his Veal Scaloppini Forrestiere, thinly sliced white veal sauted and topped with wild forest mushroom sauce. Other classic favorites include Rack of Lamb Provencal and Roast Duckling Jurassien, served with a pungent raspberry sauce.

Far from a secret, The French Cafe is often filled to capacity, even on Monday nights and reservations are highly recommended.

GIULIO'S
809 Thomas Avenue
San Diego, CA 92109
Tel.   (619) 483-7726
Hrs: Sun. - Thu.   5:00 p.m. - 9:45 p.m.
            Fri. - Sat.   5:00 p.m. - 10:45 p.m.
Visa, MasterCard, AMEX, Diners Club, Carte Blanche and Discover are accepted.

Giulio's has been a favorite in San Diego since 1961. In fact, the locals immediately think of Giulio's whenever Italian food is mentioned.

Located at the corner of Mission Boulevard and Thomas just south of Grand Avenue, Giulio's is warm and inviting inside. Decorated with burgundy and white tablecloths and lots of fresh flowers everywhere, the atmosphere is relaxed and comfortable. Giulio Peveri was an accomplished chef in Milano, Italy before he opened Giulio's in San Diego. Along with his brother Italo and brother-in-law Dennis Sheilds, he created a restaurant with a sense of tradition. No one ever leaves Giulio's hungry or disappointed. All the entrees include either soup or salad and a side dish of pasta. And all the pastas are made fresh daily by a special crew. Southern as well as Northern Italian cuisines are offered. A wonderful appetizer is a split order of Tortelloni Verdi, spinach pasta stuffed with ricotta, parmesan, and served with Funghi(mushrooms) Porcini in a cream sauce.

There are eighteen pasta dishes in all. Two of the most popular entrees include Giulio's traditional recipe of Scampi, and Valdostana Di Vitello, veal stuffed with porcini mushrooms, prosciutto, and cheeses. Top off your meal with a dessert of Giulio's famous Pera con Zabaglione, or Tartuffo, Chocolate mousse with rum and almonds. Whenever you seek a quiet intimate dinner for two or a get together for up to fifty, Giulio's will make your meal a special occasion.

THE GOOD EGG
7947 Balboa Avenue
San Diego, CA 92111
Tel.   (619)   565-4244
Hrs: Mon. - Sun.   6:30 a.m. - 2:00 p.m.
Visa, MasterCard and AMEX are accepted.

Egg lovers, you've hit pay dirt! You've found an eggs-straordinary and egg-ceptional place to eat breakfast, brunch or lunch at The Good Egg.

Not that eggs are all you'll find there. The lunch menu features some great sandwiches, such as Roast Beef Heaven and Earthquake, a combination of avocados, tomatos, mushrooms, onions and melted cheese smothered with sprouts and ranch dressing. All sandwiches are served with fresh fruit and country potatoes. Salads include the San Francisco Spinach Salad, the Dom DeLouise (ham, bacon, turkey breast, Swiss and cheddar cheese, fresh veggies, and mixed greens) and the Dynamic Trio, a choice between several salad varieties. What The Good Egg is best known for, of course, are the breakfast delights. Eight yummy omelettes are available for your selection, and it's guaranteed you'll have a hard time making a choice. Meggsican-style breakfasts include the Hot Juan Frittata, (eggs, chorizo, onion and cheese, sour cream and salsa) and the Breakfast Burrito (scrambled eggs, chorizo, onions, green chilies in a flour tortilla, covered with salsa, cheese, and sour cream). The Good Eggs Benedict is great, as is the Western Scramble, a regional favorite. If you aren't interested in eggs, enjoy Good Eggs gourmet pancakes, made from scratch with fresh ground wheat, and served with sweet butter and warm syrup. Choose from plain, strawberry, wheat germ, blueberry, apple and cinnamon, trail mix and oranges, or cashew blueberry!

The Good Egg is also located in Phoenix, Scottsdale and Mesa, Arizona, and in Boulder, Colorado. Watch for new locations opening soon. Eat there, even if you have to go an eggs-tra bit out of your way!

GUADALAJARA GRILL
4105 Taylor Street
San Diego, CA 92110
Tel. (619) 295-5111
Hrs: Mon. - Sun.   11:00 a.m. - 11:00 p.m.
Visa, MasterCard, AMEX, Diners Club, Carte Blanche and Discover are accepted.

There are few things more enjoyable than eating lunch or dinner in a good Mexican restaurant, and the Guadalajara Grill has earned the reputation of being not just "good," but excellent. At Guadalajara Grill, authentic Mexican foods are taken seriously, which means they are not Americanized, but prepared and served in the traditional style of the best restaurants in Mexico.

Through the archways of this attractive stucco 1870s style building, you'll find a light and spacious place carefully decorated with antiques and art from Mexico, and filled with the wonderful odors of corn and cumin, cheese and tomato, chilies and simmering sauces. Guadalajara Grill is popular because it offers a combination of everything that makes dining a pleasure: good foods, attractive surroundings, excellent service, modest prices and lots of people enjoying themselves. The lounge is open until 1:00 a.m., and serves cocktails and drinks from north and south of the border.

If you happen to be heading Tijuana way, don't miss the "sister" to the San Diego Guadalajara Grill, the Tijuana Guadalajara Grill at Diego Rivera 19, Tel. 1 (706) 684-2040. It's easy to see why the San Diego branch is authentic, with a "sister" in Tijuana.

HYATT ISLANDIA RESTAURANT
1441 Quivira Road
San Diego, CA 92109
Tel. (619) 224-1234
Hrs: Lunch   Mon. - Sat.   9:00 a.m. - 2:30 p.m.
        Dinner   Mon. - Sat.   5:00 p.m. - 10:00 p.m.
        Brunch   Sunday   9:00 a.m. - 2:00 p.m.
All major credit cards accepted

Capture the fresh breezes of the ocean. Add a prime portion of tasty elegance with a dash of casual tropical scenery. Serve this in a location on the Mission Bay waterfront with a side of luxury pleasure craft in the background and you have the Hyatt Islandia Restaurant.

For fine gourmet dining at its best, this restaurant has a pedigree of class and distinction. All of the kitchen staff are culinary graduates. Meals are full course gourmet dinners served by a professional dinner staff that insure a pleasant evening of dining. Daily entrees include six choices of fresh fish, shell fish, Cajun style cooking of pasta and chicken, lamb and beef. After the appetizer, salad is tossed table side prior to the main course. Many personal touches accent the service. And for those who can't get enough of a good thing, dessert features a variety of chocolate lovers delights, try the fresh fruit fondue in chocolate sauce. Saturday evenings feature a large oyster bar outside on the patio with live music performed on a nearby floating platform. Happy Hour is Monday through Friday with hors d'oeuvres. The Sunday Brunch is a sight to behold. Eighty-eight feet of choice selections. This brunch includes omelets, roast beef, pates, fruit bar, cold cuts, salads and a delectable spread of desserts. Other days of the week a scaled down yet equally delicious version is offered during lunch buffet.

At The Hyatt Islandia, fine dining is complimented by fine surroundings. All this blends to provide an enjoyable repast for you.

KANSAS CITY BARBEQUE
610 W Market Street
San Diego, CA 92101
Tel. (619) 231-9680
Hrs: Mon. - Sun.   11:00 a.m. - 10:00 p.m.
Visa, MasterCard and AMEX are accepted.

Put a tingle on your tastebuds with a real honest Midwest style barbeque sauce that'll knock your socks off!

In addition to good homemade food, Kansas City Barbeque also gained notoriety as the filming location for two scenes in the recent hit movie, *Top Gun*. It is conveniently located in downtown San Diego between Horton Plaza Shopping Center and Seaport Village. An intoxicating aroma greets you even as you park the car, as the meats are cooked slowly and basted constantly in a giant pit behind vaulted doors. The meat entrees are complemented with curled french fries, onion rings that are a work of art, or crisp cole slaw, and may be topped off with a dazzling walnut or sweet potatoe pie. Plenty of napkins are provided and you'll need 'em, as you dive in and "become one with" your zesty meal!

There are train tracks out back near the patio dining, where you can tie on a game of horseshoes while you wait. No need to dress up, the company is casual, and everyone is there for the same reason, to dig in and feast on the best barbeque this side of Kansas City!

LA SALSA
415 Horton Plaza
San Diego, CA 92101
Tel. (619) 234-6906
Hrs: Mon. - Sun.   10:00 a.m. - 10:00 p.m.
Credit cards are not accepted.

What began as a small Mexican restaurant in Los Angeles in 1979 has expanded into ten restaurants throughout southern California. To grow like this, it has to be good! La Salsa prides itself in bringing the real taste of gourmet Mexican food to California. And, authentic it is.

One of the tastiest touches of Mexico served by La Salsa is Antojitos Mexicanos. *Antojitos* translates to "little cravings," and are a must for anyone eating at La Salsa. But don't stop there. The day begins with a splendid breakfast menu including everything from Huevos Rancheros to breakfast burritos. If you're a Quesadilla fancier, La Salsa creates the best there are, melted cheese and guacamole in a hot flour, blue corn or corn tortilla, to which you add shredded beef, chicken or pork. The soft tacos are outstanding, and the lime-marinated, charcoal grilled steaks are superb, enhanced by a generous serving of Frijoles Negros (black beans), which are the best in town. You'll also find an excellent fresh salsa bar with sauces ranging from a mild Salsa Mexicana of fresh tomato, chili serrano, chopped onions and lime, to the Salsa Guego which will blow your ears off.

The staff is capable and friendly, and will gladly describe any food you may not be familiar with. If you live in the area, La Salsa offers catering services for anything, from a small event to a complete fiesta for a large crowd.

LA TERRAZA
2830 Canyon Street
San Diego, CA 92106
Tel. (619) 224-2777
Hrs: Mon. - Sun.   11:00 a.m. - 11:00 p.m.
Visa and MasterCard are accepted.

San Diego is a large city. At times, it can become so crowded and hot that all you want to do is get away and relax. Well, for your sake, the next time you find yourself in this predicament, assay your appetite and see if it isn't in need of something as well. If you find it is, make your way immediately to La Terraza for a remedy that can't be found elsewhere.

La Terraza, a restaurant specializing in authentic Mexican cuisine, is situated off the beaten path, making it a very quiet and relaxing place. Due partly to the location, but even more so to the skilled and happy people who serve you, this is one of those "in" places where you can escape on a hot weekday afternoon, have a maragarita, from a regular glass to a gallon container, and then stay for dinner. And what a dinner it is! You can choose from among many of the traditional Mexican favorites, such as the Carne Asada, a lightly marinated Filet Mignon served with a cheese enchilada, guacamole, rice and beans. This is but one of many delicious entrees served at La Terraza.

J.C. and Fred, the owners, are long time restauranteurs and have developed several landmark restaurants in the area. With this experience behind them you can be sure your visit to La Terraza will be an enjoyable one. The next time the heat, crowds and hunger start to assail you, remember this pleasant sanctuary.

MISTER A'S, 2550 Fifth Avenue, San Diego, CA 92106. Tel. (619) 239-1377. Winner of the Mobile Four Star Award, this restaurant high atop the Fifth Avenue Financial Center promises gracious European dining with a view.

MORGAN RESTAURANT, 515 Fith Avenue, San Diego, CA 92101. Tel. (619) 232-3352. An intimate and romantic restaurant in the Gaslamp Quarter, Morgan's offers the best in French and Italian cuisine. Call for dining hours.

NATI'S MEXICAN RESTAURANT
1852 Bacon Street
San Diego, CA 92107
Tel. (619) 224-3369
Visa and MasterCard are accepted.

Some businesses are so right for a place and the people who run them so right for that business, that in time it becomes almost a part of the landscape. The people who have operated Nati's since its inception in 1960 have created a landmark Mexican restaurant that incorporates continuity, consistency and elegance in the authentic Mexican dishes and setting.

Imagine Chili Rellenos made by Chef Luis from freshly roasted chilies, Chimichangas, sour cream Enchiladas and Carnitas prepared individually for each order. Other true dishes of Mexico are served and all foods are prepared from scratch from the freshest of ingredients. These are people who have a tradition of quality and service behind them. The original owner, Vern Lontz, is still an active participant in the business, and over the years the restaurant has been expanded to its comfortable 140 seat capacity in two dining rooms. The same chef who started back in 1960, and two of the waitresses, Maria and Luisa, are also part of the original "family."

A patio, shaded by colorful umbrellas by day and lit by candles and colored lights by night, makes an inviting addition to the comfortable dining rooms, particularly in view of Southern California's delightful weather. For anyone enjoying the fishing pier, Sunset Cliffs, Sea World, Cabrillo National Monument Lighthouse or other diversions of the Ocean Beach Area, the opportunity exists to enjoy the casual, authentic atmosphere and fine food at Nati's. Don't miss it.

OLD VENICE CAFE
2910 Canyon Street
San Diego, CA 92106
Tel: (619) 222-5888
Hrs: Mon. - Thu.   11:00 a.m. - 9:30 p.m.
        Friday   11:00 a.m. - 10:30 p.m.
        Saturday   4:00 p.m. - 10:30 p.m.
        Sunday   4:00 p.m. - 9:30 p.m.
Visa and MasterCard are accepted.

Everyone has experienced those occasions when they are so hungry that all they can concentrate on is the thought of food. For many, the foremost desires at times like these are things like large rigatoni noodles covered with meat sauce or a gooey pizza with all the toppings. To satisfy these cravings you must either spend a lot of time in the kitchen or go to a good restaurant. For those who choose the latter, there's no better place than Old Venice Cafe.

At Old Venice Cafe, you can either take one of the sidewalk tables, or dine indoors. But whatever you choose, you'll feel as if you were far way in the Alps on a beautiful sunny day. Like the restaurants in the Alps, the menu consists of an elegant offering of Italian dishes: lasagne, manicotti, chicken marsala, ravioli and eggplant parmesan, to mention a few. Some of the other favorites include the large antipasta salad and, of course, the pizza. You can order thick crust or, for that matter, anyway you like. The toppings are piled on and the sauces are delicious.

No Italian restaurant would be complete without a healthy selection of wines and beers. Following this tradition, you'll find that Old Venice is authentically Italian. Food apart, the ambiance here is terrific. It's soft, serene and quite romantic. All of this, the atmosphere and the food, make Old Venice Cafe a perfect haven for those who want to satisfy their hunger in style.

OLINDA'S MEXICAN RESTAURANT
2253 Morena Boulevard
San Diego, CA 92110
Tel. (619) 275-0024
Hrs: Sun. - Thu.   11:00 a.m. - 9:00 p.m.
           Fri. - Sat.   11:00 a.m. - 10:00 p.m.
Visa and MasterCard are accepted.

This is the definitive family restaurant complete with full family participation in the preparation of secret family recipes. All the authentic Mexican food is cooked from scratch on the premises and cooked to your order by the Olinda Sandoval family.

The restaurant has been operating for over six years at full tilt. One of the many attractions are the authentic Mexican fiesta costumes worn by the waitresses, brightly colored outfits that bounce with ruffles. The attire is perfect right down to beautiful matching earrings. Another attraction is the collection of lovely Spanish dancing dolls displayed in a glass case near the cashier's stand.

Bright red tablecloths lend even more "fiesta" to the environment. In the summer enormous ceramic ceiling fans gently cool the air. In the winter a cozy fireplace snaps and crackles, warming hearts and toes. A happy and relaxing restaurant, Olinda says with great sincerity that she serves "the best Mexican food in all of San Diego at family prices." You can't beat that!

PACIFIC BEACH BOATHOUSE
4325 Ocean Boulevard
San Diego, CA 92109
Tel. (619) 274-3474
 Hrs: Lunch   Mon. - Fri.   11:00 a.m. - 2:30 p.m.
           Dinner   Mon. - Sat.   5:00 p.m. - 10:00 p.m.
Also,

GROSSMONT   ENCINITAS
5500 Grossmont Center Dr.   85 Encinitas Blvd.
La Mesa, CA 92041   Encinitas, CA 92024
Tel. (619) 589-5353   Tel. (619) 944-1338

IMPERIAL BANK   HARBOR ISLAND
701 "B" Street   2040 Harbor Island Drive
San Diego, CA 92101   San Diego, CA 92101
Tel. (619) 696-0225   Tel. (619) 291-8011

This family of restaurants in the San Diego area are known by the locals as the place to go for great seafood. As a visitor looking for a fine meal, the Boathouse Restaurants are dining establishments you should frequent during your stay.

"Seafood that catches your imagination", is the descriptive phrase that forms the motto of the the Boathouse. The interior of the restaurants will also catch your imagination. Each is based on a nautical theme with beautiful sand-etched glass work and appropriate accents to the decor. Each dinner entree begins with a special house salad made at your table. Included also is fresh bread, vegetables, and choice of rice or potatoes. A great way to start your dinner would be with the appetizer sampler which is a trio of shrimp, crab-stuffed mushrooms, and potato skins. Take your pick of entrees from the shellfish section, maybe some gourmet stuffed shrimp, or select from the steak section if you prefer. The highlight of the Boathouse Restaurants are the twelve to fifteen fresh fish dishes prepared daily, each in a unique way.

With five locations to serve you there has got to be a Boathouse Restaurant near to you. Be sure to make one of them your favorite stop in San Diego.

PARADISE BAY SEAFOOD RESTAURANT AND OYSTER BAR
1935 Quiuira Road
San Diego, CA 92109
Tel. (619) 223-2335
Hrs: Lunch   Mon. - Sun.   11:00 a.m. - 3:00 p.m.
      Dinner   Mon. - Sun.   5:00 p.m. - 10:00 p.m.

The word "paradise" carries a hefty definition. It's a word that is too easily tagged on far too many places that are unworthy of the title. However, one place that is qualified to be associated with this claim is the aptly named Paradise Bay Seafood Restaurant and Oyster Bar. This restaurant, in a setting of gentle sea breeze, blue sky, sandy beaches and warm temperatures clearly evokes a state of elated bliss.

Now turn your senses inward and enjoy the sights, sounds and aromas of one of San Diego's finest dining houses. A green carpet with light floral designs combined with the soft colors of the table and booth seating, creates a relaxed and inviting dining atmosphere. All the while, the delicious scents generated by the house specialities are enough to tease anyone's appetite. Tempura shrimp, scallops, and excellent beef entrees are only a few of dishes the menu holds in store for you. After dinner, you'll want to try one of the exquisite desserts such as the Paradise Bay Pie - Amoretto with fudge ice cream in a chocolate wafer crust, covered in a wine chocolate sauce and topped with whipped cream.

On Tuesday thru Saturday night's, when your dining extravaganza is finished, you can enjoy live music in the upstairs lounge. The Paradise Bay Seafood Restaurant and Oyster Bar is the "Best Choice" for paradise this side of Heaven.

THE PENNANT
2843 Mission Boulevard
San Diego, CA 92109
Tel. (619) 488-1671
Hrs: Mon. - Sun.   8:00 a.m. - 2:00 a.m.

Since 1962, The Pennant has been the place for speciality dinners, great conversation and terrific drinks. It is the best possible example of a California beach bar, and is well worth the visit.

Upon entering The Pennant, you are greeted by low lights, a twenty by twenty square foot, wooden bar and an occasional standing room only crowd. But not to worry, if it's too crowded downstairs, just take a short hike to the roof top patio. Here, you can enjoy balmy ocean breezes, a wonderful view and some of the best burgers in town.   The owner of the establishment, Richard

Kovalchek, is a native San Diegian who has lived on it's beaches most of his life. Because of his experience, the atmosphere of The Pennant is genuine and enjoyed by locals and tourists alike.

Speciality dinners are served everyday except Tuesdays. For instance, Monday is spaghetti night. Wednesday meals vary from week to week, but might include a delicious dish of stuffed porkchops. A key attraction at The Pennant is the upside down margarita. They're served by reservation only, and you had better love tequila. If you've got a party coming up, this restaurant caters everyday except Sunday. The Pennant is an adult only experience. However, it is well managed, clean and thoroughly enjoyable. Stop by for a good meal and a good time that won't be easily forgotten.

PIRET'S MISSION HILLS
902 West Washington
San Diego, CA 92103
Tel. (619) 297-2993
Hrs: Sun. - Thu.   9:00 a.m. - 10:00 p.m.
         Fri. - Sat.   9:00 a.m. - 11:00 p.m.
Visa, MasterCard and AMEX are accepted.

It's Piret's Mission Hills where you can decide for yourself whether you want to sit down to a leisurely meal or go home with the best bag of groceries ever to go through a checkout stand. Then again, you might want both.

Piret's Mission Hills is a carryout gourmet food store as well as a restaurant. It successfully combines a gourmet food and pastry shop with an indoor cafe. The grocery products are the best of their class. There's a well-rounded assortment that just preys upon impulse buyers. There's also an extensive wine selection. A continental breakfast is popular during the week, as is the weekend brunch. Among the favorite appetizers is a great paté. Diners should always look into the special of the day. Diner menu entrees include offerings such as Scampi Provencal, Lamb in brandy sauce and sauteed chicken breast in wine and mushrooms.

This is a popular spot for local personalities, but they usually stay in the shadows, says owner Jeanne Driscoll. The place is clean and crisp, but with a warmth and ambiance that comes with each guest being made to feel welcome.

RAINWATER'S
1202 Kettner Boulevard
San Diego, CA 92101
Tel. (619) 235-5757
Hrs: Mon. - Fri.   11:30 a.m. - 12:00 midnight
          Saturday   5:00 p.m. - 1:00 a.m.
          Sunday   5:00 p.m. - 10:00 p.m.
Visa, MasterCard, AMEX and Diners Club are accepted.

In a part of the country known for unusual and trendy restaurants, it's reassuring to find there are still those that go back to the basics. Fine dining is not a matter of trends or fads, it is a matter of offering the finest meats, fish and other fresh foods and accompaniments, and preparing them superbly. Ambitious goals, but Rainwater's executes them to perfection.

Laurel and Paddy Rainwater bring a wealth of experience to their elegant restaurant through their past ownership of restaurants in the midwest. In their current location in the beautifully restored McClintock Plaza, they have fashioned their restaurant along the lines of a Chicago chophouse. They feature perfectly prepared meats selected from the finest available. The specialty is a Pepper Ribeye Special topped with sauteed mushrooms, bacon, onions and peppercorns. Traditional pasta dishes are featured, along with a good selection of fresh fish and seafood. Continental favorites of Pate de Foie Gras and fresh caviar are offered among the appetizers, and dinner wine, champagne and vintage port are available by the glass. For dessert, be sure to try the Southern Pecan Pie.

One can't help but find dining at Rainwater's a delightful experience, where everything can be enjoyed in a sophisticated yet unpretentious setting, surrounded by the warm cherryword of the restored warehouse.

REEL INN CAFE
5120 N. Harbor Drive
San Diego, CA 92106
Tel. (619) 226-0268
Hrs: Mon. - Sun.   7:00 a.m. - 10:00 p.m.
Visa, MasterCard and AMEX are accepted.

There's no better way to take advantage of San Diego's bountiful seafood than to dine right at the harbor, at the Reel Inn Cafe.

Newly opened in 1987, the Reel Inn makes everything from scratch using absolutely the freshest, best quality ingredients to be found. Locally caught seafoods are featured daily on an ever-changing fresh sheet. Often available are Yellowtail Tuna, Swordfish, and Lobster, as well as *mahi-mahi*, English Sole and Mexican White Shrimp. Produce from Chino's Farm provides the key ingredients to salads like the Vine Ripened Tomato Plate and the Mixed Garden Salad. Nothing is average here. For instance, the B.L.T. is made with Italian Bacon, lettuce and Chino's Vine Ripened Beefsteak Tomatoes. The Reel Inn has an herb garden and make fresh pesto from basil and olive oil. Homemade pastas are a real treat, and the sandwiches include a mesquite broiled fish sandwich, slow roasted brisket of beef and mesquite breast of chicken with roasted peppers. Even the French Fries are made from scratch.

Located harborside on North Harbor drive between Harbor and Shelter Island, the Reel Inn Cafe is just minutes away from downtown or the airport. It's understated elegance, nautical decor, and enthusiastic staff are part of the charm that will prevent this little gem from remaining an insider's secret for long.

RUEBEN E. LEE
880 East Harbor
San Diego, CA 92101
Tel. (619) 291-1880
Hrs: Lunch   Mon. - Sat.   11:00 a.m. - 4:00 p.m.
        Dinner   Sun. - Tue.   4:00 p.m. - 10:00 p.m.
                        Fri. - Sat.   4:00 p.m. - 11:00 p.m.
Visa, MasterCard and AMEX are accepted.

The *Reuben E. Lee* is an authentic replica of the Mississippi riverboats of the 1800s. She is 205 feet long, 55 feet wide and will carry 600 "passengers."

Tied up at the east end of Harbor Island, she actually floats on San Diego Harbor and affords a spectacular view of the San Diego skyline and the various military and pleasure craft movement on the harbor. There are two full restaurants and a cocktail lounge on board. The Sternwheeler Restaurant menu offers a variety of beef and fowl entrees with specialties such as Shrimp Scampi, Prime Rib and Roast Duckling. The Seafood Deck specializes in fresh fish and various seafood delicacies including Bouillabaisse, steamed clams and lobster. A lovely Sunday brunch is featured form 10:00 a.m. to 2:00 p.m. The cocktail lounge offers top name entertainment and dancing on selected nights. The lavish interior of *Reuben E. Lee* contains beautiful carpeting, mirrors, hundreds of windows and the dining facilities are graced with crisp linens.

Complete banquet facilities are available for private functions including weddings, receptions, professional meetings and other special events. The Texas Deck with its outside patio is perfect for larger parties, while the Wheelhouse offers an intimate dining experience for parties of two to twelve.

Both rooms feature a breathtaking view of the harbor. Enjoy an elegant step back in time aboard the *Reuben E. Lee.*

RICCI'S
1203 Garnet
San Diego, CA 92109
Tel. (619) 272-6632
Hrs: Mon. - Thu.   11:00 a.m. - 10:30 p.m.
        Friday   11:00 a.m. - 11:30 p.m.
        Saturday   4:00 p.m. - 11:00 p.m.
        Sunday   4:00 p.m. - 10:30 p.m.

When you walk into Ricci's, you feel a bit of Italy in the air. The white stucco building has large picture windows in the front and smaller panes on the sides, giving diners views of the lovely patio area outside. Vine covered trellises, an abundance of hanging plants and cheery red linen on the tables lend warmth and friendliness to the restaurant, which makes dining there especially pleasant.

And the food. Ahhh! Spaghetti you could die for. Done *al dente* with special sauce recipes you'll wish you could duplicate. Chicken, pasta and fresh fish dishes such as Calamari are specialties of the house. Excellent wines are available, and there's an espresso bar that also serves cappuccino.

For dessert, Italian ice cream and cheesecake are available. For quality Italian cuisine in a warm and inviting atmosphere, try Ricci's in San Diego.

TARANTINO'S RESTAURANT
5150 North Harbor Drive
San Diego, CA 92106
Tel. (619) 224-3555
Hrs: Mon. - Thu.   11:00 a.m. - 10:00 p.m.
                 Fri. - Sat.   11:00 a.m. - 11:00 p.m.
Brunch   Sunday   9:30 a.m. - 3:00 p.m.
Visa, MasterCard and AMEX are accepted.

When you think of Italian restaurants, do you think of seafood and a harbor setting? Most people don't, however Tarantino's Restaurant has that unusual element going for it, as well as an unusually exceptionally traditional Italian menu.

Because of its setting on the edge of San Diego Bay, Tarantino's has a wonderful view of the San Deigo fishing fleet. Cool ocean breezes fan the evening air, and during the summer months their is a special treat for restaurant patrons. Named for the owner's mother "Carmela Bella" is a small river boat reserved for guests at Tarantino's. Either after your satisfying meal or while waiting for a table, you can tour San Deigo Bay and take in a bit of sight seeing while sipping on a cocktail or wine. John Tarantino first opened his business nearly thirty years ago and still presides over the preparation of the daily meals. John is known for is his delicious fresh made pasta. The elaborate kneeding and rolling proceedure that each batch must go through before it is cut and air dried causes the finished product to take on a unique flavor. Other menu items include salads, soups, fish, veal, and chicken.

Stop in for lunch or dinner. Lunch features an extensive buffet with many memorable selections. Holidays are always a good time to make plans to visit to Tarantino's. They make a special Italian effort to put on a show. Tarantino's on the bay in San Deigo, is your "Best Choice" for Italian cuisine.

TOM HAM'S LIGHTHOUSE
2150 Harbor Island Road
San Diego, CA 92101
Tel: (619) 291-9110
All major credit cards are accepted.

The seas can be quite serene at times, yet at others they can be terrifying. The oceans of the world are one of nature's most fickle creations. The men who have sailed them are among the bravest in all history. These men would dare to tempt fate by navigating the capricious waters of the Western seas. It's in the tradition of these perilous treks that one of the most unusual restaurants in America was created.

Tom Ham's Lighthouse is more than a place to enjoy fine food and drink. It's a memorial to the dauntless men who led the way for the opening of the West. There, you'll see a recounting of the actual voyages made along our rough coast. You can appreciate the craftsmanship of fine scrimshaw or have a laugh over the innocent naughtiness of "Saucy Sally," an eminent ship's figurehead that was used to guide the ship to safety. But the lighthouse has more to offer than rich heritage and tales of the sea. You'll find it a lively place, bustling with the business and fun of contemporary California.

Music, laughter and splendid food make the atmosphere elegant yet relaxed. Finally, there's a breathtaking view of San Diego Bay and a horizon that will leave you in awe. The Lighthouse is a legend in San Diego. A legend that lives to tell it's tale proudly.

TOP O' THE COVE
1216 Prospect Street
San Diego, CA 92037
Tel. (619) 454-7779
Visa, MasterCard and AMEX are accepted.

A truly enchanting restaurant is difficult to find. However, once discovered, it becomes like a file in one's mind. It's a file that can be called upon when the holder wishes to drum up pleasant memories of a past dining experience. Or perhaps, the restaurant is recalled to make plans for another visit. Whatever the case, before you acquire this file you must first find the restaurant. The "Best Choice" around is Top O' The Cove.

At Top O' The Cove authentic charm comes home. From the time when you're greeted by the towering Morton fig trees at the entrance of this original La Jolla cottage, to the moment when you're looking through the menu, you'll notice the ambiance here is like that of no other restaurant. It has a warmth and coziness that you're sure to savor. There are many wonderful surprises on the menu including a delightful selection of hors d'oeuvres, such as fresh asparagus with caviar and Grenouilles en Vert, sauteed frog legs laced with a garlic herb dressing.

For dinner, choose from such entrees as Magret de Canard, a sliced duck mixed with black currants. Then there's the Filet Mignon au Poivre, a tenderloin of beef with a pepper sauce Madagascar. Mmmm, it makes you want to take French lessons. Okay, the restaurant has been found and the file has been established. Now you can call it up whenever you want an unforgettable dining experience.

TRADEWINDS RESTAURANT
San Diego Hilton Hotel
1775 East Mission Bay Drive
San Diego, CA 92109
Tel. (619) 276-4010
Hrs: Mon. - Sun.   6:00 p.m. - 11:00 p.m.
Visa, MasterCard, AMEX and Discover are accepted.

You'll dine as if you were aboard the Bounty with Charles Laughton and Clark Gable when you dine at Tradewinds. The nautical decor is from the actual 1934 movie set! Your surroundings are complete with original rigging, barrels, and maiden head, and you'll be seated near the very mast where Clark Gable was tied during the filming of "Mutiny on the Bounty."

A Four Star restaurant, Tradewinds enjoys the reputation of being the finest restaurant in the area. The extensive continental menu features such mouth watering selections from the sea as lobster Cinzano - tender pieces of lobster sauteed in butter and vermouth, flavored with sweet cream and served in the shell, or the brochette of seafood - scallops and lobster sauteed to perfection on a skewer. Land items include veal piccata, Marsala, or scallopini, tender Chateaubriand bouquetiere, and grenadine of beef saute with sauce bernaise.

Enhancing the main bill of fare is a wide selection of delicious appetizers, salads, soups, chowders and flambe´ desserts. Enjoy the romantic nautical setting as if aboard the Bounty, while waiters provide service fitting for a captain and his guests.

WOODSTOCK'S
6548 El Cajon Boulevard
San Diego, CA 92115
Tel. (619) 265-0999
Hrs: Sun. - Thu.   11:30 a.m. - 1:00 a.m.
        Fri. - Sat.   11:30 a.m. - 2:00 a.m.

It is Woodstock's philosophy to make the best, not the fastest, pizza in town. Each pizza is rolled by hand, piled with real mozzarella cheese, and topped with fresh meats and vegetables. The pizza dough, both white and wheat, is made fresh each morning.

Woodstock's offers sixteen different "Tasty Toppings" to create your own pizza with, including artichoke hearts, almonds, salami and garlic. If you can't decide, they also offer two combinations: The Monty's Revenge with pepperoni, mushrooms, green peppers, onions and sausage; and the Vegetarian Delight with mushrooms, olives, green peppers and onions. The Woodstock's Special gives you your choice of any five toppings for the price of four.

The menu also includes dinner salads, antipasta salads, garlic bread, mini pizzas and a great selection of tap and bottled beers, and a variety of other beverages. There are lunch specials, offered until 4:00 p.m. with salad, pizza slices and mini pizzas. Woodstock's will also deliver your 12" or 16" pizza free within their delivery area.

The employees enjoy working at Woodstock's and their attitude is reflected in the quality of the food and service you receive. The decor is comfortable and the restaurant is a fun place for both families and students.

YAKITORI II
1740 Sports Arena Boulevard
San Diego, CA 92110
Tel. (619) 223-2640
Hrs: Lunch   Mon. - Fri.   11:00 a.m. - 2:30 p.m.
                       Sat. - Sun.   12:00 noon - 4:00 p.m.
        Dinner   Sun. - Thu.   5:00 p.m. - 10:00 p.m.
                       Fri. - Sat.   5:00 noon - 11:00 p.m.
Visa, MasterCard, AMEX and Diners Club are accepted.

The rise in popularity and availability of Japanese restaurants and sushi bars has also given rise to greater levels of variety and authenticity. Yakitori, in operation since 1978, has provided consistently high quality food, a variety of dishes and appeal to the eye.

Owner Victor Murashige and his wife, Kyoko, maintain a place of quiet, peace and beauty created by the use of rice paper partitions, bamboo supports and fresh flowers in lovely arrangements by Kyoko herself. Equally stunning to the eye and the palate, are the entrees. The combination dishes allow diners to sample a wide range of Japanese specialties centered around seafood, beef, pork and chicken. One such combination includes Shrimp Tempura and tender beef morsels stir-fried with vegetables. To help in making a selection, a great number of the special dishes are colorfully shown on the menu.

As the name suggests, this is the second Yakitori for Victor Murashigi; the first having been opened on Guam in 1971. Fortunately for Southern Californians and visitors to San Diego, Victor moved here after a lengthy search for just the right place, a benefit to those who like to indulge in the finest of Japanese style and foods.

SALON

WALDON ASHE SKIN CARE CENTRE
930 West Washington Street
San Diego, CA 92103
Tel. (619) 295-7302
Hrs: Mon.. - Sat.   9:00 a.m. - 6:00 p.m.
Appointments preferred.
Visa, MasterCard and local checks are accepted.

Exclusive, state of the art pampering of your skin for both men and women happens at the Waldon Ashe Skin Care Centre. the salon is named after its dynamic owner who has spent the last fifteen years learning about how to restore skin and keep it as youthful and beautiful as possible. Waldon, who has been featured in *Gentleman's Quarterly, People Magazine* and on the *Oprah Winfrey Show,* attracts a world famous clientele.

The facial techniques used at Waldon Ashe Skin Care Centre combine European massage and South American methods of deep cleansing. the cleansing products and make up are made especially for the Centre by a leading United States laboratory. A graduate of the New York International School of Aesthetics, and a former make up artist, Waldon and his staff also perform make up magic for special occasions, such as weddings or portraits. Among the treatments offered at the salon are deep pore cleansing facials for men and women, rejuvenative treatments for mature skin, and acne alleviation. Complete body facial and Swedish body massage are also offered by his highly trained staff of professionals.

You can choose a brief and moderately priced treatment or service at this salon, or indulge yourself in the "Waldon Ashe Escape," three to six hours of unequaled pampering. Whatever package you choose, time spent at Waldon Ashe Skin Care Centre will leave you feeling luxurious and rejuvenated.

SPECIALTY SHOPS

THE MEXICO SHOP
2783 San Diego Avenue
San Diego, CA 92110
Tel. (619)298-9167
Hrs: Mon. - Sun.   10:00 a.m. - 6:00 p.m.
Closed Thanksgiving, Christmas Day and New Year's Day.
Visa, MasterCard and AMEX are accepted.

Touring Old Town San Diego is a great way to experience an important part of California's history: The Mexican Period. The Mexico Shop allows you to bring home a little of that history.

Established in 1962, The Mexico Shop was the first tourist oriented store to open in San Diego's Old Town district. Housed in one of San Diego's original Spanish dwellings, and stocking an incredible selection of South of the border treasures, The Mexico Shop seems like it could have been one of the original businesses in old time San Diego. The Mexico Shop is renowned as the place to go for pinatas and Mexican Christmas items. But that's only the beginning. The Mexico Shop is a veritable Mexican marketplace, complete with hand embroidered clothing, jewelry, baskets, hats, colored paper flowers, and onyx miniatures.

Owner Elba Moxley says many companies buy party favors and hats for their Mexican theme parties, such as Cinco de Mayo. There are many reproductions of ancient masks and figures. And the store carries special products from Spain and Central America.   Best of all the prices are the the most competitive you'll find North of the border

SILVER SEA
2527 San Diego Avenue
San Diego, CA 92110
Tel. (619) 291-0274
Hrs: Mon. - Sat.   10:00 a.m. - 9:00 p.m.
           Sunday   10:00 a.m. - 7:00 p.m.
Visa, MasterCard and AMEX are accepted.

The Silver Sea is a unique sea oriented specialty shop, featuring items to intrigue the most discriminating person. It started as a small shop that sold sea shells, and has expanded to include decorator items in brass, ceramics and durastone.

Right now it's the "Southwestern" look and the store is chock full of all kinds of items to make your home look straight out of Santa Fe.

The Silver Sea is located behind an old time storefront on Old Town's busiest street. One of the original owners was a diver and brought back rare and wonderful treasures from the ocean floor. Today the store stocks shells from around the world for both the collector and the novice. There is also a wide variety of jewelry priced for any size pocketbook and the store ships via UPS anywhere in the United States.

The Silver Sea has been growing over the past twelve years, with several expansions and has increased to 2,000 square feet, with a gift for finding new and interesting items, the buyers for the Silver Sea will always have something to intrigue the visitor as well as the folks from San Diego.

SPORTS EQUIPMENT

ADVENTURE 16
I-8 at Mission Gorge Road
4620 Alvarado Canyon Road
San Diego, CA 92120
Tel.   (619) 283-2374
Hrs: Mon - Fri.   10:00 a.m. - 8:00 p.m.
        Saturday   10:00 a.m. - 6:00 p.m.
        Sunday   12:00 noon - 5:00 p.m.
Visa and MasterCard are accepted.
Also,

143 S Cedros	Horton Plaza
Solana Beach, CA 92075	Sports Deck
Tel. (619) 755-7662	San Diego, CA 92101
	Tel. (619) 234-1751

Mic Mead's greatest pleasure is being associated and surrounded by people who love what they're doing. He also happens to be one of them. You see, Mic Mead loves the outdoors and adventure, and he's made a life's work of it.

Starting with a small workshop and retail store twenty- five years ago, Mead called his business Adventure 16. He made and sold backpacks, tents and camping gear. Today Adventure 16 has grown to six stores, an international adventure travel and outings program, a major wholesale division and an award winning factory. Adventure 16 has become an institution in the outdoor outfitting industry, offering such diverse services as ballooning classes, state park campground reservations, and a complete equipment rental program. There are clinics, seminars, classes and outings sponsored by Adventure 16 to stimulate awareness and promote sport through participation. Adventure 16 manufactures its own line of tents, backpacks and other outdoor gear, including the famous bomber hat and the world's warmest down jacket. Footprints, a publication subscribed to by over 60,000 backpackers and outdoor enthusiasts, is published three times a year by Adventure 16. And through it all, Mead has never given up his outdoorsiness. His office is a log cabin smack in the middle of one of his stores where customers both young and old wander in and out all day long.

If you have the spirit of adventure somewhere inside you, then Adventure 16's door can be the gateway to discovering the excitement of your dreams and the endless possibilities of life in the outdoors.

DIVE LOCKER
1020 Grand Avenue
San Diego, CA 92109
Tel. (619) 272-1120
Hrs: Mon. - Fri.   9:00 a.m. - 7:00 p.m.
          Sat. - Sun.   8:00 a.m. - 5:00 p.m.
Visa and MasterCard are accepted
Also,
8650 Miramar Road Suite C   405 N. Highway 101
San Diego, CA 92126   Salona Beach, CA 92109
Tel. (619) 271-5231   Tel. (619) 755-6822
                                 348 E. Grand Avenue
                                 Escondido, CA 92025
                                 Tel. (619) 746-8980

Before you plunge into Scuba Diving, acquaint yourself with the Dive Locker. Chuck and Terry Nickland are a father and son team who operate four area dive shops that emphasize service over retails sales.

You can buy anything you need, from air to air regulators, but the best comes free, good advice on where to go and what to see in what is probably the best underwater sea scape on the West Coast. They sponsor free dive trips for certified divers, and offer lessons to the next generation. They were one of the major sponsors for the creation of an artificial reef in the La Jolla Cove as a result of sinking of a Kelp Cutting ship.

During your next sea hunt, don't go off the deep end, check out the Dive Locker first.

MISSION BAY SPORTCENTER
1010 Santa Clar Place
San Diego, CA 92109
Tel. (619) 488-1004
Hrs: May - Sept.   Mon. - Sun.   10:00 a.m. - 7:00 p.m.
          Oct. - April   Sat. - Sun.   10:00 a.m. - 7:00 p.m.
Visa and MasterCard are accepted.

Here is an opportunity to play with water sports for the uninitiated and experienced alike. If you're new to supra skiboating, windsurfing, sailing, or water skiing, worry not. Owners Dee and Rich Gleason and their staff have the experience and enthusiasm to make the learning of new water sports both fun and comfortable. For those of you who know the ropes, you'll be delighted with the advanced classes and rental programs.

Located right on Mission Bay with protected water and sandy beaches met on the land side by expanses of grass, the whole family can come out and picnic right on the site before trying the water sport of their choice. All instructors are certified and safety conscious.

Attention is individual and the large inventory of equipment is clean, well maintained and ready to go when you are.

(See special invitation in the Appendix.)

STATIONERY STORES

CAMILLE'S HALLMARK
3007 Clairemont Drive
San Diego, CA 92117
Tel. (619) 275-2270
Hrs: Mon. - Fri.   9:30 a.m. - 8:00 p.m.
           Saturday   9:30 a.m. - 6:00 p.m.
           Sunday   11:00 a.m. - 5:00 p.m.
Visa and MasterCard are accepted.

Here's a shop that does everything! Located close to Mission Bay's Visitor Center, Camille's not only functions as an eclectic gift shop, but also as a post office with copier services and office supplies.

As a gift shop, however, Camille's carries a wide selection of items calculated to meet every need from gifts for brides, babies and children, to party supplies, puzzles, and gift wrappings. A huge array of greeting cards are available including those super funny ones from Gary Larsen's "Far Side" series which will meet every contingency.

And there really is a Camille. A happy lady with large brown eyes and dimples, owner Camille enjoys her store and enjoys meeting the people who visit. If there is something you need, Camille will help. There's lots of room for browsing. If you happen to visit at Christmastime, you'll be invited to join their open house. If it's Halloween, beware, you'll walk into a Boo Bazaar.

THE PAPER DOLL
11211 Sorrento Valley Road, Suite L
San Diego, CA 92121
Tel. (619) 455-5322
Hrs: Mon. - Fri.   10:00 a.m. - 6:00 p.m.
        Sat. - Sun.   12:00 noon - 5:00 p.m.
Visa, Mastercard and AMEX are accepted.
Also,

PAPER DOLL #2
1111 Prospect Mall
La Jolla, CA 92037
Tel. (619) 459-0561

PAPER DOLL #3
1523-8 E. Valley Pkwy.
Escondido, CA 92025
Tel. (619) 743-6686

PAPER DOLL #5
4373 La Jolla Village Dr.
San Diego, CA 92122
Tel. (619) 455-9591

PAPER DOLL #7
Fashion Valley Road
Bldg. 290, Suite 567
San Diego, CA 92108
Tel. (619) 296-8151

PAPER DOLL #8
947 1st St., Suite 102
Encinitas, CA 92024
Tel. (619) 436-2855

PAPER DOLL #10
Crossroads Mall #302
1700 28th Street
Boulder, CO 80301
Tel. (303) 449-5959

PAPER DOLL #11
540 South Coast Highway
Laguna Beach, CA 92651
Tel. (494) 494-8999

If it looks good on paper, you'll probably find it at the Paper Doll. Specializing in cards, gift wrap, paper goods, invitations and stationery, this store sells fun by the ream.

Owner Kathleen Germain attracts customers to each of her seven stores by doing what she calls, "creating a feeling, an experience...by putting together combinations of merchandise that work well together." Among them is stemware, elegant pieces that a customer may buy to present with a fine bottle of Champagne. There are toys for children and toys for playful adults. Among the offerings you'll find jewelry, hair ornaments, table accessories, picture frames, vases, clocks and seasonal items. Their selection of cards is one of the best and range from very elegant to very humorous. You can always find the right card to express your exact sentiments.

As a result of stocking a good selection of paper items and other gifts over the years, the Paper Doll stores have flourished. Even in recessionary times, there are plenty of people looking for inexpensive but refined and distinctive gifts. The Paper Doll, where small change turns into paper.

Visit their other locations in Fashion Valley, University Town Center, La Jolla's Prospect Square, the Lumberyard in Encinitas and Horton Plaza in San Diego and in Laguna Beach.

SUMMIT STATIONERS
1640 Camino Del Rio N.
Mission Valley Center
San Diego, CA 92108
Tel. (619) 297-0795
Hrs: Mon. - Fri.   10:00 a.m. - 9:00 p.m.
        Saturday   10:00 a.m - 6:00 p.m.
        Sunday   11:00 a.m. - 5:00 p.m.
Visa and MasterCard are accepted.

When you need to find the ultimate in stationery stores, don't miss shopping at Summit Stationers. This store is one of the most unique stationery and gift stores around. They literally have thousands of greeting cards and a huge selection of items such as party supplies, helium balloons, quality giftware and holiday needs. There are 4,200 square feet of shopping and browsing area and it is a fun place to visit.

The cards and gifts are well-lighted and displayed, and everything is clean, bright and cheerful. Some of the more unusual items found at Summit Stationers are a huge selection of top quality picture frames and stuffed animals.

This is also the special place for the office person. They feature a large selection of office supplies from pens to blackboards. The store also has a 25,000 items catalog desk for customers special orders with one day delivery. The management really goes all out for the holiday seasons too. You will find their staff smiling, warm and helpful. They welcome you to browse at your leisure and enjoy the tremendous selections fo high quality products available.

SWIMWEAR

PILAR'S BEACHWEAR, INC.
3745 Mission Boulevard
San Diego, CA 92109-7194
Tel. (619) 488-3056
Hrs: Summer   Mon. - Sun.   9:00 a.m. - 8:00 p.m.
          Winter   Mon. - Sun.   10:00 a.m. - 6:00 p.m.
Visa, MasterCard, AMEX and Carte Blanche are accepted.
Also,
PILAR'S II
108 Santa Monica Boulevard
Santa Monica, CA 90401
Tel. (213) 394-2214

Go where the stars shop for elegant swimwear. Pilar's carries sixty lines of designer swimwear for women. All styles and sizes are represented by over 10,000 suits attractively displayed by designer name. Some brand names include Yves Saint Laurent, Diva, Vollbrach, Body Glove, De La Renta, and Lisa Bruce from England.

Owner Pilar came from Barcelona to visit a sister in the United States and, liking it here so much, decided to remain. She likes to make people feel good about themselves and when she decided to open a shop, it was her flair for fashion and love of swimming that directed her toward this specialty swimwear concept. "I wanted something special and fun to do," she said.

Pilar is proud of the vast variety represented in her shop and is quick to promise special orders, as well as a willingness to ship anywhere. For the ultimate in swimwear selection and friendly service, visit Pilar's in San Diego or her new shop, Pilar's II, in Santa Monica.

TOURS

CHAMPAGNE COWBOYS TOURS
P.O. Box 203010
San Diego, CA 92120
Tel.   (619) 283-0220
          (800) 522-8488

True to their name, when you sign up for one of five exceptional Champagne Cowboy Tours, yes, your hosts are cowboys and cowgirls. There's no better way to see San Diego's best attractions than climbing aboard one of Champagne Cowboy Tours clean, modern vans or mini-buses. Each tour is distinctive and well thought out. The La Jolla, San Diego and Coronado Tour takes you to the summit of Mount Soledad for a panoramic view of the city. Then it's back to the heart of things for a swing by the Embarcadero, Gaslamp Quarter, Balboa Park, a shopping stop at Old Town and finally a tour of the famous Hotel del Coronado.

The Mexico Shopper is a taste of Old Mexico and the "most visited city in North America," Tijuana. One of San Diego's most famous attractions is Sea World, and Champagne Cowboy Tours will take you there in style. The tour includes free admission to all of Sea World's attractions. The San Diego Zoo is legendary, and Champagne Cowboy Tours considers this one of its favorite tours. Your fare includes admission, a narrated bus tour of the entire zoo and admission to the children's zoo.

For a really full day of entertainment, try the Zoo and Sea World Combination. Don't forget, they will provide personal door to door service from your hotel or resort.

OFFSHOOT BOTANICAL TOURS
1640 Monroe Avenue
San Diego, CA 92116
Tel. (619) 297-0289
Park tours are free every Saturday.

Explore with experts the impressive gardens, unique architecture and fascinating history of Balboa Park. Tour guides Dale Ward and Bonnie Poppe lead informative walks every Saturday in the Park and monthly at the San Diego Zoo.

Balboa Park, noted for its fine museums and theaters, has over 1,000 acres. Many fine gardens abound. Offshootours conducts a rotating series of one hour easy paced walks to interest almost everyone. The "Heart of the Park" tour introduces you to the museum core of the Park. During this time you will acquaint yourself with its architectural and botanical richness, while learning the inside story of the Park's history and developemnt. Other one hour walks in the weekly series highlight the gardens in great detail: The Palm Arboretum, the Desert Garden, the exotic tree collection and more.

The San Diego Zoo not only has a vast collection of animals, but has over 7,000 plant species form around the world. You will view many rare and endangered plants on the two hour botanical walks conducted by Offshootours. These special Zoo tours are free with admission or membership to the Zoo.

Offshootours is a delightful way to get to know San Diego. It's also a fun way to entertain friends and relatives that fits into almost any budget. Offshootours also provides group tours of local private gardens, North

County nurseries, the Find Japanese Garden at the Neiman Tech Center and a nature walk in Presidio Park.

(See special invitation in the Appendix.)

OLD TOWN WALKING TOURS
3977 Twiggs Street
San Diego, CA 92110
Tel.   (619) 296-1004
Hrs: Mon. - Sun.   10:00 a.m. - 5:00 p.m.
Tours leave hourly.

An Old Town Walking Tour is like strolling through 200 years of history. Director, Robert Doyle takes pride in offering a complete tour of beautiful Old Town San Diego.

Friendly, knowledgeable tour guides lead groups and individuals on forty-five minute tours of the historic Old Town. The guides are skilled at weaving vivid tales of 19th century life, often embellishing their narrations with touches of humor, and, they enjoy answering questions. Each guest of Old Town Walking Tours receives a complimentary map of Old Town's historic points.

Whether you expect visiting friends and relatives, or are planning field trips for vacationing children or you are a visitor to San Diego yourself, an Old Town Walking Tour is just the ticket for your holiday outing.

(See special invitation in the Appendix.)

TRAVEL AGENCY AND STORES

LE TRAVEL STORE
295 Horton Plaza
San Diego, CA 92101
Tel.   (619) 544-0005
         (619) 544-0800   Agency
Hrs: Store   Mon. - Fri.   10:00 a.m. - 9:00 p.m.
                                 Saturday   10:00 a.m. - 6:00 p.m.
                                 Sunday   11:00 a.m. - 6:00 p.m.
         Travel Agency   Mon - Sat.   10:00 a.m. - 5:30 p.m.
Visa and MasterCard are accepted.

Joan and Bill Keller are among the lucky few who have turned a youthful hobby into a successful business. Both were avid travelers prior to meeting in

Madame Ermenkov's French class at Grossmont College in 1973. When Bill transferred to the University of California at San Diego, he created and ran the student travel service that is still on campus. Joan and Bill opened Le Travel Store in 1976, and many of their customers are yesterdays students, now today's professionals.

Le Travel Store is both a travel agency and a store that carries travel accessories. Imagine coordinating your travel plans and finding everything you need for an overseas trip in one stop. Shopping Le Travel Store lets you avoid the frantic search for odds and ends at the last minute. The store has it all. There are practical items such as voltage converters and plug adapters for your shavers and hair dryers. Also available are dual voltage appliances, currency calculators, travel clocks, security/money belts, all sizes of packs and garment bags, raingear, walking shoes, "Let's Go:Europe" and other travel guides. Specialty items like "Wrinkles Away", the travel size steamer that makes suitcase-tired clothing look fresh again. Or Hedbed, the contoured, inflatable travel pillow. And there are hard to find books, maps, and language tapes. Le Travel Store is frequently consulted in the manufacture and design of travel gear by the makers of Dolt, Eagle Creek and Caribou.

When you're ready to travel, come to Le Travel Store, where everyone on the staff is an avid traveler ready to share their tips and experiences with you. If you can't make it to the store, send for Le Travel Store's free color catalog.

TRAVELERS DEPOT
1539 Garnet Avenue
San Diego, CA 92109
Tel. (619) 483-1421
Hrs: Mon. - Fri   10:00 a.m. - 6:00 p.m.
        Saturday   9:00 a.m. - 5:00 p.m.
        Sunday   12:00 noon - 4:00 p.m.

If traveling well is your bag, you'll find everything to ensure a *bon voyage* at the Traveler's Depot. Traveler's Depot is a complete, one-stop store for the person on the go.

There are money belts, compasses, money exchange converters, dual voltage appliances, travel clocks, Swiss army knives, voltage converters, inflatable pillows and maps from Antarctica to Zurich.

Traveler's Depot's go-everywhere suitcases and carry-on luggage tell the world you know where you're going without drawing unwanted attention.

And whether you're going to Bangor, Maine, or Bangladesh, Traveler's Depot stocks over 2,000 travel books, guides and maps to give you the information you want and need to know.

(See special invitation in the Appendix.)

THE LAMB SHOP/PACIFIC ESCAPES TRAVEL
4417 La Jolla Village Drive Suite N-7
University Towne Centre
San Diego, CA 92122
Tel.   (619) 447-9381
Hrs: Mon. - Fri.   10:00 a.m. - 9:00 p.m.
         Saturday   10:00 a.m. - 6:00 p.m.
         Sunday   12:00 noon - 5:00 p.m.
Visa, MasterCard and AMEX are accepted.

The Lamb Shop is a must for the shopper with a penchant for quality leather and lamb's wool products. Named an official 1991 America's Cup sponsor, the shop is dedicated to offering its patrons meticulously crafted and unique merchandise.

The Lamb Shop products pass stringent tests from the tanning stage to final manufacturing, to ensure high standards. Most carry the International Woolmark. Shoppers will be fascinated by the variety of unusual items carried at The Lamb Shop. Browsers will be delighted with gift ideas in the form of sheepskin covers of all kinds including those for bicycle seats, steering wheels and golf clubs. The Lamb Shop offers lamb's wool mattress pads to aid sleeping comfort in summer and winter and improve blood circulation. Beautiful one of a kind hand dyed and knitted sweaters are tastefully displayed with lovely suede clothing for the shopper. These exciting apparel items have been created by designers who have hand selected yarns for texture and color, sometimes hand spinning and hand dying the article to specifications.

An agency to keep in mind when planning your next vacation is located in the back of the Lamb Shop. Pacific Escapes Travel specializes in custom tours, from New Zealand farms to mountain climbing. Pacific Escapes Travel's theme tours include Fashion, Jazz, Golf and Sailing. All tours are exciting one of a kind trips. The congenial staff at Pacific Escapes Travel is always ready to help the traveler with such details as visa's and passports. For an exciting look at textures and travel, visit the staff at The Lamb Shop and Pacific Escapes Travel.

ALPINE

Alpine began in the 1860s as a mountain health resort. Here the dry mountain air was said to be the perfect tonic for sufferers of lung diseases. In the not too distant past Alpine was a rural outpost on a mountain at the edge of the Cleveland National Forest. Many of the residents were professionals or outdoorsmen who didn't mind being well beyond the metropolitan area and had the means to purchase some of the ranchland. Downtown is full of small charming shops and warm, friendly people. Local planners are working to maintain the mountain village character and the overall feeling is that planned growth will be positive. Alpine is a pleasant and relaxing suburban community where horse owners, ranchers, business people and professionals have come together to share an appreciation for a mountain lifestyle just thirty-five miles east of San Diego.

ANZA BORREGO STATE PARK

The Anza Borrego Desert State Park, with 600,000 acres, stretches from just above the Mexican Border and into the Los Angeles Basin, making it the largest state park in the nation and nearly two-thirds of the stat's parkland. The park is one of California's last untouched desert areas. Development has been confined to the private lands of the Borrego Valley in the northern part of the park.

Although its not exactly the same lush grandeur of Yosemite Valley, the lonely desert landscape has a unique power to evoke a sense of awe for the life forms that struggle and at times flourish in this primeval habitat. To the uninitiated, the desert may come across as a parched wasteland of hard packed clay and gravel scarred with sand blasted gullies. But the region is remarkably diverse as altitudes range from 100 feet below sea level to more than 6,000 feet above the San Ysidro Mountains. There are stands of pine among the cool heights, sparking springs bubbling from the earth, and brief burst of color when the cacti and wildflowers bloom.

The desert is far from lifeless. If you keep your eyes open you might spot a big horn sheep in some of the remote areas in the north end of the park. About 600 species of indigenous plates grow in the park. Between March and April the desert flowers bloom profusely.

A unique aspect of Anza Borrego is that you'll never have to worry about camping sites being full. Camping is allowed in the entire park. There are, however, a few restrictions: drive only on established roads, no fires on the ground and leave everything as it was when you arrived. Desert camping is best from November through May, although there may be some chilly nights and windstorms.

It would be impossible to see the entire park in one visit, so its best to pick one area, establish a base camp from which you can explore. Some of the more popular regions follow. One ting you can count on, You'll find the park's lands almost as Spanish Captain Juan Bautista de Anza saw them when he explored this area.

Borrego Palm Canyon, near the town of Borrego Springs, is where you'll find the park headquarters. The campground has all the amenities that California State Parks are known for. Campers can relax in an oasis watered by a fresh water spring and nature trails.

Blair Valley can be reached through county road S2, which was the old Overland State Route. Improved campgrounds are located at Old Vallecito Stage Station and Agua Caliente Springs.

At **Bow Willow** palm grove clusters dot the region, especially in the Mountain Palm Springs area. The region includes many roads enjoyed by four wheel drive enthusiasts.

Semi-wooded areas among huge boulders provide a scenic setting for the primitive camping areas of Culp Valley. At 4,500 feet Culp Valley often offers a cool respite from the desert temperatures. There's also a commanding view of the Borrego Valley and badlands.

Tamarisk Grove has an improved campground at the base of the North Pinyon Mountain, on slopes where there are an incredible variety of cacti. Above Tamarisk Grove is a traditional native watering spot, Yaque Well, which is among beautiful ironwood trees where abundant wildlife gathers.

BORREGO SPRINGS

When spring arrives, the desert blooms around the resort community of Borrego Springs. The settlement is right in the middle of the 600,000 acre Anza Borrego State Park in the northeast corner of San Diego County. Only a few thousand people live here. Enjoy the clean, dry air year-round, and the views of blue mist mountains rising up beyond the vast expanses of desert. Just outside of town is a luxurious La Cas Del Zorro Resort. A short hike up the Borrego Palm Canyon will bring you to a desert palm oasis. At this writing the town was pretty much unchanged from past generations, but nearby new residential resort developments are being built. Be sure to stop at the million dollar visitor center that features a slide show, and exhibits of the geology, plant life and animals of the desert.

CORONADO

Because so many kings and queens of Hollywood, political king pins and members of royal families have visited this narrow strip of land across the bay from San Diego, Coronado has earned the title of "Crown City."

A long strip of sand extends from the south end of San Diego Bay to form the west edge of the bay. In 1969 a bridge connecting San Diego with Coronado was completed. Before that visitors had to either ride the ferry or make the trip to the south bay and drive back up the sand spit.

But even with the graceful bridge that moves 20,000 cars a day, Coronado still has the feel of relative isolation from the rest of the world. It is almost as if it were still the island that it once was in the not too distant geological past. This isle has several tennis courts, an eighteen hole championship golf course, and Olympic pool, fascinating shops, boating, fishing, and racquetball courts. The city shares the island with the North Island Naval Air Station.

While other communities might have their beginnings as fishing villages or military outposts, Coronado was in the 1880s what it is today, a resort community and adult's playground. Although its history is quite a bit younger than San Diego's, every square foot of this strip has a story to tell. According to legend, the most famous romance of the 20th Century may have begun here when Duke of Windsor met Mrs. Simpson, while her husband was commander of North Island Air station.   In 1927 Charles Lindbergh took off from here on the first leg of his journey that led to Saint Louis, New York, and Paris.

Before it was developed, Coronado was the habitat of coyotes and jack rabbits. Then in 1885 railroad financier Elisha S. Babcock, and H. L. Story of Chicago paid $110,000 for for the land that they would sell off in lots, later build a hotel on, that would "be the talk of the Western world."

After a year of construction, the ornate 400 room red roofed Hotel Del Coronado, designed by Stanford White, was completed. Thomas Edison supervised installation of the wiring so that the hotel would be the first in the world to have electric lights. The hotel continues to operate today both as a luxury resort hotel, as well as a California State Historical Landmark. The grand wooden structure dominates the community and the small board harbor that's set behind it.

The city's neighborhoods are filled with historical homes. There is, for example, the spacious mansion that once belonged to John Spreckles, one of the early owners of the hotel. Located right across from the hotel, the estate covers a complete city block. The old hotel boathouse still stands on the bayside of the peninsula, but today it houses a fine restaurant. The largest mansion in Coronado is the Richards-Dupee-Van Ness House at 1015 Ocean

Boulevard. The seventeen bedroom home was build in 1902 for Barlett Richards, a wealthy rancher who sold it in 1913 to Walter Dupee.

Many first time visitors tour the local sights at the Hotel Del Coronado, p erhaps in the hope of spotting some famous person in the lobby. On Saturday afternoons, beginning at 1:00 p.m., free guided tours are conducted through the hotel. For a fee, the Coronado Touring Company will take you on a one hour tour through the historical sights of the town.

The beach along the Silver Strand is one of the finest in the country. It runs nearly the entire length of the sand spit. Tiny sea shells shine in the sunlight, which explains why the sand spit came to be called the Silver Strand. The beach provides some opportunities for clamming, surf fishing and is known for grunion runs.

BEACH

If you think you might want to visit the county's widest beach try the **Coronado Municipal Beach**. Situated on the long isthmus at the west side of San Diego Bay, the Coronado beach offers calm waters and white fluffy sand. The beach is a good family beach. The well-to-do congregate just south of the Coronado Shores condo towers. You'll find tourists from around the world near the deluxe Hotel Del Coronado. Take I-5 to the Coronado Exit and and cross the San Diego-Coronado Bay Bridge and continue to Orange Avenue, and then just follow the signs.

EVENT

The Independence Day Celebration in Coronado, is one of the larger area 4th of July events, featuring a parade, clowns, a rough water swim, Naval air and sea demonstrations and fireworks over Glorietta Bay. Tel. (619) 566-6083.

GOLF COURSE

Coronado Golf Course, 2000 Visalia Row, Coronado, CA 92118. 6,700 yards, par 72. Tel. (619) 435-3121.

NAVAL BASE

The Spanish were the first to recognize San Diego Bay as a naval stronghold and base from which to control the Pacific Coast. Three hundred years later, San Diego is probably the most heavily defended city in the nation.

The military bases offer opportunities to San Diego's visitors. Most popular are the shipboard open houses. On most weekends, visitors can board a naval vessel docked at the foot of Broadway at Harbor Drive. The hours vary, but ships are usually open between 1:00 p.m. and 4:00 p.m. For more information call (619) 235-1116.

The Naval Training Center has two attractions. One is the Naval Training Center Museum which includes models, paintings, photographs and maritime artifacts. The other is the colorful recruit graduation ceremony, held every Friday afternoon at 2:30 p.m. Entrance to the training center is through Gate 1 off Barnett street near Litton. Tel. (619) 225-4011.

At the Navy Amphibious Base at Coronado tours are available, by advance reservation, on Tuesdays and Thursdays between 9:00 a.m. and 3:00 p.m. Groups are limited to no more than ten people. There are some restrictions, which include no children under eight. For reservations or information call (619) 437-2735.

During mid-summer the Miramar Naval Air Station attracts thousand to its annual air show. Among the major events is the Blue Angels precision flying team. For information call Tel. (619) 271-3011.

ANTIQUE SHOP

CASA DE PANCHO
1349 Orange Avenue
Coronado, CA 92118
Tel.   (619) 435-0865
Hrs: Mon. - Sun.
Call for winter and summer hours.
Visa, MasterCard and personal checks are accepted.

Whether it's something from trendy and urban Guadalajara or from the home of a peasant farmer, if it has anything to do with Latin American arts, antiques or fashion, Casa Del Pancho will have it. The assortment of charming items is remarkable.

Casa de Pancho brings Latin American crafts to Coronado from the most primitive villages, in addition to works of exquisite design from the teeming and fashionable cities. The antiques range from massive pieces of furniture to unique accent pieces, some of them dating back to the middle 1700s. The fabric used for the clothing and table linens are hand woven. There are both formal and informal cruisewear only steps away from things, such as, antique branding irons, spurs and shoe lasts. There's a wide selection of jewelry ranging from stoneware beads to sterling silver. Home furnishings include hand-loomed woolen rugs, as well as furniture.

People from all over the United States seek out this shop. Clintele includes names such as Robert Wagner, Jill St. John, Stephanie Powers and Patrick Duffy. Sign the guest book yourself, and join a loyal following who have found this truly distinctive collection of South American art, crafts and antiques.

ART GALLERY

SUE TUSHINGHAM MCNARY ART GALLERY
1500 Orange Avenue
Coronado, CA 92118
Tel. (619) 435-1819
Hrs: Mon. - Sun.   10:00 a.m. - 10:00 p.m.
Visa, MasterCard, AMEX and Discover are accepted.

Prince Charles, Carol Lawrence, Dick Van Dyke, Mrs. Joseph Magnin, Mike Wallace and the Begum Aga Kahn may have little in common, but they do share one thing; all have placed in their collections art from Sue Tushingham McNary.

McNary's etchings and oils, known for a soft-colored style depicting buildings, landscapes, flowers and many other subjects, are on display at her gallery in the historic Hotel Del Coronado. Her works have been popular in corporate and military collections, as well as in the homes of private collectors. The etchings and limited editions are surprisingly affordable.

There's a variety of style that ranges from intricate oriental subjects to bold stylized southwestern landscapes, which gives the gallery a scope not found in some multi-artist galleries. The gallery is small, intimate and charming. Visitors are always met with a smile and the willing voice of knowledge about the artist and her work. Whether you are a browser or a buyer, you won't be given the brush-off.

CHRISTMAS STORE

CHRISTMAS 1888
1500 Orange Avenue
Coronado, CA 92118
Tel.   (619) 435-1045
Hrs: Mon. - Sun.   9:30 a.m. - 10:30 p.m.
Visa, MasterCard and AMEX are accepted.
Also,
Lawrence Welk Resort Village
Escondido, CA 92026
Tel.   (619) 749-1045

The wonderment and magic of a child's first Christmas are re-created every day at Christmas 1888. This fairy land of decorated trees and gifts is located in two famous landmarks: The century-old Hotel del Coronado, and Lawrence Welk's Village in Escondido.

Owners Tom and Eileen Kennedy first opened an art gallery to display Eileen's pen and ink sketches of Coronado, however the gallery grew into two separate gift shops and Eileen became a Christmas decorator and designer.

The fifteen trees, in each shop, are decorated with theme ornaments: teddy bears, old world glass, animals, sports, children, angels, Santas, German wood, mice, country and elegant, all of which can be personalized free of charge.

The shops carry, year-round, the largest selection of imported nativities in the region, such as handcarved German wood, Italian alabaster, German porcelain and Spanish ceramics, many of which are open "stock," thus enabling customers to purchase individual pieces.

The Kennedys make a yearly journey to Europe to directly purchase unique Christmas collectibles such as Nuremberg angels, miniature dolls, nativities and ornaments. However, the shops also features many handmade American-crafted items created by regional artists.

The spirit of Christmas can be shared at the Christmas 1888 shops, where one can live Christmas past while creating Christmases of the future.

RESTAURANT

MEXICAN VILLAGE
120 Orange Avenue
Coronado, CA 92118
Tel. (619) 435-1822
Hrs: Mon. - Thu.   11:00 a.m. - 12:00 midnight
      Fri. - Sat.   11:00 a.m. - 2:00 a.m.
      Sunday   8:00 a.m. - 12:00 midnight

The world famous Mexican Village Restaurant has been pleasing customers since 1945 when it opened as a small one room restaurant with a kitchen in the rear. It has since expanded to give one the feeling of being in an authentic Mexican village with plaza, dancing and more. Inside the Spanish Colonial style building with its stuccoed walls, balconies, and red tile roofs, are thick adobe walls covered with colorful murals. The original building, which once served as Coronado's first Firehouse in 1898 has been designated a Historical Landmark.

One of the the best buys here is the huge Taco Grande, an over-sized flour tortilla bursting with shredded beef, lettuce and tomatos. The Mexican Village Romaine is a salad which has been getting rave reviews for years. The Mexican Pizza was invented here; it's a crisp flour tortilla topped with refried beans, guacamole, seasoned beef, lettuce, tomatos and melted cheddar cheese. All specialities are served with refried beans and Spanish rice. If you're not in the mood for Mexican food, there's an excellent selection of standard American dishes on the menu.

Throughout the year, Mexican Village Restaurant hosts fun-filled events, such as a New Year's eve party, a Valentine's Sweetheart Dinner and a Halloween costume party with prizes and dancing. Anytime of year, the Mexican Village Restaurant offers fun and great food to the visitor.

EL CAJON

Most people think of El Cajon as the metropolitan hub of the East County Region of San Diego County. Both I-8 and State 67 go right through this city where more than 81,000 people live.

It is a city that has light industry, office complexes and a seemingly endless spread of residential neighborhoods. El Cajon lives up to the East County reputation for a hot summer temperatures.

The city is known for its Mother Goose Parade, the only parade in the nation with a theme focusing on a collection of nursery rhymes. What began as a small community event has grown to one of southern California's major events, second only to the Rose Parade. The parade is held the Sunday before Thanksgiving. For more information, contact the El Cajon City Hall at, Tel. (916) 441-1776.

ATTRACTION

Do you wanna bet? There is true high stakes bingo on the tiny **Syquan Indian Reservation** east of El Cajon. Officially the reservation is home to just forty-eight members of the tribe. But these folks have managed to raise the stakes through their love of traditional betting games by operating the 1,600 seat **Sycuan Bingo Palace** that's open seven days and nights a week. Free shuttle bus service is available by calling Tel. (619) 470-1345. You'll find the place out at 5469 Dehesa Road, El Cajon, CA 92021.

El Cajon's Parkway Plaza. is off I- 8 at the Magnolia Exit. It's open weekdays 10: a.m. to 9:00 p.m.; Saturday 9:30 a.m. to 6:00 p.m.; Sunday 10:00 a.m. to 6:00 p.m. Tel. (619) 579-9932.

EVENT

If it's the Monday after Thanksgiving, it's time for El Cajon's popular **Mother Goose Parade**. The procession of floats, bands and clowns rivals the Rose Parade as one of the big Southern California celebrations.   Tel. (619) 444-8712.

GOLF COURSE

SINGING HILLS COUNTRY CLUB AND LODGE
3007 Dehesa Road
El Cajon, CA 92019
Tel. (619) 442-3425
Hrs: Golf course daylight to dusk
Visa, MasterCard and AMEX are accepted. Reservations are required.

Have you been harboring a secret yen to test your golf game against a championship course? Singing Hills is just the place to try it. It has hosted numerous PGA, USGA and SCGA tournaments, including the 1956 San Diego Open; the USGA Junior Championships were held here in 1973 and will return in 1989.

All three of the spectacular courses are open to the public. Willow Glen is the par-72, 6,600 yard course; Oak Glen has a par-71, 6,600-yard layout, and Pine Glen offers a par-54, 3,000 yard "executive" challenge.

Ted Robinson, the internationally acclaimed golf course architect who recently redesigned the Singing Hills courses, in his own words did his "very best job" here. He has taken full advantage of a picturesque setting in the Sweetwater River Valley, where natural rock outcroppings and ancient oaks and sycamores outline themselves against rugged mountain peaks. The river meandering through the courses, plus six lakes, elevated bunkers and multi-tier greens all put a premium on strategy and shot placement.

In addition, there are two large putting greens near the unusually well stocked golf shop, plus a chipping green, practice sand bunkers and a fine golf driving range. Eighty guest rooms are available at the Lodge, with its pool, its own putting green and spacious bar and restaurant. Lodge guests may also play at the adjacent membership tennis club for a moderate fee. If you are short of time, come for one great championship day. Better yet, plan to stay. You'll find excellent instruction, congenial company, and some of the most enjoyable golfing in the West.

HARBOR ISLAND

Although San Diego has never been short of water recreational facilities, the demand for new facilities has never slackened. One product of that demand is Harbor Island. It was designed to create another tropical island atmosphere like its neighbor on the bay, Shelter Island. So successful was Shelter Island, the city started another bayside development in 1961.

After twelve years and fifty million dollars, San Diego had its second romantic island getaway, complete with palms and south sea landscapes. Visitors to the island can enjoy a spectacular 360 degree view of the water, and look out over the city's shining skyline. Lighted walkways and balmy Southern California air, make the evenings special at both Harbor Island and Shelter Island.

Harbor Island is just two minutes form the airport, and a mere five minutes from downtown San Diego. Although the island is less than a mile long, there is a lot to see and do. The island offers docking and parking facilities, hotels and restaurants. Some 1,600 private yachts and boats are berthed here.

Guests of the Sheraton East and West Hotels on the island find so much going on here, that they really have to work to see the area's other attractions.

ACCOMMODATION

ELUSIVE DREAM CHARTER
1933 Friendship Drive Suite F
El Cajon, CA 92020
Tel. (619) 258-9393
Visa, MasterCard and AMEX are accepted.
The address of this business is El Cajon, but the yacht is located in Harbor Island.

If life is but a dream when you row, row your boat, it's an elusive dream if it's on a fifty-one foot motor yacht.

"Elusive Dream" is the name of one yacht you can sail out of San Diego harbor as your dream boat. For about the price of a first class hotel room your vacation or business party can reside in luxury docked on San Diego Bay. With three state rooms and accommodations for ten, there's plenty of room. Amenities include two baths, a full galley with microwave oven, stereo and a great view of the Pacific Ocean. You can have it for an intimate moonlight cruise, a day cruise or even an extended trip to Catalina Island for an additional charge.

Step aboard and dream on with this "Best Choice" for travel in San Diego.

LA JOLLA

Luxury homes top the cliffs where residents can watch the sparkling blue sea roll into enchanting coves, as palm trees sway in the breeze. The scene could be the French Riviera, but it's La Jolla, one of San Diego County's most prestigious communities and a favorite for shoppers and beach lovers.

Technically, La Jolla is a part of the city of San Diego, but this enclave is a community in its own right. Even the US Post Office recognizes it as "La Jolla, CA." The community is known for its Mediterranean resort ambiance, magnificent homes, wide sandy beaches, enchanting coves, and fascinating underwater scenery. It is a place for active endeavors such as swimming, surfing, skin diving and excellent international shopping.

The excellent local restaurants can make your dining a truly international experience as you choose among many different national cuisines.

The fashionable restaurants, boutiques and galleries along Prospect Street and Girard Avenue, remind some visitors of fashionable Paris neighborhoods. It does retain a small town style of friendliness. Although this is a fashionable community, the milieu is casual and comfortable.

Without having to go far, you can tour tree lined roadways, sunbathe on the beach, surf, scuba dive, snorkel, play around of golf or a set of tennis. Two marine reserves make La Jolla one of the best snorkeling and scuba diving venues on the California Coast. La Jolla Underwater Park, providing a safe haven for sea life among submerged moss-covered rocks, extends from La Jolla Cove northward to the La Jolla Beach and Tennis Club. Another underwater reserve is just north of the pier and extends to Black's Beach.

A tour of this community's fashionable boulevards will show that it has remained relatively unspoiled from its original "village" atmosphere. You won't find blatant signs of commercialism or flashy neon signs. Many homes in the community cost more than $500,000. The community continues to be the focal point of many social and cultural events.

La Jolla provides a home to several biological research facilities and high-tech firms, and the people who work in those facilities. Among these are the Salk Institute and the Scripps Institute.

The town name comes from the Spanish word for "The Jewel." But even before the Spanish arrived the Indians called this "La Hoya," which referred to the caves formed by the sea into La Jolla's cliffs. It's sometimes called simply, "The Village."

La Jolla's natural amenities began luring visitors to San Diego in the 1880s. It was not easy to get here, it was a journey that required traversing long stretches of rough and bumpy roads. In 1886, Frank Botsford, loved the region and bought a 400 acre tract for $5.50 an acre. Botsford probably had more than one acquaintance try to convince him that investing in land so far out of the way was not the most prudent thing to do with one's money. However, today that land is worth literally billions of dollars, and getting here is a quick twenty-minute drive from downtown San Diego. The quickest route is to take I-5 to the Ardath Road Exit, West, but the community is also accessible by way of Mission Boulevard through the community of Pacific Beach.

ATTRACTIONS

La Jolla Cove is just one of the sights that seem to make people fall in love with this community. It is a popular spot to sunbathe on the beach, swim in azure waters, or snorkel down to colorful depths. In the summer, the beach is usually packed, and parking is difficult to find.

Ellen Browning Scripps Park, is south of the cove and offers a peaceful grassy area surrounded by palms and torrey pines.

Sunny Jim Cave, is one of La Jolla's seven sea caves. Its entrance is through a tunnel at the Cave and Shell Shop, 1325 Coast Boulevard and involves descending a stairway of more than 300 steps. A small admission is charged. Other natural caves in the rocky cliffs can be explored along the water's edge.

Soledad City Park, offers a spectacular 360 degree view of the region, including the La Jolla Coastline, from the top of Mount Soledad. Take the Scenic Drive to the top.

The Salk Institute is a world famous medical research facility. Scientists work in more than twenty laboratories doing advanced research in neuroscience, molecular and cellular biology. Docent tours through the complex are conducted Monday through Friday from 11:00 a.m. to 2:00 p.m. For information contact the Salk Institute, 10010 North Torrey Pines Road, La Jolla, CA 92037.   Tel. (619) 453-4100.

Scripps Institution of Oceanography Aquarium, see "Museums, Greater San Diego".

La Jolla Museum of Contemporary Art, see "Museums, Greater San Diego".

La Jolla Playhouse, see "Theaters, Greater San Diego."

BEACHES

Also south of the Cove is the **Children's Pool,** a place where a breakwater offers calm waters to wade and swim in, with a wide and sandy beach.

Writer Tom Wolfe made **Windansea Beach** known to readers of his book *The Pumphouse Gang,* a tale of the 1960s about a group of die-hard surfers, some of whom are still around. Today Windansea is still popular with surfers. The beach provides a good setting from which to watch the sunset. Take La Jolla Boulevard to Nautilus Street.

Scuba Divers favor **Casa Cove,** as do fanciers of spear fishing. The beach lies beyond the protected marine reserve so licensed spear fishing is legal here. Lifeguards are on duty year around. Casa Cove is just north of Windansea and about one-half mile south of the La Jolla Cove on Coast Boulevard.

Another popular scuba diving spot is **La Jolla Cove.** But it is also a draw for families with small children, as well as tourists. The cove features some caves for exploring just to the north. Lifeguards are always on duty. Take Ardath Road from I-5. You'll find the beach just south of La Jolla shores on La Jolla Shores Drive.

Locals, inland visitors and tourist all come to **La Jolla Shores.** They bring wine and cheese to picnic under the sun or to celebrate the sunset. Keep in mind that glass is prohibited, so decant that wine in a bota bag. Dogs are welcome, before 9:00 a.m. and after 6:00 p.m. as long as they remain on leashes. In the water you'll find surfers riding the waves and scuba divers emerging from the depths like creatures from the black lagoon. Joggers like to come here for early morning runs. There's also a pier, and boating is allowed on the north side of the structure. At the south end of the beach a boat launch is available for small craft. Volleyball, courts are available and lifeguards are on duty year around. Take the Ardath Road exit from I-5 to La Jolla Shores Drive and follow the signs.

Scientists and students from University of California at San Diego hang out at **Scripps Beach**. Just above the beach is the Scripps Institution of Oceanography. Note that the beach is open to the public only on weekends. Take La Jolla Shores Drive to the Scripps Institution of Oceanography.

EVENTS

The streets of La Jolla get transformed into a Monte Carlo Style bike race during the annual **Bud Light La Jolla Grand Prix**, held in early July. The race is one of the few truly international races in the United States. Other events include a celebrity race, a run and a stunt show. Tel. (619) 296-5165.

La Jolla hosts another rough water swim during the second week in September at the La Jolla Cove. This event is supposed to be the largest annual rough water swimming competition in the United States. Tel. (619) 454-1444.

Another major golf tournament of the winter season is **The Andy Williams Open**, held at the Torrey Pines Golf Course, La Jolla. Tel. (619) 281-4653.

A parade of floats and marching bands launches La Jolla's Christmas season with the **La Jolla Christmas Parade and Party**. Tel. (619) 454-1444.

GOLF COURSE

Torrey Pines Municipal Golf Course, 11480 North Torrey Pines Road, La Jolla, CA 92037. Two courses both in excess of 6,000 yards and both par 72. Tel. (619) 453-0380.

SHOPPING

La Jolla's **University Towne Centre**, offers 178 shops, restaurants and services in a outdoor European setting. The center also includes one of the region's leading museums, The Mingei International Museum of Folk Art (see Museums under Greater San Diego). Major department stores include Sears, The Broadway and Nordstrom. You'll also find an international food pavilion, theatres, child care center, fitness center and an Olympic size ice skating ring.

For more information contact University Towne Centre, 4545 La Jolla Village Drive, La Jolla, CA 92122. Tel. (619) 296-6475.

ACCOMMODATIONS

COLONIAL INN
910 Prospect Street
La Jolla, CA 92037
Tel.   (800) 826-1278 CA
        (800) 832-5525 US
Visa, MasterCard and AMEX are accepted.

If you want plush, the kind you might expect in Monaco or Naples, you can get it in La Jolla. To put it simply, the Colonial Inn is an elegant hotel, where a door man welcomes you to this refuge of old world charm.

Each of the rooms is twice the the size of most luxury hotels. The ceilings are high and windows open up to an expanse of Southern California Coast line. Although the beds are some of the best made today, the rest of the furnishings are fine antiques. The hotel is located within easy reach of some of the best shopping and dinning in La Jolla. You can also enjoy a relaxed, but elegant, meal at Putnam's Restaurant within the Inn.

So relax, enjoy Southern California, with the refined tastes of Europeans.

INN BY THE SEA
7830 Fay Avenue
La Jolla, CA 92037
Tel.   (619) 459-4461
        (800) 526-4545 CA
        (800) 462-9732 US
Visa, MasterCard, AMEX, Carte Blanche and Enroute are accepted.

Inn By The Sea has just completed a $3 million building and renovation project. Two new wings were added to the hotel bringing the total number of rooms to 134. The five story Inn By The Sea, formerly known as Royal Inn of La Jolla, was built in 1971. It was bought by a group of La Jolla businessmen in 1973, and renamed Inn By The Sea in 1984.

New terrace rooms overlooking an enlarged pool area, a spa, a conference room, and underground parking are all part of the new design.

A complete new color scheme of blue, taupe, and off-white has been used on the exterior of the hotel, as well as in its interior. Inn By The Sea now reflects the casual, comfortable atmosphere of a sea side resort. As part of the renovation, the hotel's entire operation was computerized to permit more efficient handling of reservations and commissions.

Art Thomson, general manager of Inn By The Sea, states that the moderate rates and a prime location are the hotel's most important drawing cards. "We seem to have the location vacationers and business travelers prefer, in the heart of the village of La Jolla, within walking distance of the world class restaurants and shops on Prospect Street. The beach is a few blocks in one direction, public tennis courts in the other. We're only minutes by car from San Diego's business centers and tourist attractions, but in a whole different world." For further information contact Art Thomson.

LA VALENCIA HOTEL, 1132 Prospect, La Jolla, CA 92037. Tel. (619) 454-0771. La Jolla's famous pink hotel offers the epitome in luxurious accommodations, lavish service and personal conveniences for those intent on business, pleasure, or both.

LA JOLLA MARRIOTT HOTEL
4240 La Jolla Village Drive
La Jolla, CA 92037
Tel. (619) 587-1414
Visa, MasterCard, AMEX and Discover are accepted.

Elegance and luxury are apparent when you enter the La Jolla Marriott through its two story atrium lobby with walls of glass and polished marble floor. Rich wood furnishings and Oriental art stand out against a backdrop of soft pinks and greens.   Color TV in the rooms offer pay TV and free HBO, ESPN and CNN.

The Marriott's six suites are appointed with wet bars, marble accents, and lavish spaces with separate areas for meeting and sleeping. The Concierge Level is earmarked for those accustomed to exceptional service and privacy. These upgraded rooms include morning newspapers and a private lounge for complimentary continental breakfast, afternoon hors d'oeuvres and honor bar drinks. A concierge is always available to arrange your travel or business needs.

Located on a broad mesa in the heart of La Jolla's research and business community, the La Jolla Marriott is designed with the perfect combination of classic elegance and contemporary freshness; big enough for impressive receptions yet small enough for impeccable service. A must for the discriminating traveller.

PROSPECT PARK INN
1110 Prospect Street
La Jolla, CA 92037
Tel.   (619) 454-0133
        (800) 433-1609 US
        (800) 345-8577 CA
Hrs: Lobby   Mon. - Sun.   6:30 a.m. - 11:00 p.m.
After hours there is a private entrance for guests.

If La Jolla is called "the Jewel of Southern California" then the Prospect Park Inn is the perfect setting from which to base your explorations of this engaging part of the country.

Your innkeeper, Brigitte Schmidt hails from Germany and has brought all the charms and nuances of European hospitality to the Prospect Park Inn. Her background in the hospitality industry has prepared her for her life's dream of running a small hotel with true European charm that caters to the individual wishes of each guest. Accordingly, the Prospect Park Inn is a sparkling clean bit of paradise amidst the eclectic concentration of fashionable shops, boutiques, galleries and restaurants that make up the quaint village of La Jolla. Newly decorated rooms are filled with contemporary furnishings and feature private balconies overlooking panoramas of the Pacific Ocean. All of the rooms have private baths and color TV. And there are athletic facilities available in cooperation with a nearby club. Each morning, a Continental breakfast is served on the Penthouse Terrace which also has a sweeping ocean view. Afternoons, the same terrace becomes a sun deck and site of a gracious afternoon tea service and refreshments are available in the library as well.

The Prospect Inn has facilities for meetings, conferences, and weddings of up to fifty people. And it's a truly romantic hideaway for honeymooners, too. When you come to La Jolla, put yourself right in the lap of luxury. Brigitte promises to be at your beck and call. What more could you ask for?

SUMMER HOUSE INN AND ELARIO'S
7955 La Jolla Shores Drive
La Jolla, CA 92037
Tel.   (619) 459-0541
        (800) 223-7896
        (800) 468-3245 CA
Hrs: Breakfast   Mon. - Sat.   7:00 a.m. - 11:00 a.m.
                     Sunday   7:00 a.m. - 9:00 a.m.
       Brunch   Sunday   10:00 a.m. - 2:00 p.m.
       Lunch   Mon. - Sat.   11:30 a.m. - 2:00 p.m.
       Dinner   Mon. - Sun.   5:30 p.m. - 10:00 p.m.
Visa, MasterCard, AMEX, Diners Club and Carte Blanche are accepted.

All ninety rooms in this warm, intimate hotel face the beautiful La Jolla Shores beach to give you what many consider the finest ocean views on the Pacific coast. From the spectacular seascapes to such niceties as a telephone in your bathroom, you'll find that luxury is the norm here. In addition to the swimming pool, there's a sauna and a therapy pool, plus free tennis and racquetball privileges at a nearby facility.

Elario's, the hotel's eleventh floor rooftop restaurant, offers the same gorgeous marine views from every table. A favorite with local La Jollans and hotel guests alike, Elario's offers fine   continental dining in a casual, comfortable atmosphere. The chef cures his own salmon for Gravalax and makes his own country-style paté, both favorite appetizers. Luncheon specialties feature a different pasta invention each day of the week, and the dinner menu always offers fresh Salmon, Ahi, Ono, Sea Bass and Swordfish. Other star attractions are the *Carre D'Agneau*, a succulent rack of lamb with mint apple sauce and *Medallions de Veau a La Creme de Ciboulette*, a filet of veal with foie gras and a duxelle of mushrooms, served with Port wine sauce and a cream of chives.

It's all elegant food, beautifully served, and followed by equally enticing desserts, such as homemade cheesecakes, a light as air chocolate mousse, or Devonshire cream with chocolate sauce. The bar brings you live big name entertainment nightly, and the North Shore Room is an ideal setting for receptions, cocktail parties or banquets. A truly remarkable hotel with the finest of facilities, The Summer House Inn offers you Southern California beach vacationing at its very best.

APPAREL

BAGS 'N BELTS
7864 Girard Avenue
La Jolla, CA 92037
Tel. (619) 459 -3536
Hrs: Mon. - Sat.   10:00 a.m. - 6:00 p.m.
           Sunday   12:00noon - 5:00 p.m.
Visa, MasterCard and AMEX are accepted.

Bags 'N Belts is the place where it happens. People from all over come to this fun shop.

Bags 'N Belts has one of the finest selections of leather hand bags, belts, hats, scarves, umbrellas and costume jewelry accessories in San Diego. When you enter Bags 'N Belts, the first thing you'll notice is the rich aroma of high quality leather. The advantage of shopping Bags 'N Belts is that you can select from up to ninety different design labels normally costing $5 to $600 at discounted prices. Owner Jan Borkum and her staff are happy to assist you with accessories. Be sure to ask for help if you don't find what you're looking for on the shelves; it will be special ordered for you.

The belts come in leather, canvas, as well as other materials. But the real eye catchers are the one's studded with precious stones. While you're at it you can get earrings with matching stones to go with your belt.

CUSTOM SHIRTS AND BOUTIQUE OF LA JOLLA
7643 Girard Avenue
La Jolla, CA 92037
Tel. (619) 459-6147
Hrs: Mon. - Sat.   9:30 a.m. - 6:00 p.m.
Closed on Sundays and major holidays.
All major credit cards are accepted.

Owner Gerhard Bendl says his love for high collar shirts put him into the custom shirt business. Previous to beginning business in San Diego, Gerhard worked for custom shirt stores in New York and Beverly Hills. Wanting his wife. Elisabeth, to be with him at the store, he encouraged her to add a fine women's line of clothing to his shirt business. Today they have an expanded mixture of fine European/American clothing for men ard women.

The Bendls specialize in custom shirts and custom suits for men. Customers measurements are kept on file making ordering by phone or mail a convenience for out of town customers. Gerhard will make "house calls" and helps coordinate his male clients wardrobes by coordinating existing clothing in the customers own closet. Using their carefully selected customer files, the Bendls will call a patron when something particularly unique or suited to the customer arrives in stock. An unusual array of European and American sportswear is available for women customers.

The interior of Custom Shirts and Boutique is modern yet elegant with soft couches, a wet bar from which coffee or wine is served as customers browse or shop. Everything is displayed with a grace and style that reflects the Bendls attitude in business.

IGELMAN AND COMPANY
7643 Girard Avenue
La Jolla, CA 92037
Tel.   (619)   454-9699
Hrs: Mon. - Fri.   9:30 a.m. - 6:00 p.m.
            Saturday   9:30 a.m. - 5:30 p.m.
Visa, MasterCard and AMEX are accepted.

Igelman and Company offer the kind of quality, selection and service in men's clothing that no large department store can rival. From the moment you enter the elegant store and see the burgundy, Ralph Lauren wallpaper, oriental rugs over polished oak floors, and deep leather chairs where you may enjoy a drink of your choice, you know you've found The Place.

Owner Ron Ingelman has been in the industry of quality men's clothing for over twenty-nine years and has the best selection in the La Jolla area. Included with the usual array of suits, slacks, formal jackets, ultra soft suede jackets and cashmere sweaters, you'll find accessories to compliment your choices. These include fine, hand-sewn ties, imported cotton shirtings, leather belts, umbrellas, antique watches, English socks, cummerbunds and unique sets of brass buttons and silk braces.

Ron has an expert tailor on the premises, where most alterations are made at no extra charge. Even if it means the unusual remaking of pants or the shortening of coats, you will not be turned away. You can also have your own monogrammed label added to your selections.

For the best in men's clothing, from suits to sportswear, Igelman and Company certainly is the place.

JIG SAW
7948 Herschel Avenue
La Jolla, CA 92037
Tel. (619) 456-1605
Hrs: Mon. - Sun.   10:00 a.m. - 6:00 p.m.
Hours are extended in the summer.
Visa, MasterCard and AMEX are accepted.

Imitation is the highest form of flattery, and the folks at Jig Saw are feeling pretty flattered these days. When Brian Borkum opened Jig Saw with its international look of causual and comfortable clothes, for men and women, his store was the only one of its kind in La Jolla.

Now there's about twelve with a similar look, but with out the keen sense of fashion and quality. Many of the clothes are cotton, silks and washed rayons, the kind of threads people feel comfortable in whether at work or play. There are contemporary fashions with exclusive designs from Japan, Italy, France, England, Scandinavia, Germany and "The States." Brian is known around town as someone who really cares about his customers.

So for fashions that flatter, try Jig Saw. It's where all the pieces will fit in your picture.

NATASSIA'S CLOSET
7643 A Girard Avenue
La Jolla, CA 92037
Tel. (619) 459-KIDS
Hrs: Mon. - Sun.   10:00 a.m. - 6:00 p.m.
         Sunday   12:00 noon - 5:00 p.m.
Visa, MasterCard and AMEX are accepted.

Both kids and parents will enjoy a shopping trip to Natassia's Closet, where they will find an exclusive selection of children's clothing from newborn to age fourteen, as well as children's furniture and bedding. The shop was named after owner, Melanie Ray's daughter, who was born in 1984.

Adults come to Natassia's Closet because they want the very best for their children. Children like to come because they are made to feel so welcome here and they have a wonderful time. White walls, with a plush green carpet and wicker, brass and wood furniture set the tone for the shop. You'll be delighted with the name brands such as Jean Bourget of France, Cache-Cache, Gear Boys and Fix of Sweeren. The baby layettes, toys and clothes always elicit "ooohs and aaahs" from shoppers.

Melanie herself, is such an interesting person, be sure to take a few minutes to become aquainted. She has her private pilot's license and has flown a Cessna 172 all over the US; she holds a geology degree, has been a system's analyst and owned a professional dance studio. Look for Natassia's Closet across the street from Sak's in the original part of La Jolla Village.

UP YOUR ALLEY
7717 Fay Avenue
La Jolla, CA 92037
Tel. (619) 459-7977
Hrs: Mon. - Fri.   9:30 a.m. - 6:30 p.m.
          Saturday   9:30 a.m. - 6:00 p.m.
          Sunday   11:00 a.m. - 5:00 p.m.
Visa and MasterCard are accepted.
Also,

620-A Grand Avenue   2632 Del mar Heights Road
Carlsbad, CA 92008   Del Mar, CA 92014
Tel. (619) 729-5595   Tel. (619) 259-5151

Quality discount designer and top brand clothing is what Up Your Alley is all about. Owner, Cathe Bjorklund has a knack for knowing just what to buy to keep a great turnover of merchandise happening in her stores. Some customers are so eager to get their hands on the weekly arrivals, they even show up to "help unpack" the delivery truck.

At Up Your Alley, over 200 new items arrive weekly, keeping a fresh selection of designer and name brands always available. You'll find Esprit, Diane Von Furstenberg, Diffusion and other popular designer clothes here at greatly discounted prices. Dresses, blouses, pants, leisure wear and accessories such as belts and jewelry are featured. Cathe and her staff love helping customers put together great fashion looks and always make a visit to Up Your Alley more than just a shopping experience.

The store keeps its prices reasonable by not going in for a lot of fancy store frills and displays, just good value. A "Best Choice" for your next shopping excursion is Up Your Alley.

(See special invitatation in the Appendix.)

ART GALLERIES

GALLERY OF TWO SISTERS

1298 Prospect Street
La Jolla, CA 92037
Tel. (619) 459-7119
Hrs: Mon. - Sat.   10:00 a.m. - 5:30 p.m.
       Sunday   11:00 a.m. - 5:00 p.m.
       Thu. - Sun.   7:00 p.m. - 10:00 p.m.
Summer evenings extended hours.
All major credit cards are accepted.

Gallery of Two Sisters is La Jolla's most unique art gallery, with one of the largest selections of sea and area related art and fine crafts on display, predominantly from California artists.

Yes, there really are two sisters. Linda and Sue, originally from Texas, started their dream in this beautiful La Jolla setting over seven years ago, and have built up their gallery to a renown excellence, with many customers returning year after year to repeat the experience.

A sampling of exhibits are bronze sculptures by Wah Chang of Carmel; etchings, lithographs and miniatures by Sue T. McNary of Coronado; oils by San Diego artist, Irene Lumigair; photography by Dallas Clites; wood carved pelicans and seagulls by Ellis; and watercolors by many accomplished California artists.

The Gallery also features a fine selection of Austrian crystal, carvings of soapstone and ironwood, Torrey Pine baskets, kaleidoscopes, assorted notecards and much, much more. You won't see the artists exhibiting in every La Jolla gallery; the sisters strive for exclusiveness, and their quest is unending for unique, original art, crafts and gifts. What's even better, all purchases can be shipped worldwide from the gallery. The two sisters really take pride in presenting a gallery where the customer feels at home while browsing for that special purchase. Stop by for a visit to see just how unique they are!

(See special invitation in the Appendix.)

KENNEDY STUDIOS
7856 Girard Avenue
La Jolla, CA 92037
Tel. (619) 459-6818
Hrs: Mon. - Sat.   10:00 a.m. - 6:00 p.m.
            Sunday   12:00 noon - 5:00 p.m.
Visa, MasterCard and AMEX are accepted.

Wish you could take a bit of La Jolla home with you? You can do just that with one of the colorful prints offered by this cozy gallery that specializes in local land and seascapes. Rachel Murray and Louise Marshall started the shop in 1986 to meet an ever growing demand for contemporary art depicting the Southern California scene. Their goal was to present a collection of fine, affordable art and their idea has proven immensely successful.   The gallery now serves not only tourists, but also the wider La Jolla community, as well as many interior decorators.

You will find a wide range of serigraphs, monotypes, originals, paper sculpture and limited edition prints, the most popular of which are the serigraphs by John Botz, Max Hayslette and Eric Kitchell.

Framing is an important specialty and it's all done on the premises with the staff taking pride in its creative custom framing service. In addition, the gallery offers art locating services and provides art consultation to area businesses. Located on the main shopping street of La Jolla, Kennedy Studios is a bright and inviting gallery that offers warm, friendly service.

Be sure to come in and find that perfect California memento. You'll treasure it for a lifetime.

RIGGS GALLERIES, INC.
875 Prospect Street
La Jolla, CA 92037
Tel. (619) 454-3070
Hrs: Sun. - Wed.   9:00 a.m. - 6:00 p.m.
             Thu. - Sat.   9:00 a.m. - 10:00 p.m.
Visa, MasterCard and AMEX are accepted.

The subtle colors, dark carpeting and excellent lighting show off the artworks in Riggs Galleries to their best advantage, t testimony to owner Mary Riggs' taste and eye for beauty and style. After a foray to the Midwest, where she found the winters to be long and cold, Mary returned to the sunny South coast and along with Bill Strand, who has over twenty years experience in the art world, created this showplace.

More than a place to hang pictures, the gallery works with both private and corporate collectors, and is established in the commissioning of art pieces. Riggs Galleries do their own framing and on-site inspections. Although such important artisits as Francoise Gilot are represented the gallery encourages talented but unknown artists and makes their work available to the public. Many media are represented including oil, watercolor, pencil and charcoal, tapestry, bronze and clay among others.

Despite the variety and quality of the pieces in the ever changing collection, prices are reasonable. Making a visit to the Riggs Galleries is an important step for anyone interested in art.

BED AND BREAKFAST INN

THE BED AND BREAKFAST INN AT LA JOLLA
7753 Draper Avenue
La Jolla, CA 92037
Tel. (619) 456-2066
Visa and MasterCard are accepted.

This is an inn you can love. The former residence is listed   on San Diego's Historic Registry and once was home to John Philip Sousa and his family in the 1920s. Each of the sixteen bedrooms is elegantly appointed and contains a veritable treasure trove of art and expensive furnishings. Many of the rooms have a fireplace and ocean view. Not only are there two balconies, a sundeck, and an excellent library, but all kinds of special extras are provided for your comfort in the rooms, plush towels, scented soaps, fresh   fruit, complimentary sherry, books and magazines, and fresh   flowers.

Breakfast is a treat, owner Betty Albee sees that each guest   receives freshly squeezed orange juice and a selection of fresh pastries enhanced with delicious condiments, and a choice of coffee, tea, cocoa and fresh fruit.

Just steps away from the ocean, the inn is right in the middle of La Jolla's cultural area and all the galleries, shops and best restaurants are at hand. Perhaps even better than the luxury, comfort and convenience offered by the inn is the warm welcome you can be sure to receive from Betty. She is an attractive woman with beautiful laughter that bubbles right from   her heart.

BOOK STORES

BUTLER AND MAYES BOOKSELLERS
8657 Villa La Jolla Drive
La Jolla, CA 92037
Tel. (619) 450-1698
Hrs: Mon. - Fri.   10:00 a.m. - 9:00 p.m.
        Saturday   10:00 a.m. - 6:00 p.m.
        Sunday   12:00 noon - 5:00 p.m.
Visa, MasterCard, AMEX and Discover are accepted.

Your mouth is literally watering over the latest best seller. Alas, it's only out in hard cover and you have a paperback budget. Of course the waiting list at the local library is a mile long, and the book will probably be out in paperback by the time your name comes up anyway. What to do? Get thee to Butler and Mayes Booksellers, where one of the many unusual services is daily rentals, discounted best sellers and books on tape.

For a nominal fee, Butler and Mayes will rent books on tape, hard covers and best sellers by the day. The light comfortable shop, with its soft carpeting, floor to ceiling wooden bookcases and fragrant bowls of lavendar buds create a soothing ambiance for literary pursuits. There is an outstanding collection of international periodicals and newspapers including China, Russia, Japan, Europe and more. The staff will appropriate out of print books for you. You'll find a splendid selection of all types of books in all categories from history to mystery, science fiction to humor. There is a children's section as well as an area containing discount paperbacks. The shop carries one of the best selections of Windham Hill tapes and compact discs in the area.

Located in the La Jolla Village Square on the ground level, Butler and Mayes is one of the most successful independent bookstores in a major mall in San Diego. And, it is above all else a biblophiles dream.

D. G. WILLS BOOKS & COFFEE HOUSE
7527 La Jolla Boulevard
La Jolla, CA 92037
Tel.   (619) 456-1800
Hrs: Mon. - Sun.   10:00 a.m.-10:00 p.m.

If you are looking for a best seller, pick it up at the supermarket. But if it's the the works of the world's greatest minds you crave, head for D. G. Wills Books & Coffee House.

Stacked high among the comfortable clutter of school desks, barber chairs and an old gas pump, are the kinds of books with ideas that can change your life. Owner Dennis Wills should know, it was books such as *The Razor's Edge* and *Lost Horizon* that led him to give up the life as an intelligence specialist. It's a writer's and thinker's book shop modeled after Oxford booksellers, where owner Wills studied for a year. It has one of the best selections of philosophy books found anywhere.

Like any great bookstore, it is an exchange for ideas, where artists and writers can get stimulation from a cup a coffee, or from browsing the pages of an esoteric journal. Poetry readings and lectures are conducted periodically. D. G. Wills is a place for the meeting of minds.

JOHN COLE'S BOOK SHOP
780 Prospect Street
La Jolla, CA 92037
Tel. (619) 454-4766
Hrs: Mon. - Sat.   9:30 a.m. - 5:30 p.m.

How many bookstores have autograph parties with horses and dogs on a palmed and grassy front lawn? How many have special rooms for children with toys, books and windows overlooking the Pacific Ocean? How many have open patios where you can sit, drink tea and think? How many are located in an eighty-year old cottage with a sixty foot arbor entry replete with gnarled wisteria vines and creative pottery? Only one, John Cole's Book Shop in La Jolla.

Specialty books include those for children, cooking, an extensive "how-to" collection, as well as those on the subjects of art, antiques, travel, including current European maps, Baja California, nautical themes, adventure, classics, and one-of-a-kind editions. In short, at John Cole's everything is a specialty and each specialty seems to have its own room. Among the many customers to pass down the arbor have been such notables as J. Edgar Hoover, Charles Laughton, Red Skelton and Ted Geisel, a local resident better known as Dr. Seuss.

A customer's enjoyment and love of literature are treasured characteristics. Variety and fun are uppermost, as is specialized service. The knowledgeable staff will do its best to find or order limited editions and specially requested books. John Cole's Book Shop is a must for the eclectic reader and collector alike.

WARWICK'S
7812 Girard Avenue
La Jolla, CA 92037
Tel.   (619) 454-0347
Hrs: Mon. - Sat.   9:00 a.m. - 5:30 p.m.
          Sunday   11:00 a.m. - 4:00 p.m.

Open for business since 1902, Warwick's is "The oldest continuing businesss in La Jolla," says manager Barbara Christman. Physically, Warwick's is almost two stores, occupying two adjacent buildings with a section cut out of the common wall to unite them. The sense of division serves a purpose as Warwick's makes available office supplies in one section,serving over 2000 office supply customers, and books and gifts in the other.

With an inventory of over 30,000 books, they specialize in hardback fiction, mysteries, biographies, travel and gardening. "Fifty percent of our business is in hardback," says Barbara. They also offer sale books and seasonal promotions, such as back to school books. An art section has been included that features high quality Russian lacquer boxes, unusual cards, and an extensive and unique selection of glass eggs and paperweights.

Service, selection and friendliness are what have made Warwick's such an enduring tradition in La Jolla. As Barbara says, "You can always meet a friend at Warwick's."

THE WHITE RABBIT CHILDREN'S BOOKS
7755 Girard Avenue
La Jolla, CA 92037
Tel. (619) 454-3518
Hrs: Mon. - Sat.   9:00 a.m. - 5:30 p.m.
Visa and MasterCard are accepted.

The White Rabbit was opened in 1978 in response to a perceived need in the community for a bookstore providing a truly extensive selection of books for children of all ages. Owners Louise Howton and Susan Malk feel that the overwhelmingly positive response they've received from their clientele over the years is due mainly to two key ingredients: broad title selection and personal service. In a warm and welcoming atmosphere, books on every subject imaginable, in both paperback and hardcover, are attractively displayed. Extremely knowledgeable staff members are there to assist customers in finding just the right books for any particular child's needs. If a requested title is not in stock, it will rapidly be special ordered.

Autographing parties are held as often as possible, featuring some of the most notable authors and illustrators of children's books in the nation.

These parties often include a special reading or drawing board program by the guest of honor.

In the past few years, The White Rabbit has also sponsored concerts for children, featuring well-known artists, such as Raffi and Sharon, Lois and Bram. The store's selection of recorded materials for children has increased dramatically over the same period of time. The store also sponsors various workshops, teaching rubber stamp art, Origami (the art of Japanese paper folding) and doll making, as well as a twice-monthly storytime for preschoolers. News of all these events, as well as reviews of notable new and forthcoming books, are contained in The White Rabbit's newsletter, published three times a year and available to the store's large mailing list.

CHILDREN'S STORE

GEPPETTO'S
4405 La Jolla Village Drive
University Town Center
La Jolla, CA 92122
Tel. (619) 457-3401
Hrs: Mon. - Fri.   10:00 a.m. - 9:00 p.m.
         Saturday   10:00 a.m. - 6:00 p.m.
         Sunday   12:00 p.m. - 5:00 p.m.
Visa, MasterCard and AMEX are accepted.
Also,
2754 Calhoun Street
Bazaar Del Mundo
San Diego, CA 92110
Tel. (619) 291-4606

Santa Claus would be impressed with the marvelous array of choices of quality toys and clothing found in each Geppetto's store. Loni Rush is the owner of Geppetto's and her logo is "a child's fantasy," this store more than lives up to its reputation. Walk into the sleek, contemporary La Jolla shop, or the vibrant colorful shop in Old Town and you are likely to be greeted by a cuddly barking (toy) puppy who does tricks to delight children of all ages. There are fascinating model train layouts featuring the LGB trains which are true collector pieces. Many of the products at Geppetto's are made in Germany, true craftsmanship and durability their hallmark. Loni and her staff are dedicated to providing safe, quality toys. There are top line model cars and Brio wooden toys, and hundreds of stuffed animals.

As well as toys, Loni has a wide selection of tapes, books, puzzles, paint and crayon books. Geppetto's line of dolls is fantastic, including dolls from all over the world, France, Germany and Italy. Featured is Madam Alexander plus cuddly rag dolls, Gorham musical dolls, and even anatomically correct dolls. A special edition of the famed Charleen Kinser design animals must be seen to be believed. This store also carries handpicked clothing for newborn to toddlers size four. Patchez and Boomers brands are in high demand.

There are unique sleeping bags designed like clowns and colorful animals as well as Fantasy Furniture, all hand painted and special. From Beatrix Potter china figurines, baby picture frames to rubber picture puzzles, you'll find it here. And if you can't find what you are looking for, Loni or her staff of friendly people will help you find ti. There is a lot of joy, pride and love evident in Geppetto's. People are constantly telling her that shopping in her store makes them happy.

CHRISTMAS STORE

ALL ABOUT CHRISTMAS
1298 Prospect Street
La Jolla, CA 92037
Tel. (619) 454-1925
Hrs:　Mon. - Sat.　　10:00 a.m. - 5:30 p.m.
　　　　Sunday　　　　12:00 noon - 4:00 p.m.
Visa, MasterCard, AMEX and Discover are accepted.

Don't let their name fool you. All About Christmas' slogan is, "Handmade gifts for all reasons and all seasons." When this shop began, over twenty years ago, it was open only in the fall. All About Christmas was the creation of six women who were tired of running rummage sales and school carnivals. They pooled their talents, resources and entrepreneurial spirits and opened an outlet for the gift items they had made by hand all year. It was a great success, and has grown since then under the guidance of the present owner, Evelyn MacCarthy. She has added more local crafts, handmade gifts and souvenirs to the already wonderful variety of items which made the store well known in the first place.

Despite the variety of "non-Christmas" items, it is the ornaments, nativity pieces, bells, Santas, handknit, personalized stockings and other Christmas holiday gifts and goods, which proves it's never too early to shop for this grandest of holidays. Speaking of ornaments, they're a house specialty. You can find them for special people, like mom or dad or teachers, soccer players, musicians and many more. You can even have one made up specially. There is gift wrap, and gift wrapping and mailing to anywhere.

A teenager once remarked, "It's just like stepping inside a Christmas stocking." As Evelyn MacCarthy observes, "No one ever leaves my store without a smile on their face." No wonder All About Christmas is such a popular spot.

FITNESS CENTERS

FITNESS IS FUN
7614 Fay Avenue
La Jolla, CA 92037
Tel. (619) 455-1225
Hrs: Telephone for class schedules.
Visa, and MasterCard are accepted.

If you still think exercising is a drag, you haven't experienced the energizing effects of a workout at Fitness Is Fun. Now is the time to find out why so many people are doing it. Conveniently located in downtown La Jolla, its the perfect spot for travelers to stop and really stretch, or for a mid-day respite to add energy to your work day.

One session will convince you "We don't sell memberships, we sell results" is an apt slogan for this fitness center. Owner, Lee Clark, with nineteen years experience in aerobic fitness conditioning and resistance exercise and manager Jack Clark with a background in kineseology, physiology and nutrition, and former associate of television personality Richard Simmons, are equipped to see you get the conditioning program just right for you. They offer the choice of high or low impact aerobic classes, hand weights and rubberband workouts. A key feature of the center is its reputation of personal service, with a ratio of almost one to one training.

Whether you want to shed a few pounds, tone up, release tension or just do something nice for yourself, Fitness Is Fun is the place for you. Both men and women are invited to enjoy the energetic atmosphere and personalized training offered at Fitness is Fun. Please call for specific class times, hours and prices.

(See special invitation in the Appendix.)

PERSONALIZED WEIGHT TRAINING OF LA JOLLA
5697 La Jolla Boulevard, # C
La Jolla, CA 92037
Tel. (619) 456-2595
Hrs: Mon. - Fri.   7:00 a.m. - 7:00 p.m.
           Saturday   8:00 a.m. - 5:00 p.m.

Many people attracted to weight training don't have enough knowledge of their own physical potential or limitations to approach it with competence or confidence. At Personalized Weight Training, a program is designed exclusively around your own physical parameters. This will give you the confidence needed to pursue the program knowing that you have the physical ability and stamina to succeed.

Resting heart rate, girth measurements, body composition, relative percentages of bone, muscle and fat, and the endurance of your cardiovascular system are all measured and taken into account in designing your specific program. Weight loss or gain, muscle toning and strengthening, and improved stamina are addressed according to your individual needs, incorporating the most advanced equipment and refined methods available anywhere.

Privacy and a personalized workout area provide you with the most benefit from your instruction and equipment to gradually maximize the progress in your program. After eight weeks you'll be totally re-measured, and you'll be able to see for yourself the extent of the benefit to you. All of this takes place in a private atmosphere. To get in top shape, visit Personalized Weight Training in La Jolla.

RENAISSANCE FITNESS TRAINING
4660 La Jolla Village Drive
Suite 1100
La Jolla, CA 92122
Tel.   (619) 546-0711
Hrs: Mon. - Sat.   7:00 a.m. - 7:00 p.m.

Looking for the ultimate workout, the fastest and safest way to get in shape and stay that way?   Look into a private fitness program from Renaissance Fitness Training.   Located high above La Jolla at the top of the California First Building, Renaissance Fitness Training has been working one on one with satisfied clients for over ten years. These are people who saw dramatic results from the personalized attention they received at Renaissance Fitness Training.

Nick Holslag, Jr., owner and manager of Renaissance Fitness Training is proud of the fact that the prestigious Scripps Clinic refers clients to Renaissance. Nick, and his father before him have been consistently dedicated to high quality equipment and instruction, proper education, and a total fitness approach for a permanent transformation to your new fitness level. Your personal fitness instructor will tailor your workouts especially for your personal goals. You'll waste no time waiting for your instructor's attention. At Renaissance Fitness Training, it's just you and your trainer. You'll meet at least three times a week for a minimum of six weeks. If you wish, your trainer can meet you at your office or home. Each workout will be unique to avoid boredom. You'll have the advantage of the latest high tech exercise equipment and evaluations.

While Renaissance is a very exclusive private club, the expense is well worth it. After all, haven't you worked hard to get where you are today? Give yourself the private treatment you deserve at Renaissance Fitness Training.

FURNITURE STORES

THE DINING ROOM SHOP
7645 Girard Avenue
La Jolla, CA 92037
Tel.   (619) 454-8688
Hrs: Tue. - Sat.   10:00 a.m. - 5:30 p.m.
Visa, MasterCard and AMEX are accepted.

An ever changing kaleidoscope of ideas for attractive dining awaits you here. Dedicated to the idea that "great food and good friends deserve the perfect setting," owners Judith Smith and Joan Fisher have collected in their imaginative store all the ingredients you need to do your entertaining in style, your own style, as as individual and creative as you wish to make it. Much of the merchandise they have assembled is as comfortably at home on a holiday table for twelve, as it is on a picnic table for four. Antiques have been found in the back rooms of London shops, the Paris flea market, Italian emporiums, Hong Kong side streets and American craft shows.

Contemporary wares include hand colored prints, as well as custom made dinnerware and pottery. The shop is the exclusive Southern California representative for Patrick Frey linen, Puiforcat fine china from France, Taitu dinnerware from Italy and Cartier china, crystal and giftwares.

Come in any time to share a cup of tea and browse through the shop's idea sparkling collection of books on art, food and wine, antiques, decorating, entertaining and gracious living. You'll find good company and helpful advice on designing a feast for the eyes of your family and guests.

ROCHE-BOBOIS
7611 Girard Avenue
La Jolla, CA 92037
Tel. (619) 459-0297
Hrs: Mon. - Sat.   9:30 a.m. - 5:30 p.m.
Sundays and evenings by appointment.
Visa, MasterCard and AMEX are accepted.

Sometimes only the best will do. When that time is here, come to Roche-Bobois. As purveyors of the finest home furnishings and accessories anywhere, Roche-Bobois seeks out original designers whose styles combine the utmost in quality and comfort. All the lines carried by Roche-Bobois are exclusive. Contemporary European furniture for the living room, dining area and bedroom is designed with practicality, as well as beauty in mind.

Displayed imaginatively in the showroom, this exceptional furniture is a celebration of timeless beauty and devotion to sheer comfort. Roche-Bobois carries the Nec Plume Ultra line of leather sofas. Combining the finest leather upholstery with one hundred percent goose feather stuffing, these sofas are the absolute ultimate in luxury.

In addition to leather, you'll find a collection of fine lacquered pieces, modular wall units, tables, and designer bedroom sets. Italian marble, the Les Coloniales rattan collection, available in a spectrum of twenty-five colors, and the the casual Les Informels creative fabric collection are there to mix and match with exquisite lamps vases, pillows, mirrors and rugs to create extraordinary collections for your home. When you are ready for the creme de la creme in home furnishing, it's got to be Roche-Bobois.

GIFT SHOPS

LONDON ASSOCIATES SHELLS
1137 Prospect Street
La Jolla, CA 92037
Tel. (619) 459-6858
Hrs: Mon. - Sat.   10:00 a.m. - 5:30 p.m.
       Sunday   11:00 a.m. - 5:00 p.m.
Visa, MasterCard and AMEX are accepted.

Shells galore! From glowing golden cowries and sea cones for displaying on your end tables to large pieces that are so wonderful for decorating an avant garde home, like giant clams, up to 260 pounds, delicate coral, Australian trumpets, and Pacific tritons, this shop has them all.

Shells from all over the world also include many rare samples for the conscientious collector and prices range from fifty cents to $2000. Entering London Associates Shells is like entering an oceanic museum. Live palm trees and sand pebbled floor complement the marble display areas where they also have one of the best collections in the West of sea fossils and decorative minerals. The fossils include ancient shark's teeth, seashells and fish, but the most impressive are 500,000 million year old trilobites, water bug like creatures, from Utah. There are decorative minerals, such as deep purple amethyst from Brazil, white quartz clusters and brown selenite from Mexico. When polished, geodes, septarian and Brazilian agate make most extraordinary bookends. Over twenty stands are also available for displaying your own collection.

They also carry a selection of exquisite semi-precious mineral jewelry of unique designs. All fine silverwork is done by Navajo Indians. Also available is a nice selection of coral jewelry. London Associates Shells will ship anywhere and their carefully packed merchandise is fully insured. For an unusual experience that will titillate your creative urges, visit London Associate Shells today.

OUT OF THIS WORLD
1298 Prospect Street, 2E
La Jolla, CA 92037
Tel.   (619) 459-4070
Hrs: Mon. - Thu.   10:30 a.m. - 6:00 p.m.
         Fri. - Sun.   10:30 a.m. - 10:00 p.m.

Overlooking the La Jolla coves and the Pacific Ocean, you'll find a delightful shop named, Out of This World. This store specializes in ladies apparel made from original hand loomed fabrics, imported European fashions and ethnic jewelry, as well as fascinating art objects from the far corners of the world.

Out of a love of travel and a love of collecting folk art, John and Diane Ooms began this La Jolla gift shop. Visitors sometimes spend hours looking over the handmade items as John and Diane explain the history and use of each. How else might you find out about a 300 year old African mask or Indian dowry chest. There are bowls and baskets from Botswana, a loom from Mali and nut boxes from Tibet.

For someting from a place far away, and a long time ago, step into Out Of This World, your "Best Choice" for unique gifts.

PANACHE
8657 Villa La Jolla Drive
La Jolla, CA 92037
Tel.   (619) 450-9017
Hrs: Mon. - Fri.   10:00 a.m. - 9:00 p.m.
        Saturday   10:00 a.m. - 6:00 p.m.
        Sunday   12:00 noon - 5:00 p.m.
Visa, MasterCard, AMEX and Discover are accepted.

Panache is the French word for "flair" and "style." Yet the translation doesn't quite do justice to the extra special collectibles to be found at this delightful shop on La Jolla Drive.

When you step across the marble entry and see the waterfall, candelabra and fireplace, you get an immediate sense that you'll be impressed with the merchandise in this 5000 square foot store. Inside, you'll find one of a kind articles. Panache specializes in comtemporary oil lamps, candles, candle holders and fresh flowers. There are fine lines of crystal, art glass and an extensive collection of paperweights and picture frames.

If you are unsure of how a particular selection might look in your own environment, consultants from Panache are glad to provide free consultations in your home or office. Gift boxes and gift wrapping are also complimentary and shipping can be arranged anywhere. For a little bit extra in elegant accessories for your home, visit Panache in La Jolla.

PILI
7839 Girard Avenue
La Jolla, CA 92037
Tel.   (619) 454-3339
Hrs: Mon. - Sat.   10:00 a.m. - 5:30 p.m.
Visa, MasterCard and AMEX are accepted.

When you walk into Pili you feel you have entered a beautiful contemporary and high-tech museum, where you can enjoy and find wonderful things, from unusual fun pencils for less than .50 to the most elegant designs in home accessories or jewelry. You'll find items by SWID POWELL, ZANI&ZANI, ALESSI, IITTALA, BRAUN and many other well-known names. There is china, silver, stainless steel, glassware, unusual clocks, mirrors, lamps, glassware, luggage and many other things for the contemporary home or office including practical and useful kitchen items.

The collection at Pili is vast and beautifully displayed. it promises to delight everyone.

Pili and her experienced and friendly staff will help you choose the perfect gift for your special occasion. Pili's ideas, knowledge, and wonderful sense of humor are apparent in her shop. Her smile and enthusiasm make visiting Pili a rewarding experience. "Wow!," is the frequent expression heard from many visitors....

JEWELRY STORE

THE COLLECTOR
1274 Prospect Street
La Jolla, CA 92037
Tel.   (619) 454-9763
Hrs: Mon. - Sat.   10:00 a.m. - 5:00 p.m.
Visa, MasterCard and AMEX are accepted.
Also,
912 South Live Oak Park Road
Fallbrook, CA 92028
Tel. (619) 728-9121

The Collector is known by connoisseurs throughout the world as the source for fine colored gemstones. The Collector is the only North American company with extensive mining interests in Africa and Asia, and collaborates with many of Europe's and America's most famous jewelry designers to create original masterieces of exceptional quality.

Owner Bill Larson was responsible for the famous rubellite tourmaline discovery in Northern San Diego County in 1972. According to Vince Manson, curator of the Museum of Natural History in New York, the strike was "...the find of the century in terms of color and perfection."

Located on the upper level of the "Coast Walk," shops overlooking the Pacific, the store's display of original jewelry, minerals, natural gemstones and tourmaline figurines is breathtaking. Join the international visitors who flock to this glamorous shop. It is an education in itself in terms of quality and well worth visiting to see the variety of beautiful items other than jewelry.

LINEN STORE

EVERETT STUNZ COMPANY
7644 Girard Avenue
La Jolla, CA 92037
Tel.   (619) 459-3305
Visa, MasterCard and AMEX are accepted.

Discerning shoppers know that truly fine quality bed linens are hard to find. Thankfully, there is one store that wants nothing less than to provide top quality adjustable beds, linens and accessories for shoppers who want only the best. Everett Stunz Company was the first adjustable bed specialty store in San Diego County, opening is doors twenty-four years ago. Purchased six years ago by Lynn Ripley, the store has grown form a source for high quality adjustable beds to La Jolla's premiere bed, bath and table linen shop.

The trend is toward exciting contemporary designs in bed and bath linens, and Everett Stunz leads the way with product styling offering a fashion forward look as will as classic, elegant bed ensembles. Recent exclusive introductions are by popular Australian artist Ken Done, inspired by the flowers, coral, fish and waters of Australia's Eastern Coast, and Fran DeBellas, prominent East Coast artist, who designs in florals and intricate impressionist stripings. Both are at the forefront of this exciting art form.

Everett Stunz has extensive resources, enabling them to bring to La Jolla virtually any of the fine home linens which previously required travel to New York or Europe. What is not immediately available in stock is quickly located through special orders. Why not treat yourself like royalty with luxurious Egyptian cotton bed linens from Everett Stunz?

PERFUME AND COSMETICS

ALEXANDER PERFUME AND COSMETICS
7914 Girard Avenue
La Jolla, CA 92037
Tel.   (619) 454-2292
Hrs: Mon. - Sat.   9:00 a.m. - 5:30 p.m.
Closed Sundays.
Visa, MasterCard, AMEX, Diners Club, Carte Blanche and Discover are accepted.

You'll find the perfume that best complements your lifestyle at Alexander Perfumes and Cosmetics, because owner Alexander Bende will custom blend the scent for you! Alexander's shop is unique in the world of fragrance and beauty.

The boutique features three areas of personal enhancement. The first is fragrances for women and men. Alexander specializes in difficult to locate perfumes. He will find a source for you if the fragrance is not already on his well stocked shelves. The newest European lines will appear at Alexander's a year or more ahead of any other store. Cosmetics are under the purvey of Corry Bende, Alexander's wife. Corry is a trained aesthetician and is expert in her knowledge of cosmetic lines. Her skills have made her one of the best cosmetic advisors in the business. The crowning jewel of Alexander's is the perfume laboratory. Here, Alexander creates custom designed fragrances. Alexander consults with you privately and considers aspects of your life style, how you currently use fragrance, what are your favorites, what works for you, tests your skin and then creates a scent that personifies you. A secret number is given to your special perfume which makes it yours exclusively. Consultation requires about an hour to hour and half of time.

"A perfume should be as individual as the person wearing it," according to Alexander Bende. Turning words into reality, Alexander goes about creating special scents for his many appreciative customers.

RESTAURANTS

THE COTTAGE
7702 Fay Avenue
La Jolla, CA 92037
Tel. (619) 454-8409
Hrs: Mon. - Sat.   7:00 a.m. - 4:00 p.m.
Breakfast   Sunday   9:00 a.m. - 2:00 p.m.

People watching was never so scrumptious!   Nancy Long has created the perfect place for nibbling, spectating and catching up on the latest news. The Cottage is the essence of hominess right down to the charming white picket fence and friendly, attentive service.

Stop by for a quick breakfast or a leisurely interlude sipping gourmet coffee. Skim the newspaper after deciding which kind of devastatingly delicious homemade pastry to order. King Kong muffins and Very Berry muffins are baked fresh every morning as well as daily specials from the baker's imagination such as Poppyseed or Applesauce Spice muffins. Imaginative omelette combinations make The Cottage a wonderful breakfast spot. Huevos Rancheros is a popular weekend breakfast favorite.

The Cottage is a natural for people watching at lunchtime. Sit on the patio under blue and white umbrellas. Dig into a marvelous Oriental Salad, romaine and iceberg lettuce, breast of chicken, cashews, crisp oriental noodles, and mandarin oranges in a sesame seed dressing. Save room for Triple Chocolate Fudge Cake and a Cottage Cafe Mocha and settle in for a perfect afternoon in the California sunshine.

EL CRAB CATCHER
1298 Prospect Street
La Jolla, CA 92037
Tel. (619) 454-9587
Hrs: Mon. - Sat.   11:30 a.m. - 3:00 p.m.
                                     5:30 p.m. - 10:00 p.m.
            Sunday   10:30 a.m. - 3:00 p.m.
                                     5:30 p.m. - 10:00 p.m.
Visa, MasterCard and AMEX are accepted.

What is naughty hula pie? It's an extravagant dessert featured at El Crab Catcher which consists of macadamia nut ice cream pie, chocolate sauce and whipped cream. Before jumping into that, however, you might want to try the crab legs saute,   maybe the Hawaiian specialty Mahi-Mahi, or veal oscar. The selections are as delicious as they are varied.

Sunday brunch includes complimentary champagne and offers such delightful culinary choices like crab custard quiche, crab benedict, or machaca - an egg dish containing shredded beef, tomatoes and special seasonings.

Located in "Coast Walk" along the La Jolla shoreline, El Crab Catcher offers the best view in the San Diego area, a most stunning panorama of the La Jolla waterfront and caves. There can be nothing better than spending a lazy afternoon at El Crab Catcher, choosing delicacies from the Oyster and Wine Bar menu, experimenting with tropical drinks and watching the interesting shorelife.

THE FRENCH PASTRY SHOP
5550 La Jolla Boulevard
La Jolla, CA 92037
Tel. (619) 454-9094
Hrs: Lunch   Mon. - Sun.   11:30 a.m. - 4:30 p.m.
            Dinner   Sun. - Thu.   4:30 p.m. - 8:00 p.m.
                                Saturday   5:30 p.m. - 12:00 midnight

A regular Noah's Ark of pastry. How else do you describe The French Pastry Shop, where the bakery goods look like animals? Some of the breads and rolls look like rabbits, pigs, mice, birds, alligators, frogs and crabs.

That's just one of the features of this combination pastry shop and restaurant that has people coming back over and over again. For a luscious breakfast try any of the fifty plus pastries with espresso or fresh squeezed orange juice.

As a "Best Choice" lunch try Fettuccini St. Jacques, or Tourte' Minaaise, which is a ham, cheese, spinach, red pepper in an omelete layered with pastry crust and Hollandaise sauce. For dinner indulge in a L'entrecote de Boeufaux Poiures Verte. For entertainment, ask to see chef Paul Perrie's book of cakes.   Superb meals and friendly service are only two of the reasons to enjoy French Pastry.

HARRY'S CAFE GALLERY
7545 Girard Avenue
La Jolla, CA 92037
Tel. (619)   454-7381
Hrs: Mon. - Sat.   6:00 a.m. - 7:30 p.m.
           Sunday   6:00 a.m. - 2:00 p.m.

As Thomas Wolf said, "You can't go home again." But at Harry's you can still get good down home cooking. Harry and Cathy Rudolph, secret lies in part with "Mom Rudolph," who's in her eighties, but is on the job seven days a week.

Harry's Cafe Gallery is known for great breakfasts, where everyone always gets an extra free egg. When you order a cup of coffee, you get a pot. The raisan walnut French toast and pancakes have become legendary. Lunches feature juicy hamburgers that really stack up, especially the "handicapper." Specialties for dinner are petite fillet and teriyaki chicken. Take note of the art work. The walls are decked out with Bateman wildlife paintings, Paul Calle western prints, and original sports photographs of Babe Ruth and old Dodgers players, the pictures are for sale. Be sure to ask Harry about what it was like being a bat boy for the Brooklyn Dodgers.

Whether you make it to just breakfast, or all three meals Harry won't let you strike out here.

ISSIMO AT THE PASTA PLACE
5634 La Jolla Boulevard
La Jolla, CA 92037
Tel. (619) 454-7004
Hrs: Lunch   Tue. - Sat.   12:00 noon - 2:30 p.m.
          Dinner   Tue. - Sat.   6:00 p.m. - 10:00 p.m.
          Store   Mon. - Sat.   10:30 p.m. - 7:00 p.m.
                          Sunday   12:00 noon - 6:00 p.m.

There's hardly more elegant food to be found in San Diego than provided by Issimo at The Pasta Place. Using only the finest and freshest ingredients available, many of which are flown in directly from around the world, Issimo specializes in classic Northern Italian and French cuisines.

Issimo offers elegant dining in the evening. "There is hardly more elegant food to be had anywhere" praises the *LA Times Magazine*. The menu features appetizers such as Lobster and Truffle Parfait with a Tomato/Sherry Mousseline sauce and Fresh Oysters with horseradish cream and black and golden caviar. Cream of Sweet Red Pepper or Cream of Asparagus with morels are only two of several dozen homemade soups offered. Choose an entree of Noisettes D'Agneau Madere (medallions of lamb with a reduced Madeira, thyme and garlic sauce), Scampi on a bed of spinach and leeks served with sherry beurre blanc, or Osso Buco (braised veal shanks). Try an outstanding pasta dish such as Seafood Cannelloni with Crab and Scallops, or Agnolotti (a stuffed pasta with fresh wild mushrooms).

Don't miss Issimo's sensational selection of freshly prepared desserts. Their award winning desserts include Torta di Mezzanotte (a very dense chocolate cake filled with Mocha Buttercream and covered with Chocolate Ganache), La Reina Nobile (layers of light sponge cake alternated with Lemon Curd filling) and their ever popular Hazelnut Ravioli.

Issimo also offers pasta, entree items, antipasto and a great variety of marvelous sauces prepared to take home for your enjoyment. Try Paupiettes de Poulet, Pesto or Stuffed Eggplant. You'll also find a wealth of gourmet products and an outstanding selection of wines from many countries. Ask for recommendations as the owners and staff are always helpful and very knowledgeable.

This charming restaurant with its attractive cafe and sophisticated main dining room featuring wall murals by Wing Howard, offers everyone an exceptional experience. Reservation are recommended and it's best to plan at least two weeks in advance for special occasions.

Chef Will Howard and Anne Slattery truly offer the best in elegant dining, catering and gourmet foods. You'll be delighted! This remarkable restaurant in La Jolla offers Europe a challenge with its world class standards.

LA JOLLA SPICE COMPANY
7556 Fay Avenue
La Jolla, CA 92037
Tel.   (619)   454-4662
Hrs: Mon. - Sat.   7:00 a.m. - 5:00 p.m.
          Sunday   7:00 a.m. - 2:00 p.m.

More and more people in this day and age are beginning to realize the importance of healthy eating. They are consuming less of what's not good for them and eating more of what is. Reasons like these and several others make the La Jolla Spice Company so popular.

The owner of this cafe-style restaurant, Eileen Ingram, always dreamed of owning her own restaurant and even played restaurant as a child. This, in conjunction with her cooking education in New Orleans, is probably what makes La Jolla Spice Company so delightful. Its courtyard with striped umbrellas and its interior with soothing blue walls and plenty of sunshine, give this restaurant a definite air of charm. But ambiance apart, the food is another cherry on the cake for this fine establishment. On the breakfast menu you'll find a delightful assortment of goodies, such as Sweedish Oatmeal pancakes, whole wheat waffles and eggs served with fresh fruit and muffin of your choice.

Perhaps you didn't come for breakfast, maybe it's lunch you want. Well are you in luck. Quiche Maison with garden salad, a Bay shrimp sandwich and a grilled tuna melt, not to mention all the wonderful salads, are only a smidgen of the lunch menu. There are also over thirty blends of coffees available and waiting for your approval. So, bring a friend and see why La Jolla Spice Company is a wonderful place to relax, enjoy healthy food and have a terrific time.

(See special invitation in the Appendix.)

LA JOLLA TOUJOURS CAFE
828 Prospect
La Jolla, CA 92037
Tel.   (619) 456-2944
Hrs: Wed. - Sat.   7:30 a.m. - 11:00 p.m.
          Sun. - Tue.   7:30 a.m. - 7:00 p.m.

The motto here is "Gourmet coffees and desserts." Also known as "The 'Biggest Little' Jazz Coffee House in San Diego," the aim of owner Jim

McKee is to provide a place where people can relax, meet other people, and enjoy good food. They've certainly succeeded.

Decorated in the European style with glass topped tables both inside and outside on the brick patio, the atmosphere is intimate and cozy. Along with fifteen varieties of coffee and sumptuous desserts, the La Jolla Toujours Cafe also offers gourmet Belgian waffles, sandwiches, salads and homemade soups. Desserts are their specialty, however, and you can choose between brownies with caramel, fudge, and macadamia nuts, or Rocky Road, New York style cheesecake, or apple crunch pie, to name a few.

Local and national live jazz musicians are featured in the evenings from Wednesday through Sunday. Just follow the delicious aroma of freshly brewed coffee and you'll find a good time at La Jolla Toujours Cafe.

LA PLAYA GRILL, 1298 Prospect Street, La Jolla, CA 92037. Tel. (619) 454-9033. Exquisite Mexican cuisine can be enjoyed on the patio overlooking the La Jolla coastline.

MANHATTAN OF LA JOLLA
7766 Fay and Silverado in the Empress Hotel
La Jolla, CA 92037
Tel. (619) 454-1182
Visa, MasterCard and AMEX are accepted.

It is easy to understand the success of Manhattan, but not the secrets of accomplishing it. From the moment you enter you are fascinated by the brilliantly colored tropical fish peering at you form ten large salt water tanks. The tanks help retain privacy without closing you in when you are seated in the large, comfortably upholstered booths, no plastic at Manhattan.

The Northern Italian or New York style Italian cuisine is the main event at Manhattan. Start with the freshly made Cannelloni created by Manhattan owner, "P. J." Macaluso. Next, the most incredible Ceasar Salad concocted at your table by your talented, tuxedoed waiter. You can be wearing a sport shirt, but he will always be in a tuxedo. This is part of the charm of being classy, but at ease. If you are not a Caesar Salad lover, there is also a delicious fresh Spinach Salad with hot bacon dressing.

P. J. is not the chef. He is more the artist who oversees the work of art of his craftsmen in the kitchen. His Scampi P. J. is fabulous, just dip your fresh bread into that sauce. The Filet of Sole is not like any you have ever tasted, great!

As your companion to order the Veal Oscar, Scallopini, Marsala or even the unbelievable rach of lamb so you can share. Manhattan also features Steak

Florentino, a treasure of flavor and other selections using only fresh prime beef.

Ah, but wait. Now comes dessert. Fresh and rich Cannoli, Italy's answer to the egg roll, filled with rich chocolate mousse, or Zabione, which is an egg white fluffy cream and ripe strawberries, or the Apple Fritter lightly cookied in brandy and rum sauce and topped with ice cream. Manhattan is quite a restaurant. Ask for P. J. and tell him you love good food.

NECTAR JUICE BAR
6830 La Jolla Boulevard Suite 101
La Jolla, CA 92037
Tel. (619) 454-7110
Hrs: Mon. - Sat.   8:00 a.m. - 8:00 p.m.
      Sunday   9:00 a.m. - 8:00 p.m.
Personal checks are welcome.

Take a trip to the tropics Southern California style. Located just one block from the ocean, this tropical paradise offers exotic, healthy food "from soup to nuts" made the way you like it.

While surrounded by lush flowers and muraled walls you can enjoy fresh squeezed carrot, wheat grass or bee pollen juice, fruit or garden salads, or choose one of the seven "natural" sandwiches. Specialties include a soup of the day, fresh Albacore Sandwich with chips, and home baked Bran Muffins. Top your meal off with one of the seven natural ice cream smoothies which can be made super-healthy by adding extras such as protein powder, acidophilus, lecithin and more. The Da-Kine Smoothie made with secret natural fruit ingredients is available for the more adventurous connoisseur. If your timing is right you may run into Cliff Robertson who regularly enjoys the healthful, tropical ambiance and delightful foods offered at the Nectar Juice Bar. The freshest in produce includes a crisp Kiwi fruit salad to enjoy as a main course or for dessert.

If you're looking for the freshest ingredients made especially for you, stop by and experience the Nectar Juice Bar. If the saying, "what you eat you are" is accurate then eating at the Nectar Juice Bar means you're pretty special.

(See special invitation in the Appendix.)

SEA GRILLE RESTAURANT, La Jolla Marriott, 4240 La Jolla Village Drive, La Jolla, CA 92037. Tel. (619) 587-1414.   Intimate and elegant, this restaurant features fresh local seafood.

SOUP EXCHANGE
7777 Fay Avenue
La Jolla, CA 92037
Tel. (619) 459-0212
Hrs: Mon. - Sun. 11:00 a.m. - 9:30 p.m.
No credit cards are accepted.
Also,

7305 Clairemont Mesa Blvd.
Kearny Mesa, CA 92111
Tel. (619) 576-0622

7984 La Mesa Boulevard
La Mesa, CA 92041
Tel. (619) 697-8561

1840 Garnet Avenue
Pacific Beach, CA 91745
Tel. (619) 272-7766

2665 Vista Way
Oceanside, CA 92054
Tel. (619) 433-7687

Sometimes a hot, steaming bowl of homestyle soup would just hit the spot. Other days a fresh salad with every vegie you can think of is what you crave. When the soup or salad urge befalls you, walk, run or jog to the Soup Exchange. With it's five locations in the San Diego area, the Soup Exchange offers a wonderful alternative in dining. Offering fresh soup, salad, bakery and fresh fruit dessert bars, the restaurant aims for customer awareness about health and nutrition.

The Soup Exchange serves six freshly prepared homestyle soups daily. You may choose from over sixty garden fresh and prepared salad entrees with many dressings and condiments. Specialty muffins, breads, and pastries as well as fresh fruits and dessert are included with soup, salad or soup and salad main item purchases. A variety of beverages, including both domestic and imported beers and wines are also offered. Quantity and return privileges are unlimited.

An atmosphere of tile, glass, light and airiness make The Soup Exchange a pleasant place to eat. Seniors and children are very welcome here and are extended discounts. If you are in a hurry take advantage of their special "express service." And, if you are interested in more information about this consumer friendly, health oriented operation, the Soup Exchange distributes a monthly newsletter, *Pot' Pourri*. If it's soup and salad you want, put on your walking shoes and make your heart happy at the Soup Exchange.

VIC'S RESTAURANT
7825 Fay Avenue
La Jolla, CA 92037
Tel. (619) 456-3789
Also,
FISHERMAN'S GRILL
7825 Fay Avenue
La Jolla, CA 92037
Tel. (619) 456-3733
Visa, MasterCard and AMEX are accepted.

If it's an evening of fine dining and wonderful entertainment you're planning, then you've turned to the right page. Vic's and Fisherman's Grill are the experiences you're fishing for and they're both in La Jolla.

Vic's Restaurant, in the Merrill Lynch building is the companion restaurant to the Fisherman's Grill, which is next door. Vic's serves great old-fashioned American cooking with a touch of California Modern. You can get everything from chicken pot pie with homemade mashed potatos at lunch, to huge slabs of aged Angus prime rib of beef at dinner. Jack Monaco has created a superb menu to accompany the clubby atmosphere with curving booths and tables set with comfortable padded chairs. Vic's upstairs lounge offers live entertainment Wednesday through Saturday evenings.

At the Fisherman's Grill, where the fish is fresh, the atmosphere is bright and casual. Featured are a large, attractive oak oyster bar and outside tables in the courtyard for fair-weather dining. The menu, although innovative, includes an extensive selection of traditional seafood favorites. Vic's and Fisherman's Grill, two of the best places to go when looking for something different.

SALON

SALON GENITO FULL SERVICE SALON AND DAY SPA
7712 Fay Avenue
La Jolla, CA 92037
Tel.   (619) 454-2771
Hrs: Tue. - Wed., Fri. - Sat.   9:00 a.m. - 6:00 p.m.
       Thursday   9:00 a.m. - 9:00 p.m.
Visa and MasterCard are accepted.

A first look at the black and white awning that graces the entry to Salon Genito, will cause you to suspect that inside, a treat is waiting. After entering the spacious black and white art deco salon, your suspicions will be confirmed: You're about to be pampered. Whether man or a woman, you'll enjoy the feeling of being taken care of, and knowing it will be good for you. This is a salon for skin, hair and body care, and you can't help but enjoy it all.

The salon and spa is divided into separate specialty areas, including a make-up department, retail center featuring fine European skin and hair care products, and a manicure/pedicure area where they offer a new hot wax treatment which restores moisture to hands while it provides deep conditioning and relief to joints. There is also a styling area, and a chemical department where permanents and coloring are done, plus the spa area where you'll find a passive exercise room, steam rooms, massage rooms, facial rooms and panthermal room. The steam room is complimentary to anyone who comes in for a treatment or service. But, if you want a complete body cleansing and detoxifier, try the steam tub in the panthermal room.

This quintessential salon and spa has everything: The masseur and masseuse are masters of their work, as are the friendly, internationally trained hair stylists. Have you ever tried an herbal body wrap? Here's your chance. You'll find manager Nicole Ungaro and her entire staff to be capable, helpful and very friendly.

SPORTS EQUIPMENT

LA JOLLA SURF SYSTEMS
2132 Avenida De La Playa
La Jolla, CA 92037
Tel. (619) 456-2777
Hrs: Mon. - Sun.   10:00 a.m. - 6:00 p.m.
Visa, MasterCard and Discover are accepted.

La Jolla Surf Systems provides everything one needs for surfing, swimming and snorkling as well as casual cruise wear for both men and women.

A stock of 5,000 suits fills the upstairs women's swimwear boutique. California casual wear by Gotcha, Quiksilver, Jimmy'z Jag, Too Hot Brazil, Speedo and more line the racks. Wetsuit brands include Rip Curl and O'Neil. Competitive swimwear and gear are top of the line, for the serious swimmer or casual beach lounger. T-shirts, suntan products and other beach articles round out the sun worshipper's wardrobe needs. Surfboards by Rusty Boards, Linden and Al Merrick's exclusive Channel Islands are for purchase. La Jolla Surf Systems also rents surf videos! The shop is across from the famous La Jolla Beach and Tennis Club on the Avenida De La Playa.

La Jolla Surf Systems is a surf shop and more. By the way, it's the only surf shop with an annual catalog, sent free anywhere in the world.

MATCH POINT, INC.
2156 Avenida de la Playa
La Jolla, CA 92037
Tel. (619) 459-2831
Hrs: Mon. - Sat.   9:00 a.m. - 6:00 p.m.
           Sunday   10:00 a.m. - 5:00 p.m.
Visa, MasterCard and AMEX are accepted.

Newspapers and magazines bombard us with information alluding to the benefits of an exercise program or sport. Rarely is mention made of the equipment or special clothing you need to participate. Whether a neophyte or veteran of a sport, you'll appreciate the complete line of equipment and clothing displayed at Match Point which will make shopping fun, before the game or exercise begins.

Match Point has been assisting sports and exercise minded people in selecting the appropriate equipment, clothing and accessories for over fifteen years, serving professional and novice alike. All major brands are represented, such as Head, Prince, Izod, Reebok, Tretorn, Timandra and all your other favorites.

It might be said, "It's not whether you win or lose, but how you look when you play the game"; a bit tongue-in-cheek, but the point is that if you are properly outfitted for your activity, even if it's just walking, you'll feel better about doing it, and will enjoy it more. This conveniently located store across from the La Jolla Beach and Tennis Club offers racket stringing, monogramming, free gift wrapping, and a post office substation. All you need to do is name your game.

WINDANSEA BEACHAN'SURF
6830 La Jolla Boulevard
Suite 102
La Jolla, CA 92037
Tel. (619) 454-4433
Hrs: Winter   Mon. - Sat.   10:00 a.m. - 6:00 p.m.
                     Sunday   10:00 a.m. - 5:00 p.m.
      Summer   Mon. - Sun.   9:00 a.m. - 7:00 p.m.
Visa and MasterCard are accepted.

The motto of Windansea Beachan'surf is "Buy the best and shine the rest." Owners Eric Huffman and Ernest Higgins offer only top name surfing and beach accessories.

Windansea features custom surfboards by Rusty, Frye, Caster and others. Their wet suit line includes O'Neill, Rip Curl and Peak. Actionwear is by Quiksilver, Billabong, O'Neill and more. Boogie boards and skate boards are available to rent or buy. Lessons for first timers to surfing sports provided. Eric and Ernest have a combined forty-five years of experience between them and are willing to share their knowledge with beginners and old-timers alike.

Windandsea Beachan'surf believes in providing the best equipment and seasoned advise to help make your surf sport adventure the best ever. Call (619) 454-4433 for the current surf report and ask for "Bird."

(See special invitation in the Appendix.)

WINE SHOP

THE BOTTLE SHOP
7660 Fay Avenue
La Jolla, CA 92037
Tel.   (619) 454-6115
Hrs: Mon. - Sat.   9:00 a.m. - 7:00 p.m.
Visa, MasterCard and AMEX are accepted.

One of the finest reservations wine and fun lovers make in La Jolla is with The Bottle Shop for one of their Friday evening wine tastings. The atmosphere is friendly and casual, the staff is knowledgeable, but never intimidating. Each tasting focuses on a particular group of wines, perhaps a collection of Vintage French Bordeaux, California Chardonnay's, Spanish wines or even a tasting of French Champagnes! Considered the best place to buy wine in La Jolla as The Bottle Shop has been a part of La Jolla since the early '60s.

Because The Bottle Shop tastes every wine before they make a decision to purchase, you can be certain you will enjoy any wine you choose from their exceptional inventory. Partners Jack Thornton and David Reynolds make annual pilgrimages to wine country on both continents to bring back the finest wines available, and promise that they buy no wine until it has passed their own private tasting.

Well-informed staff members will gladly help you coordinate wines for your next event and will also arrange temperature-controlled private wine storage. An informative monthly wine report published by The Bottle Shop offers excellent guidelines for buying fine wines plus delightful reports on The Bottle Shop's endless search for extraordinary values in wine. To recieve The Bottle Shop newletter on a monthly basis simply call The Bottle Shop or better yet, come in person. You'll enjoy your visit and walk out the door with a great bottle of wine. The Bottle Shop also has a terrific selection of beer and spirits. The Bottle Shop offers free delivery in La Jolla and will gladly ship wines anywhere in California.

LA MESA

If you have a good idea of what a midwestern All American city might look like, you have a picture of this community. The city of 54,000 has a "home town" ambiance. In 1987 film director Richard Benjamin brought crews here for the filming of *Little Nikita*, a movie set in the midwest. As a matter of fact, many of the residents have roots in America's heartland. The community enjoys a crime rate so low that it ranks as one of the ten safest cities in the nation.

The city plays host to some 200,000 visitors for its big fall celebration, Octoberfest. This is traditional German festival featuring Bavarian bands, street dancing and Germanic food and games.

La Mesa had its beginnings in the 1800s on this brush covered mesa where sheep were brought to graze near natural springs. For more information about La Mesa, contact City Hall at Tel. (619) 463-6611.

SHOPPING

Enjoy shopping at the **Grossmont Center** in La Mesa. This major regional shopping center has more than 145 shops and services, a post office and four department stores, including The Broadway and Montgomery Ward. Grossmont is open weekdays 10:00 a.m. to 9:00 p.m.; Saturday 10:00 a.m. to 6:00 p.m.; Sunday 12:00 noon to 5:00 p.m. Take Interstate 8 to Jackson Drive. For more information, contact the Grossmont Center, 5500 Grossmont Center Drive, La Mesa, CA 92041. Tel. (619) 465-2900.

LAKESIDE

Lakeside is just east of Santee and is home to some 44,000 residents. This diverse unincorporated area is known for its annual April Western Days, its professional Rodeo and the Labor Day Chili Cook-off. But it's best not to be deceived by reputations. This is also a community of young and professional families who sought out this region of East County as one of the last bastions of affordable housing.

LEMON GROVE

The lemon groves are gone from the region just south of State 94, but Lemon Grove still has not given up its rural ambiance. It is one of the few incorporated cities in the county where a family can keep horses and livestock on their property. Some citrus trees remain along the quiet streets and commercial areas. The community has continued to display its trademark, a giant stucco lemon in the center standing in the middle of town that boasts "the best climate on earth." Lemon Grove City Hall can be reached at Tel. (619) 464-6934.

PACIFIC BEACH

Pacific Beach is a community between Mission Bay and La Jolla. For those who were around ten years ago, they may remember Pacific Beach as a quiet beachfront community. Like many other San Diego area communities, Pacific Beach underwent massive changes in the last ten years as developers began looking for more oceanside properties to improve.

Pacific Beach has a reputation for being a Yuppie community and something of a party town. It is one of the trendiest places in San Diego County. Demand has fueled the growth as ritzy townhouses have sprung up on every available lot. Even established neighborhoods are undergoing a lot of remodeling.

Pacific Beach is not simply residential; it's fashionable night clubs also draw people for the increasingly popular night life. Most of the clubs are clustered around the intersection of Garnet Avenue and Mission Boulevard. You one can get a sampling of rock, jazz, blues and even comedy. For more information about Pacific Beach, contact City Hall at (619) 483-6666.

Sometimes Pacific Beach is called "Little Arizona" because of all the visitors from California's neighbor to the southeast that find their way here. But it's really something of a melting pot of beach-goers. In the winter, the beach is populated mostly by locals. During most times of the year the area near Crystal Pier is usually tourist and young family territory. To the south, the crowd is much younger. Sundown usually sets off a noisy night long party. The sand is considered good here, and many come for spear fishing and surf fishing. Swimmers and surfers are separated from each other and lifeguards are on duty. Dogs are allowed on leashes during the early morning and in the evenings.

POINT LOMA

Point Loma extends into the ocean like a long index finger pointing to the passing ships and whales who make their way to Mexico. The 400 foot tall promontory protects San Diego's harbor from rough seas, and breaks the wind that sweeps across the city.

To the visitor it offers a panoramic view of San Diego Bay, the mountains to the north and south, and the distant Coronado Islands off the coast of Mexico. Standing at the tip of Point Loma is one of the nation's smallest national monuments, but one of the most visited. Cabrillo National Monument surpasses even the Statue of Liberty in the number of visitors it receives each year. A statue of the Portuguese Navigator, Juan Cabrillo faces the bay he discovered for Spain. The statue was a gift from Portugal in 1949.

The visitor center contains exhibits that describe and recount Cabrillo's discovery. A picturesque light house built in 1854 stands at the tip of the point.

The monument also has a nature trail where you can see an extraordinary variety of native plant and marine life. The abundant marine life in the tide pools at the monument make them among the best tide pools remaining in Southern California. And during the winter migration of whales, Point Loma is just about the best place on the coast to watch.

Another portion of Point Loma is an old and prosperous community. The bayside neighborhood of Roseville is mainly populated by Portuguese fishermen. Not far away, a neighborhood called La Playa, or sometimes "The Wooded Area," is populated with residents and ocean view homes. And then there's Sunset Cliffs, right on the ocean.

Point Loma is the final resting place for some 43,000 military personnel buried at the Fort Rosecrans National Cemetery, through which Cabrillo Memorial Drive passes. Some of the graves are more than a century old.

Also on this land mass are military and research installations. Among the most ambitious projects, was a sea water desalination project. Back in the 1960s the Navy pulled out all the stops to find an economical way to convert sea water into fresh water. (At that time, Fidel Castro was threatening to shut the water supply off at the US Naval station in Guantanamo Bay.) Research continues today at the U.S. Naval Electronics Laboratory Center where, men and women work to improve technology relating to communications, navigation and optics.

RAMONA

North of the I-8 corridor, and a little southeast of Escondido, is the geographic center of San Diego County, otherwise known as Ramona. Ramona is a picturesque community set in a valley thirty-eight miles from the central city. Poultry, especially turkeys, was once its biggest business. Residents once claimed the distinction of living among the world's largest concentration of egg laying hens. Now country estates, ranches and real estate developments make Ramona a small modern city.

SANTEE

The newest East County Region city, Santee built up around the commercial strip along Mission Gorge Road. The community of 47,000 has managed to keep much of its rustic feel. Families go trout fishing at the

Santee Lakes, or picnic at nearby Lindo Lake. In the last several years since it was incorporated, the city has developed a prosperous commercial district.

SHELTER ISLAND

Shelter Island, with its palm-lined pathways and Polynesian style buildings may be about as close to the South Seas as one can get and still be in Southern California. Shelter Island is one of two man-made islands in San Diego Bay. Have no fear of being marooned, because each is actually connected to the mainland.

Shelter Island is a boater's paradise, where there are 2,700 boatslips and a wide variety of marina oriented businesses including sailboat dealers, marine mechanics and marine insurance brokers. It's a good place to watch those million dollar yachts pull into their berths, or sea-going ships passing through the bay channel. The elite San Diego, Silvergate and Southwest yacht clubs operate out of Shelter Island.

The island has a free municipal fishing pier on the southeast side. Yokahama Friendship Bell Park on the southwest end of the island offers green grass and beaches. San Diego's sister city, Yokahama, Japan, gave the bell to the people of San Diego as a token of friendship. Several hotels and motels operate on this narrow strip of land. Restaurants offer a variety of cuisine, music and entertainment.

Shelter Island started out as a rock and rubble build up that flowed out of San Diego River. In the 1930s more mud from dredging operations was dumped on the growing land mass. Seeing the opportunity for another water recreation facility, the city built roads, parking areas, a boat launch and landscaped the area in 1950. Businesses began operating in 1952, but it was not until 1966 that the last of the island leases were snatched up.

To reach Shelter Island by land, take the Shelter Island Drive leading of Rosecrans.

EVENT

Beginning in May and continuing throughout the summer is **Humphrey's Concerts By the Bay**. Live Jazz concerts are performed outside at Shelter Island's Humphrey's Night Club. Tel. (619) 299-8518.

NORTH COUNTY

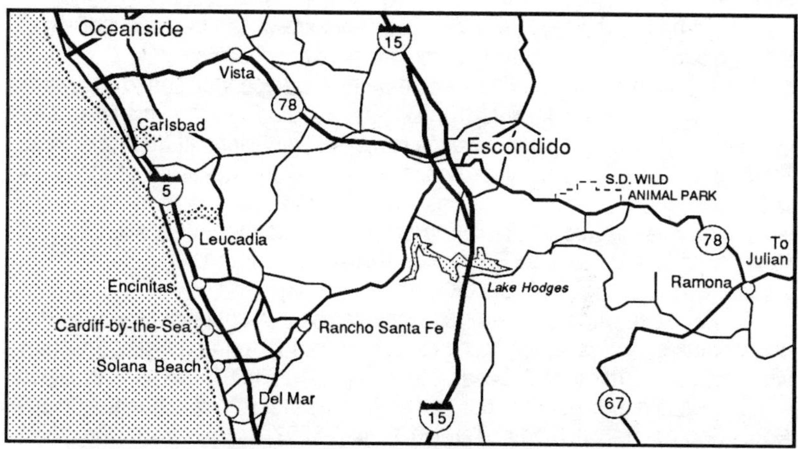

San Diego's coast is where many find the good life, a lifestyle among ocean beaches and white sand. Tourists stroll the streets of beach community commercial districts sporting sunglasses, broad straw hats and t-shirts with the message, "Life's a beach." Overlooking teeming beaches are one and two million dollar homes clinging precariously to cliffs and bluffs. On summer afternoons popular beaches become a patchwork of blankets, towels, and well-oiled bodies.

Along the North Coast, busy cities and tiny beach villages are strung along the shore line from Del Mar, just above La Jolla to Oceanside. A wealth of year round sea and beach related activities are plentiful for the welcome visitors. Shoppers find fine works of art and crafts that range from the practical to the purely decorative. The restaurants offer everything from hot dogs to the very best of international cuisine.

Each community has its own identity, all set along the ocean frontage, estuaries, cliffs and rolling hillsides. Each of them is accessible by way of I-5, which runs about two miles inland. More scenic is Highway SR21, but is usually referred to as "Old Highway 101" by locals who refuse to acknowledge a designation that could have only been dreamed up by a highway engineer.

Like almost any route through San Diego County, the contrasts one sees along "Old Highway 101" can be staggering. North of La Jolla one emerges from an industrial park and a strip of medical research facilities, only to be struck by the shimmering Pacific and maybe a formation of carnival colored hot air balloons drifting through the clear sky. Closer to ground the gnarled trunks of Torrey pines clutch the rocky cliffs, forming a veritable bonsai forest. And below, the wetlands of Los Penasquitos Creek swarm with flocks of shore birds as condominium towers rise out of lush hillsides.

It's no wonder that San Diego residents are willing to pay hundreds of thousands of dollars for housing in this extraordinary setting.

Although the region offers some of the best opportunities to indulge in fine overnight accommodations, the pleasures of camping are also available for those who plan far enough in advance to make reservations at South Carlsbad State Beach and San Elijo State Beach. Both offer campsites on ocean bluffs with stairway access to the beaches. Reservations are available up to eight weeks in advance through Ticketron outlets. For further information contact California State Parks and Recreation Department, San Diego Coast Area, P.O. Box 38, Carlsbad, CA 92008.

For those who would like to explore the coast by some means other than car, Amtrak operates seven trains daily from San Diego and Orange County with stops in Del Mar and Oceanside Tel. (619) 239-9021. The San Diego Transit System will get you out to Del Mar where you can transfer to the North County Transit District Tel. (619) 433-8202, which covers the entire North County. For further information about the region contact the San Diego North Coast Visitors Center, 550 Via de la Valle, Salona Beach, CA 92110. Tel. (619) 237-6770.

ATTRACTIONS

Among the companies that offer balloon excursions are: **Pacific Horizon Balloon Tours,** Tel. (619) 456-2719; **A Beautiful Morning,** Tel. (619) 481-6225; **Curved Air/Elegant Ballooning,** Tel. (619) 457-1544; **Aerostatic Balloon Tours,** Tel. (619) 438-9518; and **Dawn Balloon Flights,** Tel. (619) 244-3511. Keep in mind the balloon can carry no more than four people and most operators require that reservations be made at least two days in advance.

Golfing is another North County pursuit. There's plenty of green to keep even the most avid golfer happy. North Coast has about two dozen golf courses. Among them are the **Oceanside Municipal Golf Course**, an eighteen hole, par seventy-two course at 825 Douglas Drive, Oceanside. Reservations are required. Tel. (619) 433-1360. **Rancho Carlsbad Golf Course**, an eighteen hole, par seventy-one course at 5200 El Camino Real, is another popular North County course, Tel. (619) 438-1772, as is **Lomas Santa Fe Executive Golf Course**, an eighteen hole, par fifty-six, just east of I-5 in Solana Beach. Tel. (619) 755-0195.

The classic blend of Moorish, Spanish and Mexican styles of **Mission San Luis Rey** near Oceanside make it the "most perfect architecturally" of all of the California Missions. Because of its size and importance in the development of the state it has long been called the "King of the Missions." Spanish Franciscan fathers first established the mission here in 1798. It would be one in a chain of twenty-one along the California Coast, each being no more than a day's ride from the next.

Construction of the building began in 1811. Upon completion, the complex of buildings covered six acres. This building is the largest California mission. Sections of the great adobe wall that once encircled the complex remain today. Also on the grounds is a small fruit orchard and gardens, one of which contains California's first pepper tree.

By 1827 the mission was flourishing, servicing an Indian population that numbered 3,000. The mission's land and livestock holdings were extensive. Records showed that at one point the mission owned more than 22,000 head of cattle, 27,000 sheep, 1,120 goats, 280 hogs and 1,500 horses. Today the mission continues to serve as a parish church and retreat. In July the Fathers lead an annual Blessing of the Animals in celebration of the Mission's birthday. The Mission if open Monday through Saturday from 10:00 a.m. to 4:00 p.m. and from noon on Sunday. For information call Tel. (619) 757-3651.

Torrey Pines State Preserve offers trails through twisted trees that exude an air of unbelievability that will make you feel as if you are in an enchanted forest. The 110 acre preserve offers spectacular vistas of the coast line and the sand stone cliffs on which these trees cling. The preserve is just one of two places on earth where this rare tree grows naturally; the other is Santa Rosa Island, 125 miles to the northwest. They were discovered in 1850 by Dr. C.C. Perry, a botanist doing working for the International Boundary Society. He was rather pleased with himself for having found the only conifer with five needles to a bundle. Just for the trivia record, nearly every other conifer has two, three of four needles to a bundle. The Preserve is along Old 101 at Carmel Valley Road, just south of the city of Del Mar.

A restored historic town is one way to peek into the past, but the scientist who looks through the lens of the giant Palomar Observatory looks at objects so far away that the light is a billion years old. Set in the mountains of northeast San Diego County, the **Palomar Observatory** is America's largest optical telescope. The 200 inch mirror weighs a total of sixteen tons. The facility was built in 1920 to provide a clear sky observation point away from the haze and lights of the city. Today astronomers continue to use the instrument, although visibility is not what it once was. In most cases scientists use the telescope to take time-lapse pictures of faint nebulae, star clusters and other objects. For visitors there's a small museum featuring astrophotography and a twenty-five minute video presentation explaining the observatory's operations.

After taking a look at the photographs and exhibits in the visitors' gallery, your appreciation of the heavens may make you want to camp out under the stars at the **Observatory Campground**. A two mile trail leads from the camp to the observatory, affording awesome views of the southern California landscape.

The sixty-six mile drive to the observatory is a scenic tree lined route along State 76 and the windy County S6. The observatory is open 9:00 a.m. to 4:00 p.m. For more information contact Palomar Observatory, Palomar Mountain, CA 92060. Tel. (619) 742-3476.

Just fifteen miles north of downtown San Diego is the **Los Penasquitos Canyon Reserve**, a favorite of local hikers. The hike down into the canyon is an easy five miles. Enroute you'll see a restored adobe dating back to 1868, and if you visit following a recent rain, there will be a waterfall. Take I-15 to Black Mountain Road.

The Antique Steam and Gas Engine Museum, is not your usual museum. It is a great place to putter around and see one of the largest collections of antique steam and gas engines and farm equipment on the coast. You'll find it just North of downtown Vista at 2040 North Santa Fe Drive, open 10:00 a.m. through 4:00 p.m. daily. Tel. (619) 941-1791.

At **Deer Park** you can buy your wine and cheese and picnic on the grounds of this pleasant private park near Escondido. Deer Park includes an antique car museum, gift shop and a wine tasting room featuring wines of Deer Park's Napa County winery. The car museum includes forty restored convertibles, roadsters and touring cars, everything from a 1915 Studebaker Touring Car to muscle cars of the 50s and 60s. From I-15 take the Gopher Canyon Road Exit East to Champagne Boulevard. The park entrance will be at 29013 Champagne Boulevard. The park is open daily. Tel. (619) 749-1666.

Live Oak County Park is one of the major attractions in the heart of this agricultural region. The park has set aside a natural wooded area for hiking and picnicking. You'll find it just West of I-15 on Reche Road.

Dixon Lake, Northeast of Escondido, invites many a visitor to pack a fishing pole, pack a picnic lunch, and load the kids into a mini-van bound for these peaceful waters. A children's playground keeps the restless little ones happy as others enjoy quiet lounging under the trees where the breeze blows off the lake. For information Tel. (719) 741-4680.

San Diego Wild Animal Park, where the elephants never forget, so riding one is an unforgettable experience for both parties. That's just one of the memorable adventures in store for visitors of the San Diego Wild Animal Park in North county's San Pasqual Valley. The San Diego Zoo first established the facility to provide a more peaceful and secluded breeding area for the zoos animals.

The park contains a vast number of exotic animals in natural looking surroundings. It houses the world's most celebrated collection of hoofed animals, which include rhinoceroses, elephants, giraffes, antelopes, as well as forty endangered species, within the 1800 acre sanctuary.

A fifty minute monorail ride takes visitors on a comfortable safari of the simulated habitats. Elsewhere in the park, visitors ride Asian elephants and there's a self-guided walking safari that's nearly two miles long. In the African village animal shows are produced. The park is Southeast of Escondido at 15550 San Pasqual Valley Road, Tel. (619) 234-6541.

BEACHES

Like everything else, beaches come in a variety of shapes, sizes, styles and textures offering an outstanding array of choices. There are crowded beaches that rumble to the sound of music, and beaches where the beat of the surf is surpassed only by an occasional squawk of bickering gulls. There are beaches where you run your dog and beaches where you need have no fear that a ninety-eight pound German shepherd will kick sand in your face. There are beaches that stretch for miles and some that offer a cozy retreat from the expanses. For some, the sand is smooth, but others offer a rocky terrain. What follows is a description of North County beaches, beginning with those closest to Greater San Diego and working up the coast.

Black's Beach might best be described as "unsuitable." Although nudity at this beach, just north of La Jolla, is officially prohibited, the restriction has not been enforced in recent times. During the 1960's and 1970's a tolerant "bathing suit optional" policy was in place. But several years ago the local authorities decided to change that rule. The trouble was, however, the policy did little to legislate behavior that had become well established. Take I-5 to Genesse Avenue and head south at North Torrey Pines Road, then west at Torrey Pines Scenic Drive. You can park at the Torrey Pines Glider Port. Access requires negotiating a steep trail down the bluff.

Adjacent to Black's is the **Torrey Pines State Beach**. Here the sand is smooth and the beach offers spectacular views with the back drop of the pine covered cliffs.   The beach is popular with hikers. Note that prohibitions include dogs, glass containers and fires. From I-5 take the Carmel Valley Road Exit.

Along the 700 block of Del Mar's South Sierra Avenue is **Del Mar Shores**, a small beach popular with local yuppies and offers ideal conditions for snorkeling. Spear fishing is popular, but a license is required. Fire rings and volleyball courts are available and lifeguards patrol the area in the summer.

A popular spot of the young affluent families with small children is **Seascape Shores and Seascape Surf**. Be forewarned, however, these are among the busiest beaches in the county, especially during Del Mar's racing season when free parking places fill up around 10:00 a.m.   The sand is about the best on the coast and lifeguards are on duty during summer. A volleyball game is almost always underway. You can have a beer, but Bowser is not at all welcome. From I-5, take the Lomas Santa Fe Drive and head over to the 500 block of South Sierra Avenue in Del Mar.

For she who would like to sell sea shells by the sea shore there's **Solana Beach**, a delight for beach combers and shell collectors. Water conditions are just right for wading or for less than an expert swimmer who likes to keep a toe or two touching bottom. The breakers are small and the beach offers plenty of soft white sand to sun it. The view is so splendid that couples occasionally hold weddings and receptions at the community center. Fire rings are available for barbecues, other amenities include restrooms and volleyball courts. Take the I-5 exit at Lomas Santa Fe drive and head west until it becomes Plaza Street in the city of Solana Beach.

Joggers, surfers, snorkelers and scuba divers flock to **Tide Park Beach** in the community of Solana Beach. There's also a fair number of people who come here just to walk and take in the breathtaking view of the coastline. The tide pools are teeming with marine life and spear fishing is allowed for those who have a State Fish and Game Department License. Dogs are prohibited, as are glass containers. You can get there from I-5 by taking the Lomas Santa Fe Drive exit to the Coast Highway, then north one mile to the parking lot.

A mix of local teenagers and Beach Boy era surfers is likely to be found at **Cardiff State Beach**. For those in the know, the beach has a reputation for both good surf and sand. It is one of the lesser known beaches to outsiders, and locals would just as soon keep it that way. A drawback is that it has one of the most hazardous rip currents on the coast. Dogs are allowed on leashes and alcohol is allowed in cans. Facilities include restrooms, showers, fire rings and lifeguards. From I-5 take the Birmingham Drive Exit and head south one mile from San Elijo Beach State Park.

The nearby state campground and relative closeness to beach communities makes **San Elijo Beach State Park** the place where out of area visitors mix with locals. Surf fishing is among the more popular pastimes along this one and a half mile stretch of fine sand and surf. Dogs are strictly prohibited, as are fires on the beach and glass containers. Take the Birmingham Drive Exit from I-5 south of Encinitas.

For good karma try **Swami's Beach**, so named because it lies below the bluff that's home to the gold domed Self-Realization Fellowship, a philosophical sect founded by an Indian dedicated fellowship of surfers. A long wooden stairway winds down the sandstone bluffs from Sea Cliff Roadside Park. To get there, take the Encinitas Boulevard exit and head west to First Street, the left through town until you reach the Sea Cliff Roadside Park.

For solitude there is **Boneyards Beach**, located at the north end of Swami's Beach. It's a great place at low tide for cozy alcoves. Lifeguards warn that the surf is unpredictable. Access is through Swami's Beach.

D Street Beach in Encinitas is a popular "hang out" beach for surfers and others. The beach is located 200 yards south of Encinitas Boulevard and is a continuation of nearby Moonlight State Beach.

The once rowdy reputation of **Moonlight Beach** has changed now that rules are enforced by an armed lifeguard. It's now more of a family beach where concession stands offer food, drink and recreational equipment. The sand is plentiful and soft, which is one of the factors that has contributed to its popularity. Picnickers will find tables and fire rings and for active people, there are two volleyball courts. Both alcohol and dogs are prohibited.

Just north of Moonlight State Beach is one stretch of sand and surf seldom seen by tourists, although a few have been fortunate to stumble upon **Stonesteps Beach**. Almost everyone on this beach is local. There's limited parking, but good sand and surf for those who make the effort.

A one mile isolated beach that's skimpy on sand and generous with rocks is **Encinitas County Beach**. The one mile street has limited public access and is used primarily by locals. The surfing is good and lifeguards are on duty during the summer. Take the Leucadia Boulevard Exit from I-5.

Like any hangout, **Leucadia State Beach** has a variety of regulars, many of which know each other by name. It's a varied mix of people from yuppies and affluent teens in designer beach wear, to grandparents and retirees with rolled up chinos. On this two mile length of beach, dogs are allowed on a leash. Facilities are limited; there are no lifeguards or restrooms.

Retirees from the Winnebago set mix with the teenage surfers who congregate on **South Carlsbad State Beach**. It's a beach for surfing and walking, rather than lounging, because sand is in short supply. As one of two state beaches with campgrounds in North County, there's usually a mix of retired travelers as well as well as families here. The surf is gentle enough for good swimming and neophyte surfers and sail boarders. Lifeguards are on duty during the summer. Prohibitions are enforced against dogs, alcohol and glass containers. From the freeway take the Palomar Airport road and drive south on Carlsbad Boulevard.

A volleyball game is always in play and someone is usually tossing a frisbee through the breeze at the active **Carlsbad State Beach** where surfing is popular all year round. The crowd is usually comprised of locals, tourists and families. It is the most cosmopolitan of the North County beaches, the kind of place where one is likely to meet visitors from several different states, and maybe a foreign country or two. To better enjoy our barbecue, fire rings are available to those who arrive early enough to claim one.

For the whitest sand that the North Coast has to offer, head for **Oceanside's Pier Beach.** Lifeguards are on duty during the summer. Dogs are prohibited, as are glass and alcohol. Overlooking the beach is the famous pier on which one can fish, shop or dine. To get there take I-5 to Oceanside's Mission Avenue. Head east to Hill Street, then north one block for a left on Third Street.

Oceanside's Harbor Beach is a favorite with young surfers who ride the breakers next to the north Jetty. The beach has fine white sand with very few rocks and is the widest beach on the North Coast. Lifeguards are on duty and there are prohibitions against dogs, glass and alcohol. Take Harbor Drive in Oceanside.

WINERIES

The Mediterranean climate has made North county a good place for wine production. At this writing the North county region had six wineries, some of which operate tasting rooms and conduct tours. And three of these wineries are near San Marcos.

The oldest of the local wineries is Bernardo, located in the **Bernardo Winery Village Shops**, 13330 Paseo del Verano Norte, just outside of Rancho Bernardo, which make it one of the nearest to San Diego. It's nearly 100 years old and has been in the same family since 1928. Also in the complex is a deli and a picnic area. Wine tasting and self-guided tours are available 9:00 a.m. to 5:00 p.m. daily, Tel. (619) 487-1866.

The San Pasqual Winery, is known for award winning Muscat, Canelli and Sauvignon Blanc. The tasting room is open 11:00 a.m. to 5:00 p.m. daily and tours are conducted weekends at 1:00 p.m. and 3:00 p.m. San Pasqual is just a stones throw from the San Diego Wild Animal Park and can be reached by taking the Via Rancho Parkway exit from I-5, the East to 134 San Pasqual Road.

Founded in 1932 by Gasper Ferra, the **Ferra Winery** at 1120 West 15th Avenue, Escondido, is still run by his son, daughter-in-law and four grown grandchildren. The winery operates a tasting room daily and self conducted tours are available on the weekends.

San Diego County has a unique breed of young, upwardly mobile professional: the professional hot air balloon operator. These FFA licensed pilots comprise a growing number of enterprising individuals who cater to visitors and residents looking for an uplifting experience. Imagine floating 3,000 feet above the coast, suspended from the brightly colored seven story balloon, and watching the sun set into the sea, or rise over the distant mountains. During the three hour flight you can pick out the communities that dot the coast. Passengers have a choice of a sunset flight or sunrise flight. The breeze is also consistent enough to give the balloons the lateral movement they need. First timers who are skittish about heights are often surprised to find how secure they feel riding in the small gondola basket. The fears that set in upon examining the simplest of aircraft on the ground, seem to remain there. The experience of floating is peaceful and serene, but the experience goes beyond that. Passengers usually take an active part in the adventure, everything from assisting in the balloon set up, helping to pack up, to uncorking the champagne in celebration of a first flight.

BONSALL

About halfway between the coast and I-15 past rows of orange trees and stands of eucalyptus is Bonsall. A mere stop on the windy State 76, Bonsall has long been the butt of small town jokes. But this cluster of stores and rural homes is renown for its fresh produce stands and an annual chili cookoff.

CARDIFF-BY-THE-SEA

Cardiff-By-The-Sea is a small beach community in the northern area of San Diego County, between Solana Beach and Encinitas, and is easily accessible by I-5. It is home to the popular Cardiff State Beach where there is a reef break and frequent surfing contests. Excellent seafood restaurants and beautiful architecture are highlights of this town.

RESTAURANT

THE TRITON RESTAURANT
2530 South Highway 101
Cardiff-By-The-Sea, CA 92007
Tel. (619) 436-8877
Hrs: Lunch   Mon. - Fri.   11:30 p.m. - 2:30 p.m.
       Dinner   Mon.- Fri.   5:00 p.m. - 10:00 p.m.
Visa, MasterCard and AMEX are accepted.

If you want new wave, there's plenty of them every minute at The Triton Restaurant. No, we're not talking about orange hair, but the real thing: ocean waves lapping up a few feet from your dining table.

Located right on the Pacific Ocean shoreline, you can enjoy an elegant dinner outside on the terrace, or inside the building, with its distinctive sand castle design. The mood is romantic both inside and out. As you step into the dining room, you will see a sculpted wooden shark mounted over the huge fountain, setting the mood for a memorable seaside dining experience. At your tiletop table are fresh flowers, but you will probably be gazing at the ocean through the beautiful stained glass windows. Before ordering from the menu, ask for the day's specials. The offerings change every day to take advantage of what the sea has just served up fresh. Among the favorites are marinated white sea bass and cioppino for lunch, and the chummer's delight, a dinner combination featuring shrimp, scallops, fish and crab charbroiled on a skewer. If you don't have your sea legs yet, there's still an outrageous prime rib, as well as New York Steak and a Hawaiian chicken.

All dinners include a choice of fresh vegetables, a basket of sourdough and raisin pumpernickel bread, and salad bar or tossed green salad served at your table. With the ambiance, the service and the food at Triton, it's no wonder that this restaurant enjoys a steady tide of happy diners.

SPORT - LACROSSE

SPORTS LACROSSE PLUS
618 Faith Avenue
Cardiff-By-The-Sea, CA 92007
Tel. (619) 436-6111
Hrs: Mon. - Sat.   9:00 a.m. - 6:00 p.m.
Checks are accepted

What is known as the fastest game on two feet, began as warrior training for North American Indians, and was named by the French for its resemblance to the crosier? If you answered Lacrosse, you're right. The game has been gaining popularity in the U.S. since teams were first established in 1868 at Harvard University. In order to meet the demands of growing numbers of local Lacrosse enthusiasts owner Jack Mangelsdorf opened the first store of its kind in the San Diego area, Lacrosse Plus.

Both the dedicated Lacrosse player and the novice will enjoy talking to Jack about this exciting sport. During his ten years in business Jack has introduced Lacrosse to many potential players. His biggest accomplishments to date are the introduction of Lacrosse to San Diego and the coaching of the most successful junior high and high school Lacrosse teams in San Diego County. As well as first hand information from a pro, a trip to Lacrosse Plus will enable you to observe demonstrations and exhibitions. All Lacrosse equipment and accessories are available, as well as T-shirts, shorts and other Lacrosse wear.

Jack has done such a good job spreading the word of Lacrosse he's planning on opening another store in the San Diego area. Much of his success is based on the fact that he offers his enthusiasm for the sport to anyone who will listen. For the novice, stop by and learn more; for the coach, outfit your entire team at any level; for the pro, stop by and swap stories. There's something for everyone at Lacrosse Plus.

(See special invitation in the Appendix.)

CARLSBAD

A touch of color, a touch of history, and plenty of deep blue sea make Carlsbad a popular North Coast beach community and the pride of some 41,000 residents. Drive by in spring and you'll find the fields around Carlsbad ablaze with broad swaths of market ready flowers in hues of red, orange and yellow. Restored buildings give the community an old time accent. Carlsbad has much of the charm of a New England seaside community.

The townspeople have made it a point to retain the history that springs from the discovery of mineral waters which made the community an early resort. The Twin Inn, a huge blue and white towered Victorian structure is one of the most impressive structures along the main drag. There were once two twins, but the identical building across the street was torn down in 1950. The remaining building houses a restaurant today.

A sense of community identity has long been important to the people of Carlsbad. The people were so proud of the mineral waters discovered here that they decided to name their community after the famed European mineral water resort of Karlsbad. When the railroad arrived it shortened the name of the town to Carl, so as not to confuse it with Carlsbad, New Mexico. But the townspeople objected to the point that the railroad felt compelled to give the town back its name.

But when World War broke out, the town found itself with a name that sounded far too Germanic for most people's tastes, thus the town became Carl again. And then with the allied victory, the town again became Carlsbad.

A little inland from town is the elegant La Costa Country Club Hotel and Spa. Several major tennis and professional golf tournaments are staged here, including the PGA's "Tournament of Champions."

More information about Carlsbad is available from the Carlsbad Convention and Visitors Bureau, Old Train Depot on Elm Avenue, Carlsbad, CA 92008. Tel. (619) 729-1786.

ATTRACTIONS

Buena Vista Lagoon, just south of the business district on State 78, is home and sanctuary for more than 200 varieties of birds. Bird watching and feeding the friendly ducks are popular pastimes here.

Agua Hedionda Lagoon, is bisected by I-5 just south of downtown. Bathing, fishing and jet skiing make it a popular spot.

The Old Santa Fe Depot, near Elm and Washington was built in 1887, and served as a Wells Fargo Post Office and General Store. When the railroad arrive, it then became the town's depot. Today the depot houses the Carlsbad Convention and Visitors Bureau.

Magee House and Park, at 258 Beech Street, was the home of Samuel Church Smith, the town's founder. The house serves as a museum and the offices of the Carlsbad Historical Society. Tel. (619) 434-5575.

The Alt Karlsbad Hanse House, 2802-A Carlsbad Boulevard, is built on the site of the original mineral water well and includes a museum and gift shop.

The building follows the steep roofed, plaster and timber architectural style of medieval Germany, but it was built in 1964. It's open Tuesday through Saturday 10:00 a.m. to 5:00 p.m. and Sundays 1:00 p.m. to 4:30 p.m. Tel. (619) 729-6912.

In North County the **Plaza Camino Real Shopping Center,** in Carlsbad, offers 140 shops within an enclosed Spanish-style mall. Department stores include Bullucks, May Co., Broadway and J.C. Penney. Hours are 10:00 a.m. to 9:00 p.m. weekdays, weekends close at 6:00 p.m. Tel. (619) 729-7927.

EVENT

Carlsbad's major PGA golf tournament is the **MONY Tournament of Champions** at the La Costa Club. It's held in the first or second weekend in January. Tel. (619) 236-1212.

ACCOMMODATIONS

CARLSBAD INN
3075 Carlsbad Boulevard
Carlsbad, CA 92008
Tel. (619) 434-7020
Hrs: Open year-round
Visa, MasterCard and AMEX are accepted.

Picturesque old world architecture, a spectacular stretch of the Pacific Coastline, rolling surf and warm sandy beaches, are only a few of the delights at the Carlsbad Inn. This bit of European elegance on the California Coast offers you and your family a self-contained vacation village with enough comforts to pamper you so that you never have to leave the property to have the vacation of a lifetime.

Stroll the lushly landscaped grounds. Browse and shop in the retail shops. Sip your tea under the thatched roof of the gazebo. Play in the pool, surrounded by gay umbrellas at pool side tables. Get in shape by taking advantage of the fully staffed health club at Carlsbad Inn. The central courtyard is often the spectacular setting for afternoon concerts and art festivals. You can dine at award winning Fidel's Norte, or enjoy delightful bakery treats at Norby's, a Danish bakery. Of course, there's a beauty salon., All of this, and more, next to miles of beautiful beaches.

To get away from it all, come to picturesque Carlsbad Inn, with its wooded sloped roofs and carved lattice work draped with fragrant foliage. You'll enter another time, another world. You'll want to stay.

ANTIQUE SHOP

PAST TIMES ANTIQUE MALL
2922 State Street
Carlsbad, CA 92008
Tel. (619) 729-6443
Hrs: Mon. - Fri.   10:00 a.m. - 5:00 p.m.
     Saturday   10:00 a.m. - 5:00 p.m.
     Sunday   12:00 noon - 4:00 p.m.
Visa and MasterCard are accepted.

Proprietor Barbara McDaniel is a fifth generation Californian who has been collecting and studying antiques for years. She loves to share her treasures and her knowledge with customers. In fact, Barbara is one of the treasures of Past Times Antiques. If you can't find what you are seeking there, Barbara will hunt for it and ship it to you later.

Past Times Antiques is a spacious, airy shop with merchandise displyed attractively. You'll find quality antiques, furniture, glassware, jewelry, tools, kitchenware, art, nautical items, records, linens and lace and much more.

Past Times Antiques is located across from H. Gladstone Stores in the heart of old Carlsbad.

APPAREL

H. GLADSTONE FOR MEN AND WOMEN
2945 State Street
Carlsbad, CA 92008
Tel. (619) 434-4332
Hrs: Mon. - Fri.   10:00 a.m. - 5:30 p.m.
     Saturday   10:00 a.m. - 5:00 p.m.
Visa, MasterCard and AMEX are accepted.
Also,
121 North Freeman Street
Oceanside, CA 92054
Tel. (619) 722-1453

For the elegance and sophistication of upscale traditional clothing, you need look no further than H. Gladstone--the ultimate in prestige!

In 1950, Howard Gladstone began this company in Oceanside. In the early seventies, he expanded his efforts to the coastal community of Laguna Niguel. In 1985, his sons, Paul and Matthew, carried on the tradition of his success with another beautiful store nestled in the village of Carlsbad. Grown from the roots of traditional, professional wardrobing, H. Gladstone for Men and Women offers today's executive the unique opportunity to shop in an atmosphere with people in "the know."

H. Gladstone is known far and wide for providing the clientele with the finest quality, upscale merchandise available. Couple this with extensive, relaxed service--have a cup of coffee or a snack--and the result is this fun place to shop.

The front of the store is a pleasant, sea-foam green with matching awnings and large windows highlighting creative display work and beautiful antiques. The interior invites you to a warm, friendly ambiance which combines solid oak fixtures with accents of antique furniture. The array of menswear includes suits, jackets, shirts, ties, shoes, slacks, sweaters and a variety of special gifts. Women can choose from dresses, skirts, blouses, suits, purses, scarves and other great accessory ideas.

You will recognize the popular names found at H. Gladstone: Norman Hilton Clothes, Polo by Ralph Lauren, Cole-Haan, Ruff-Hewn, Robert Talbott ties, Barry Bricken and many others. Join those who travel from Los Angeles, Phoenix, San Francisco and New York to find the ultimate in style and quality here at H. Gladstone.

SHARON WILSON SHOES AND CLOTHING
2810 Roosevelt Street
Carlsbad, CA 92008
Tel. (619) 729-4517
Hrs: Mon. - Fri.   9:00 a.m. - 5:30 p.m.
        Saturday   9:00 a.m. - 5:00 p.m.
Visa, MasterCard and AMEX are accepted.

From furniture to fashion seems like a long step, but owner Sharon Wilson has done it beautifully. After thirteen years in the furniture business with her husband, they opened a Papagallo shoe store in the strip mall in Carlsbad, and shortly afterward expanded it by adding fashion clothing and accessories, making it a complete and stylish boutique. That was over ten years ago, and the size of her satisfied regular clientele attests to Sharon's skill and taste.

Sharon, and her assistant, Sharon Wilte, emphasize buying according to the tastes and desires of their regular customers. Designers such as Adrienne Vittadini and Mondi are well represented, and you'll also find clothing created especially for the store by Southern California designers who know the styles of the area. Clothing runs from sportswear to special occasion designs, and all the accessories to go with them are available, as well as a complete line of shoes.

Sharon observes, they offer customers a complete head to toe look, and that includes a good selection of fashion jewelry. The attractive store itself, makes a fashion statement. Once you've stepped into the light and airy interior, you'll know you've found a place to fill all your needs in clothing, shoes and accessories.

(See special invitation in the Appendix.)

BED AND BREAKFAST INN

PELICAN COVE BED AND BREAKFAST INN
320 Walnut Avenue
Carlsbad, CA 92008
Tel. (619) 434-5995
Visa and MasterCard are accepted.

Pelican Cove is a very special Bed and Breakfast Inn. Set in a glorious location with endless beaches only a few hundred yards from its doorstep, Pelican Cove offers delightful amenities and a chance to relax in the charming village of Carlsbad. The Inn is an easy stroll from the fine restaurants and pleasant shops of Carlsbad. It's a vacationer's delight. It has no car-filled streets nor crowds of people.

Accommodations at the Inn feature individual baths, private entries and fireplaces, optional Scandia feather-beds and down-comforters, televisions, and a charming blend of antique and contemporary furnishings. Gardens of flowers and trees surround the Inn. Continental breakfasts are excellent. You may enjoy breakfast at the inside nook or take a tray to your room, the garden patio or sun porch. Added amenities include beach chairs and towels for relaxing on the sand. Picnic baskets can be arranged too. Courtesy pickup from Amtrak in Oceanside is available.

Pelican Cove is located near San Diego with all its vacation attractions. The Inn combines the best of both worlds: Quiet seclusion in the village of Carlsbad within a short distance to exciting San Diego.

COLLECTIBLES

COPPOLA'S
630 Grand Avenue
P. O. Box 1309
Carlsbad, CA 92008
Tel. (619) 729-0256
Hrs: Mon. - Sat.   10:00 a.m. - 6:00 p.m.
        Sunday   11:00 a.m. - 4:00 p.m.
Visa, MasterCard, AMEX and Diners Club are accepted.

In a world where mass production seems the norm, it's nice to find a store where "one of a kind" still rings true.

Coppola's is a garden of delight for the discriminating shopper. Specializing in collectible and limited edition plates from Europe and Scandinavia, Coppola's also has a very large selection of music boxes from around the world.

But that's not all. The store is packed with a dizzying array of quality items. Things that are destined to become family heirlooms. Lithographs, Hummels, Chilmark pewter, Wee Forest Folk, Rockwell plates, Belleek china and Duncan Royale Santas and Clowns are but as tiny fraction of what is available there. Coppola's is located in the charming Old World Center, and began as a family business. A sign near the entrance says, "Please touch." And they mean it. As manager Louise Dosdourian says, "We don't have anything locked up here. The music boxes, the stuffed animals, these are things that should be touched to be fully appreciated."

The mail order catalog department makes it possible for everyone to experience shopping at Coppola's. So go ahead. Enjoy!

INTERIOR DESIGN

COUNTRY ROOMS
585 Grand Avenue
Carlsbad, CA 92008
Tel. (619) 434-9598
Hrs: Mon. - Sat.   10:00 a.m. - 5:30 p.m.
        Sunday   11:00 a.m. - 3:00 p.m.
Visa and MasterCard are accepted.

If you love country decor, Country Rooms is the find of your trip. Owner Carol Anne Bailie specializes in country interior items such as wreaths, quilts, braidied rugs, hand dipped candles, quaint dolls, placemats and more. The aroma of teas and sachet fills the air here. Merchandise is color coordinated and one has the feeling of being in a country home.

Carol Ann is always glad to assist a customer in creating a special look for his/her own home and provides lay away, gift certificates and shipping. For a "Best Choice" in quality country interior items, visit Country Rooms in the center of Carlsbad Village.

(See special invitation in the Appendix.)

RENTAL MANAGEMENT

BARBARA MCLAIN PROPERTIES
2715 Carlsbad Boulevard
Carlsbad, CA 92008
Tel. (619) 434-6161
Hrs: Mon. - Sun.   9:00 a.m. - 5:00 p.m.
24 hour answering service.

Imagine listening to waves gently caressing a sandy shore line, or envision the most gorgeous sunset kissing the horizon, its pink and orange tendrils of fire reaching out towards you as you begin to relax and unwind from your hectic day. All of this just inches away from your doorstep.   If you thought this could never be possible from your own living room, you haven't tried Barbara McLain Properties.

Barbara McLain has had eighteen years experience in real estate sales and property management. Originally from Connecticut, where she excelled as a real estate broker, she has spent the last fifteen years specializing in beach front property for vacationers and those looking to make their dream home come true. If you have ever wanted to rent a house by the beach for the summer, but just couldn't make the right connections, Barbara McLain Properties can locate those contacts for you. Barbara McLain's expertise in beach front properties is invaluable when it comes to listing properties for sale. Marketing her listings nationally and internationally allows for a broader base of exposure to prospective clientele.

In addition to the extensive management of beach front property, Barbara McLain Properties also lease and fully manage single condominiums, apartment complexes, condominium associations and industrial and commercial enterprises. Whether you are wishing to rent a perfect vacation home or wish to make your dream house come true, Barbara McLain Properties is your "Professional with the Personal Touch."

RESTAURANTS

DOOLEY McCLUSKEY'S
Old World Center off Elm Street
P.O. Box 1575
Carlsbad, Ca 92008
Tel. (619) 434-3114
Hrs: Lunch   11:30 a.m. - 11:30 p.m.
         Dinner   5:30 p.m. - 10:00 p.m.
Visa and MasterCard are accepted.

Dooley's has dedicated itself to restoring the old time ale house atmosphere of fun and good times, and from the look of things, is succeeding very well.

If you're looking for peace and quiet and a bite to eat, better not choose Dooley's. But if you want to bring the whole family out for a rousing good time, excellent saloon snacks, lunches and dinners, and a bit of authentic English brew, then head on down. At Dooley's grandparents and toddlers mingle happily with the rest of the crowd and a good time is had by all.

No one goes away hungry. Try the legendary iced shrimp bowl with Dooley's own Ale House Beer Muffins, or the Pasta Portofino, with shrimp, scallops, and crab in a Marinara cream sauce, or the best Prime Rib around, complete with a second slice on request! Nobody goes away hungry.

And don't forget the Dooley McCluskey's Pro-Am Golf Tournament, held each year to benefit Carlsbad parks and Recreation Youth Organizations. A better bash has never been thrown anywhere. Dooley McCluskey's! Dedicated to fun times for all.

NEIMAN'S
2978 Carlsbad Boulevard
Carlsbad, CA 92008
Tel. (619) 729-4131
Hrs: Lunch   11:30 a.m. - 11:30 p.m.
         Dinner   5:30 p.m. - 10:00 a.m.
Visa and MasterCard are accepted.

Housed in the recently renovated, historic Twin Inns, Neiman's has carved a niche for itself as the place where anyone can feel at home. Upwardly mobile types mix with senior citizens and boisterous toddlers on the expansive veranda and by the massive mirrored bar.

Comfort and style are the bywords here. And, of course, fine food and spirits. The newly remodeled kitchen features both a mesquite broiler and an oakwood smoker. Heady aromas waft through the cavernous dining room and set taste buds a hoppin'! The menu is a blend of contemporary favorites and old standbys and leans toward Cajun and Southwestern cuisines. Highly recommended are the Baby Back Ribs and Cajun Chicken Pasta. Oakwood Smoked Chicken comes with avocado, feta cheese, mixed greens and Cilantro Sesame Seed Dressing.

Neiman's regularly features an impressive selection of seasonal fresh seafood, including shark, snapper, ono, sole catfish, salmon, mahi-mahi, scallops, trout, halibut and yellowtail among others.

The bar at Neiman's is as well stocked as any you'll find. Thirty feet in length, it elegantly displays hundreds of spirits. And the beers! It's possible to circumnavigate the globe in a few hours by sampling only a few of the fifty-six imported and domestic varieties on hand. Also available are twenty-four kinds of mineral waters from around the world.

Be sure to bring the kids when you come. Everyone is welcome at Neiman's!

PEA SOUP ANDERSEN'S
850 Palomar Airport Road
Carlsbad, CA 92008
Tel.   (619) 438-7800
Visa, MasterCard and AMEX are accepted.

Since 1924, Andersen's the home of Split Pea soup has been a famous landmark, noted for excellence in dining. Now Pea Soup Andersen's at Carlsbad, California is continuing this fine tradition and is located directly off I-5 just outside the city of San Diego. The Chef, Ulrich Rieder, is famous for creating dinners around a featured winery, and their wines, once a month with his Winemaker Dinners. These are exquisite five to seven course meals served with the appropriate wines from a different winery every month.

The restaurant has the decor and ambiance of a European cottage with gift stores, large bakeries and gourmet items located just off the lobby. And besides the famous soup, every items served is fresh and of top quality. For breakfast try the delicious sugar cured ham or bacon, eggs, and buttermilk biscuits.

The dinner specialty of the house is pot roast, smooth, tender and seasoned just right. Danish pastries are rich and varied, a never to be forgotten treat to put the finish to a superb meal. Be sure when visiting

Carlsbad, that you have breakfast, lunch or dinner at an historic landmark, Pea Soup Andersen's. You'll want to return again and again!

DEL MAR

Del Mar is known for its famed horse races, near perfect beaches and unique shops. It's a community of 5,000 people living twenty miles north of San Diego on a coastal terrace.

Anyone stopping here will find it a community of galleries, boutiques, shopping areas, condominiums and a world famous horse race track. A half mile of small shops and offices line the old highway.   Two lane roads wind into the lush hillsides to the west and east.

Between July and mid-September the quiet village draws the rich and famous to the annual Del Mar Fair Grounds for the annual horse racing season. This was once the home of Bing Crosby, Oliver Hardy, Gary Cooper and Rudolf Valentino. It was Bing himself who was most responsible for Del Mar becoming the place where "Turf meets Surf." After a major flood in 1938 Crosby and others bankrolled development of the Del Mar Thoroughbred Club and the race track.   Today's residents are a mixture of affluent retirees, successful business people, academics from the University of California at San Diego faculty, and even some students. Martin Milner and Burt Bacharach also live here.

The railroad runs right along the coastal bluffs. The station is busy each morning taking commuters to Los Angeles and San Diego. Prior to 1900 the railroad line ran about a block inland from the coastal bluff. Because of steep terrain, the line was re-routed to the bluff. Over the years the eroding bluff suddenly deposited several trains on the beach below. Fortunately, the last such occurrence was January 1, 1941.

A Tudor style building at the north end of Old Highway 101 houses Stratford Square, which features specialty shops and a museum that pays tribute to Del Mar's golden age as a community of Hollywood celebrities. Also among the community's shopping areas is the Flower Hill Mall, located at Via De La Valle and I-5. It's set among lush landscaping and flower laden walks and is filled with one of a kind shops.

Across from the mall are specialty shops, a four screen theater and a restaurant that features live music. For additional information on the community contact the Greater Del Mar Chamber of Commerce at (619) 755-4844.

ATTRACTION

Flower Hill Shopping Center of Del Mar is another popular north coast shopping area. It's located at 2626 Via de la Valle and is open 10:00 a.m. to 6:00 p.m. Monday through Saturday, 12:000 noon to 5:00 p.m. Sunday. Tel. (619) 481-7131.

EVENTS

Many folks like to hop on over to the **Jumping Frog Jamboree** in Del Mar in late April. Events include jumping contests as well as frog beauty contests. Frogs are available for rent. Tel. (619) 755-4844.

Beginning in Late April, **The National Horse Show** is held at the Del Mar Fairgrounds. Tel. (619) 755-1161.

The Del Mar Jazz Festival offers a wide variety of jazz during mid-May. Tel. (619) 297-8480.

The Del Mar Fair, held in late June and early July is San Diego's county fair and features outdoor flower and garden shows, art in all media, gem and mineral displays, home arts, livestock shows and carnival rides. Tel. (619) 259-1355.

The Del Mar Thoroughbred Club Racing Season begins in late July and continues through the middle of September. Nine races are held daily, except Tuesday at the Del Mar Fairgrounds. Tel. (619) 296-4777.

APPAREL

CHARLIE'S PLACE
2670 Via del la Valle, Suite A210
Del Mar, CA 92014
Tel. (619) 481-5891
Hrs: Mon. - Sat   10:00 a.m. - 6:00 p.m.
            Sunday   12:00 noon - 5:00 p.m.
Visa, MasterCard and AMEX are accepted.

If quality clothing is an investment in yourself, then a store called Charlie's Place has become a bull market in women's fashion. Charlie's specializes in traditional, timeless clothes, a classic look, but never dull.

Owner Marlyn Nickoff considers her clothes more like an investment than a commodity. Quality and thoughtfully selected clothes should have a place in your wardrobe for many years, and not be so trendy that the initial novelty soon becomes well-worn. Since Marlyn first went into business nearly ten years ago, a very loyal following has grown to depend on her selections. Her clientele are women who know what they want and don't need the label of a famous designer to feel confident that they have made a good choice. The shop has a comfortable ambiance with its antique armoires, oak furniture, brass clothes hangers and potted plants.

Marlyn loves the shop and the feeling that she is being of service to her customers. She and her staff are pleased to help out with wardrobe consultation, and will do special alterations and shippings. For selection and classic fashion, this is one investment market where customers can buy long, but never want to sell short.

GUDI'S
2690 Via De La Valle
Suite D110
Del Mar, CA 92104
Tel. (619) 755- 5337
Hrs: Mon. - Sat.   10:00 a.m. - 6:00 p.m.
            Sunday   12:00 noon - 5:00 p.m.
Visa, MasterCard and AMEX are accepted.

Owner, Gudi Lauffenburger travels to Europe each year to select much of the gorgeous foundations and designer lingerie sold in her shop. Out of town clients make annual buying visits to take advantage of the shimmering, sensual and elegant items to be found at Gudi's. Design, fit and qualtiy are priorities here.

Aside from Gudi's female customers, men love shopping for gifts, as Gudi's friendly staff knows just how to put the male shopper at ease and to assist with his purchases.

Whether you are looking for something in a simple cotton design, an exquisite silk or lace ensemble, it's sure to be at Gudi's. Choose from well-fitting bras, panties and bodysuits sizes 32-36 A through DD, as well as the highest quality teddies, chemises, pajamas, robes, and specialty hosiery.

Located on the lower level of Flower Hill Mall, #D-110, Gudi's is a small shop that should not be missed when you are in Del Mar.

BOOK STORE

THE BOOK WORKS
2670 Via de La Valle
Del Mar, CA 92014
Tel. (619) 755-3735
Hrs: Mon. - Thu.   10:00 a.m. - 9:00 p.m.
        Friday   10:00 a.m. - 11:00 p.m.
        Saturday   10:00 a.m. - 10:00 p.m.
        Sunday   10:00 a.m. - 6:00 p.m.
Visa and MasterCard are accepted.

One of the most beautiful and unique bookstores in Southern California is The Book Works located in the Flower Hill Mall in Del Mar. This is not a typical shopping mall book store. Here you will find rare collections of books not easily found elsewhere. There are many old books, that Milane Christiansen, the owner, buys from England. There are wonderful travel books, quality fiction, books in French and Spanish, art cards and special humor cards, and so much more. Art, photography, literature and children's literature are featured.

The store is artistically decorated with antique Persian carpets, fresh flowers, wood plank floors, plants and paintings. She also has displayed her personal collection of "Carousel" horses and other folk art. Milane always had a dream of doing something she loved and enjoyed. After many successful years in the corporate business world she decided to fulfill her dream.

This book store has become a center for attracting famous authors and musicians, a community gathering place for jazz, prose readings, book signing and classes. Milane's Book Works has won "Best Book Store Window in America" award and has had her way paid to the India book fair. The welcome mat is always out to come in and browse at The Book Store in Del Mar.

CANDY SHOP

A CHOCOLATIER
Flower Hill Mall
2710 Via de la Valle
Del Mar, CA 92014
Tel.   (619) 755-1600
Hrs: Mon. - Sat.   10:00 a.m. - 6:00 p.m.
             Sunday   12:00 noon - 5:00 p.m.
Visa, MasterCard and AMEX are accepted.

When it comes to chocolate, A Chocolatier is sure to make you snicker, or at least raise a smile, when you see something like a chocolate-dipped pretzel. This new twist on an old flavor is just one item in a store that has mounds of unusual and imaginative chocolate confections.

At A Chocolatier you can have your chocolate by the single bite, by the box or molded into almost any shape. There are chocolate cigars and baby booties for the new parents on the block, tennis balls and golf balls for the athlete who likes to have his sport and eat it too, and chocolate musical instruments for the musician with a sweet tooth. For that person on the go, there are cars, boats and ships. Chocolate becomes the medium for a message when a customer orders a chocolate message bar. Likewise, a chocolate plaque will commemorate just about any worthy endeavor. The shop also offers imaginative gift containers, as well as a vast array of non-chocolate confections.   The staff will custom-make almost anything to order for individuals or organizations. For example, businesses have had their logos done in chocolate for special events.

Owner Hildy Mignone has noticed that the shop is such fun that some people come in as often as two to three times a week just to see what is new. Their eyes light up with the thrill of seeing their favorite flavor shaped into the unexpected. So kiss ordinary chocolate goodbye and sink your teeth into something different from A Chocolatier.

HOT AIR BALLOON RIDES

A BEAUTIFUL MORNING BALLOON COMPANY
1342 Camino Del Mar
Del Mar, CA 92014
Tel. (619) 481-6225
Hrs: Mon. - Sun.   9:00 a.m. - 5:00 p.m.
Visa, MasterCard and AMEX are accepted.

Balloon rides, where romance, fantasy and fairy tales are the stock in trade. From the moment you climb in the basket of the giant rainbow colored hot air balloon you'll know you are living one of your greatest fantasies.

These romantic excursions take place twice daily and last approximately one hour. Early risers and breakfast lovers will want to experience the morning flight departing one hour after sunrise and culminating with a champagne brunch. Equally romantic and satisfying is the evening flight which leaves approximately one hour before sunset. Champagne and scrumptious hors d'oeuvres are waiting as the balloon lands. Everyone goes home with a Polaroid snapshot as a souvenir, a flight certificate and a cloisonne balloon pin.

A Beautiful Morning Balloon Company is one of the largest and most experienced balloon companies in the world. Advance reservations and a deposit are required. Bring a warm coat and don't forget your camera. Because you'll never want to forget the day you flew with the clouds.

A SKYSURFER BALLOON CO.
14072 Rue d'Azur
Del Mar, CA 92014
Tel. (619) 481-6800
Hrs: 8:00 a.m. - 8:00 p.m.
Visa, MasterCard and AMEX are accepted.

The quiet is intense, the feeling of peace is absolute, and you are completely at one with nature as you float with the breeze in a colorful hot air balloon--first cruising close to the ground through the twisting canyons of inland Del Mar, then soaring   with the air currents up and out over the gorgeous coastline. What better way to celebrate the "awakening of mother earth" at sunrise or glory in the vivid radiance of the sun setting over the pounding Pacific surf? Owners Conni and Tiemo von Zweck have hosted kids from five to ninety-three on their exotic forty-five minute to one hour flights.

The balloons carry either four or six passengers, in addition to a fully qualified FAA certified commercial pilot. Ground crews stay in constant radio contact as you fly and meet your balloon on return to make sure your landing is gentle. Then they'll whisk you back to Del Mar, where you will rejoin other passengers for champagne and hors d'oeuvres and receive a first ascension certificate, as well as a lovely cloisonne balloon pin and photograph of your flight.

Air temperature in this temperate climate is similar to ground temperature here, so you'll be comfortable in ordinary sport clothes with a light sweater or jacket. Don't forget to bring still or video cameras; the photo opportunities are extraordinary. Make your reservations early for this refreshing adventure in the sky, and be sure to inquire about the incredibly beautiful spring wildflower flights.

(See special invitation in the Appendix.)

LINEN STORE

COUNTRY DOWNS
1302 Camino Del Mar
Del Mar, CA 92014
Tel. (619) 481-1356
Hrs: Mon. - Sat.   10:00 a.m. - 6:00 p.m.
           Sunday   11:00 a.m. - 5:00 p.m.
Visa, MasterCard and AMEX are accepted.

On the outside, it looks like a country English cottage. On the inside, it's a continuation of that countryside charm, the perfect place to display the fine linens, hand crafted furniture and plush bedroom accessories.

Country Downs specializes in fine linens and a unique line of lodge pole furniture recently featured in *Architectural Digest.* Much of the linen is by paper white, which is known for fine handmade lace and the highest quality linen. You'll find stuffed animals, gift baskets, specialty teas, jams and soaps. There is a line of children's furnishings that includes a wicker tea table and chairs. Also special is the natural pine furniture by John Clark, who made a few pieces for actor Robert Redford. Clark's furniture is made from burner or dead trees from the Rockies, never from trees that were cut while still alive. Country Downs is also the exclusive exhibitor of paintings by English country artist Rhonda Cobb.

Shopping here creates a mood, an experience in comfort. Visitors love this shop with its soft scents of pine wreaths, potpourri and candles filtering through the fresh ocean breeze that wafts through the windows. Bringing something home from County Downs promises pleasure and down home comfort.

RESTAURANTS

CAFE DEL MAR
1247 Camino Del Mar
Del Mar, CA 92014
Tel. (619) 481-1133
Hrs: Breakfast   Mon. - Fri.   8:00 a.m. - 11:00 a.m.
                    Saturday   8:00 a.m. - 11:30 a.m.
      Brunch   Sunday   9:00 a.m. - 2:30 p.m.
      Lunch   Mon. - Sat.   11:30 a.m. - 2:30 p.m.
      Dinner   Sun. - Thu.   5:00 p.m. - 9:30 p.m.
                    Fri. - Sat.   5:00 p.m. - 10:00 p.m.
Visa, MasterCard and AMEX are accepted.

In Del Mar, the locals choice for fine food and great atmosphere is the Cafe Del Mar. Located on Camino Del Mar in the heart of Del Mar, it's *the* place to go for breakfast, lunch and dinner.

As Del Mar's premier sidewalk cafe, the Cafe Del Mar is always busy, pleasantly romantic, and delightfully casual. The Cafe Del Mar offers the best of California cuisine, including pastas, veal, fresh fish, salads and sandwiches. The produce comes from Chino's Ranch and the owner's boat catches the swordfish! Breakfasts are special here with fresh squeezed orange juice, homebaked pastries and omelettes like the Garden Spanish Omelette with avocado, cilantro, jalapeno, tomato, green onions, and topped with sour cream. Or the Spinach Omelette with fresh spinach, sauteed onions, bacon, cheddar and parmesan cheese , topped with sour cream. At lunch time Cafe Del Mar excels with stupendous salads. Try the Prawn Salad tossed with spicy Lemon Vinaigrette, or the Shredded Chicken Salad with Shell Pasta. Classics like Caesar and Spinach salads are always as popular. Dinners at Cafe Del Mar are worth getting excited about. Appetizers like Ravioli with Salmon Mousse in Light Dill Sauce, Baked Brie, and an inventive assortment of pizzas with topping combinations like Pesto, Shrimp and Pine Nuts, or Tomatillos and Three Cheeses, or Marinara, Mozzarella, Fresh Basil and Shiitake Mushrooms. Equally unique are salads like Hearts of Palm with Chino's Ranch Lettuce, and Fresh Sea Scallops Salad with Chinese Vinaigrette.

A selection of fresh seafood pastas and grilled seafood entrees with such trimmings as Raspberry Vinaigrette and Mint Butter Sauce make dining at Cafe Del Mar a special experience. Take a drive along the Pacific Coast

Highway and make the Cafe Del Mar your stopping off point. It may well be the highlight of your day!

JAKE'S, 1660 Coast Boulevard, Del Mar, CA 92014. Tel. 755-2002. Enjoy the best fresh seafood and succulent steak while dining beside the sandy beaches of California.

ENCINITAS

Encinitas is truly a mix of the old and new. First settled by a group of German families from Chicago in 1854, the community is surrounded by new, planned, residential communities. It was not until 1986 that the community was incorporated. Although much is new, the community retains a quaint flavor along Highway 101. The community is favored for its relatively uncrowded beaches, scenic bicycle routes and antique shops. A common sight are sail planes gliding through the thermals above the community.

Surrounding the community are still some flower farms and green houses, once so numerous that many believed the region produced more flowers and bulbs than Holland. But all is not lost. A good share of the flowers that grace the Rose Bowl floats are produced here, and local grower Paul Eycke still is the world's largest producer of poinsettias.

A point of interest is the golden domed temple of the Self Realization Fellowship, a religious order founded by an Indian yogi in 1920 that's currently enjoying a popularity among today's affluent and educated New Age followers. The beautifully maintained gardens within the retreat are open to the public. The original temple was constructed thirty feet back from the cliffs, but storms in 1941 caused the bluff to fall, taking the original temple along with it, down to to beach.

To the south is the community of Cardiff-By-The-Sea, which consists of a cluster of homes, a shopping center, excellent restaurants and nightly entertainment. Many talented people in the community are artists and renowned crafts people.

ATTRACTIONS

A combination of bluff and canyon terrain at **Quail Botanical Gardens** creates a variety of micro climates on thirty-one acres allowing one of the largest variety of plants of any botanical garden in the world. Walk through trails where you will find desert cacti, exotic flowers and stands of eucalyptus. There's also a bird sanctuary. The quail and a few other feathery friends love to be fed. Follow the signs from the I-5 exit at Encinitas. Open daily 8:00 a.m. to 8:00 p.m. Tel. (619) 565-3600.

On the north coast is **The Lumberyard,** a specialty shopping center known for its rustic architecture and thirty-four shops and restaurants. The Lumberyard is open weekdays 10:00 a.m. to 9:00 p.m.; Saturday 10:00 a.m. to 6:00 p.m.; Sunday 11:00 a.m. to 6:00 p.m. You'll find the shopping center right along Old 101 in Encinitas. For more information, contact the Lumberyard Shopping Center, 937 First Street, No. 210, Encinitas, CA 92024. Tel. (619) 943-8629.

APPAREL

BONNIE'S
127J North El Camino Real
Encinitas, CA 92024
Tel. (619) 436-5321
Hrs:　Mon. - Fri.　　10:00 a.m. - 6:00 p.m.
　　　Saturday　　　10:00 a.m. - 5:00 p.m.
　　　Sunday　　　　12:00 noon - 5:00 p.m.
Visa, MasterCard and AMEX are accepted.

Most department stores devote only a tiny proportion of their space to the needs of the larger women. Bonnie Scoffin wanted to give these women the opportunity to wear the same gorgeous fashions usually available only in smaller sizes. That's how Bonnie's came about.

Bonnie's is a store full of chic, top quality fashions exclusively for larger women. Instead of one or two choices in sizes 14W to 24W, you'll find an excellent selection of all types of apparel. Bonnie's carries quality name brands such as Pendleton, Albert Nipon, Cali, French Vanilla, Bonnie Boerer, Beverly Hills Polo Club and Argenti. Choose from a wide selection of career apparel, week end wear and special occasion dressing. There are many garments made of natural and blended-fiber fabrics, as well as fine quality man-made fabrics.

Bonnie takes pleasure in helping her customers put together contemporary and flattering ensembles from the many excellent designs she has on hand. Her reward is seeing her well-dressed clientele all over town. Located in a large open air neighborhood shopping center with plenty of free parking, Bonnie's has a long list of satisfied customers who return again and again. Prices that reflect the value of the merchandise, make a visit to Bonnie's worthwhile. Why don't you become one of Bonnie's happy and satisfied customers?

C'EST SOULE´
The Lumberyard Center
897 First Street #103
Encinitas, CA 92024
Tel. (619) 436-8118
Hrs: Mon. - Sat.   10:00 a.m. - 6:00 p.m.
           Sunday   11:00 a.m. - 5:00 p.m.
Visa, MasterCard and AMEX are accepted.

Want a lift? Try bubble clothing. If you haven't heard about this one, imagine a jacket made of plastic packing bubble wrap, accented with various bobbles and bangles.

It all started at C'est Soule´, where owner Nancy Soule´ continues to offer unusual creations, as well as other lines of "regular" clothing. All of the clothing has something unique to offer, as do the shoes, hats and jewelry, much of it made and designed by local artists. Imagine the look of a hand painted silk dress, or the sensibility of hosiery that won't run.

Although Nancy has appeared on several network television shows, she continues to give personal service to her customers, helping them maximize their fashion potential, so that each person can achieve a positive image. Experience shopping that's full of fun and style and suited to your particular needs.

(See special invitation in the Appendix.)

KIRSTELLE
937 First Street, #109
Encinitas, CA 92024
Tel. (619) 753-0100
Hrs: Mon. - Sat.   10:00 a.m. - 6:00 p.m.
           Sunday   12:00 noon - 6:00 p.m.
Visa, MasterCard and AMEX are accepted.

You might need a program to know the players, but if you pull something off the rack of Kirstelle, the chances are good that its label is worthy of an entry in *Who's Who*. You can be sure that what you find there is among the latest fashion trends.

These are casual clothes with style and class. If you want to know about the designers whose names grace these labels, just ask co-owners Michele Pease or Kirsten Marvin. At the drop of a hat, they will rattle off names such as Metropole for clothing, Joseph Boris for semi-precious metal jewelry, Sarah

Arizona for sweaters and the full Laise Adzer and Karen Alexander lines. For that little extra accessory, take a look at the Avion or Doppia Vita belts and the collection of Jane Yoo hand painted bags.

You will find the shop in the Lumberyard Shopping Center off the picturesque Coast Highway 101. The shop is an attractive and pleasant place to be, with its pale pink colors, mauve carpet, huge plants, rattan couch and arched doorways. By the time you leave, you might just be ready to name names, too.

ROMANTIQUE
123 North El Camino Real
Suite D
Encinitas, CA 92024
Tel. (619) 944-6376
Hrs: Mon. - Thu.   10:00 a.m. - 7:00 p.m.
          Fri. - Sat.   10:00 a.m. - 5:30 p.m.
Visa and MasterCard are accepted.

Sisters and co-owners Jackie Tafoya and Judy Meyerhoff run a wonderful bridal shop wherein love-struck brides to be can fulfill their fondest wedding dreams.

Lovely bridal ensembles are displayed on mannequins ond on the walls of the small, but complete shop. At Romantique you can also find formal wear for the other female members of the wedding, including styles appropriate for mother of the bride. If you don't see what you want here, a special order can be made when you point out your hearts desire in *Bride's Magazine*.   In addition to wedding wear, Romantique carries formal wear for special occaisions such as proms and balls.

Because of the complexity of planning a formal wedding, Jackie and Judy suggest a bride start planning her wedding at least six months in advance. They are good at assisting with plans, ordering invitations and other necessary arrangements. Custom fitting is also done in the shop.

When the stress of the big event gets you down, take inspiration from Morris the shop cat, who can usually be found snoozing in the window. If you are planning a wedding, there's no better place to begin than at Romantique.

BAKERY

MARVELOUS MUFFINS BAKERY CAFE
632 1st Street
Encinitas, CA 92024
Tel. (619) 753-7742
Hrs: Mon. - Sun.   8:00 a.m. - 5:00 p.m.
Also,
15568 Brookhurst Street   10178 Adams Avenue
Westminister, CA   Huntington Beach, CA
                                 2530 Vista Way
                                 Fire Mountain Center
                                 Oceanside, CA

Nothing spells breakfast like the aroma of freshly baked muffins, hot from the oven. Add fresh drawn butter, sweet honey, or fruit jams and you have a treat this is hard to beat. Now a new bakery that specializes in all varieties of muffins is open for business. These are the Marvelous Muffin Bakery Cafe, a very successful new idea that is expanding as fast as people can get the muffins. Special muffins and secret recipes such as banana chocolate ship, carrot spice bran, cinnamon apple and lemon cheese cake are made fresh daily.

Marvelous Muffins Inc. was founded four years ago by Karen Heyman. She received a small loan and opened a storefront muffin shop a couple blocks for the Pacific Ocean in Encinitas. The plans for rapid expansion include twelve stores throughout Southern California. Karen is a remarkable woman. Prior to opening her muffin business, she was an FAA air traffic controller at San Diego's Montgomery field and also holds a Master's Degree in Educational Psychology.

Over one hundred and one recipes for special muffins and unique cookies have been perfected and what makes Marvelous Muffins so unique is the use of natural products and no preservatives. Nor is any expense spared in providing the best. For instance, cookies are made with Ambrosia chocolates, the best available, and the use of sweet unsalted butter. New menu items will include "Bake-Overs" filled with tasty combinations of fruits, meats and cheese, including cheesecakes in luscious flavors such as chocolate chip, lemon, chocolate and New York style, cheesecake brownies and sour cream coffee cakes. If you're tired of the same thing for breakfast, stop by this wonderful bakery and experience the wonderful fresh taste of a hot muffin. You will know what is marvelous about Marvelous Muffins.

FURNITURE STORE

BOWEN AND KERN
1010 1st Street
Encinitas, CA 92024
Tel. (619) 943-8333
Hrs: Mon. - Fri.   10:00 a.m. - 8:30 p.m.
        Sat. Sun.   9:30 a.m. - 6:00 p.m.

Walk into Bowen and Kern, and you might feel as though you stepped into someone's home in Santa Fe, New Mexico. Your first impressions are of soft colors, warm woods and textures, and a wonderful sense of casual living. Calling it "informal merchandising," owners Diane Bowen and Brent Kern say they want a relaxed, comfortable atmosphere, much the way you might find in your own home. "Our biggest compliment," laughs Diane, "is when customers tell us they would like to move right into our store."

Ask a question of origin on some item, and you're likely to find out it's Ironwood furniture from Argentina, Lodgepole furniture from Utah, or custom willow from the high Sierras in Northern California, Pastel Turkish Kilim rugs, Tarahumara Indian pottery and ladders, or brightly colored Di Simone dishware from Italy; all seem to blend and create a decidedly eclectic look that lends itself to many styles of Southern California living. "While primarily a Southwestern store, much of our furniture and accessories can easily cross-over into the Western, Country, or Mediterranean looks," explains Brent.

Need some help in achieving this look, or have a question on what best suits your home? Bowen and Kern has an in-house designer, Alison Paul, who enthusiastically says she will assist you, from placing that certain antique Mexican table, to choosing just the right fabric for your Lodgepole sofa and loveseat.

With over 4,700 square feet to wander through, including an upstairs mezzanine, it's hard to see everything on your first visit. "We really want our customers to feel welcome, and have found many are returning just to see what new merchandise has arrived that week." says Brent. Add that to the complimentary fresh coffee or herbal teas offered while you browse and it's hard not to come back and decide which live cactus or painting form an up-and-coming artist would look best in your home.

GIFT STORE

THE CORAL BRANCH
In The Lumberyard
745 First Street, Suite 102
Encinitas, CA 92024
Tel. (619) 436-6411
Hrs: Mon. - Fri.   10:00 a.m. - 6:00 p.m.
          Sat. - Sun.   12:00 noon - 5:00 p.m.
Visa, MasterCard and UPS shipping are accommodated.

Don't miss this unique shop when passing through the North County area of San Diego. While browsing at The Coral Branch, you'll find a wonderful collection of sea shells and corals from common to rare specimens.

On display is an ever changing selection of masks and spirit carvings from Indonesia, New Guinea, Mexico and the Pacific Northwest --with a most interesting display of fossils and minerals from remote areas of the world.

A selection of handmade jewelry rounds off the eclectic atmosphere of The Coral Branch; American Indian silver work, shell jewelry, pearls plus custom peices made from precious metals and gems. The knowledgeable, courteous salespeople will help you with your purchases of .50 cents to $3,000.

KITCHEN WARES

KITCHEN WITCH
127 North El Camino Real, Suite D
Encinitas, CA 92024
Tel. (619) 942-3228
Hrs: Mon. - Fri.   10:00 a.m. - 6:00 p.m.
          Saturday   10:00 a.m. - 5:30 p.m.
          Sunday   1:00 p.m. - 4:00 p.m.
Visa, MasterCard and AMEX are accepted.

People who are serious about what they do in their kitchens will have lots of fun at the Kitchen Witch cooking supplies and gourmet shop.

Owner Marie Benson has stocked the Kitchen Witch with every kitchen gadget imaginable, plus a professional line of heavy-duty professional aluminum cookware called Calphalon. There are over thirty kinds of gourmet coffee beans from which to choose, fifteen exotic teas, spices and specialty foods. To brew the perfect cup of coffee, you'll find well known coffee makers and accessories, such as Krups, Melitta and Bodum. Imported tea kettles are featured, as well as tea balls and spoons for making just one cup. Crepe-makers, canisters, food processing equipment, salt/pepper grinders, peelers, thermometers, spatulas, graters, molds and pie and cake pans make up another selection of merchandise there. And, of course, there are cookbooks. Cooking classes are scheduled regularly with guest chefs. Any item not stocked will be ordered for you, and shipping is available.

For quality kitchen and gourmet supplies, the Kitchen Witch is a "Best Choice" in Encinitas.

LINEN STORE

THE WHITE SALE
214 C North El Camino Real
Encinitas, CA 92024
Tel. (619) 436-8004
Hrs: Mon. - Fri.   10:00 a.m. - 6:30 p.m.
       Saturday   10:00 a.m. - 6:00 p.m.
       Sunday   12:00 noon - 5:00 p.m.
Visa and MasterCard are accepted.
Also,
630 Nordahl Road
San Marcos, CA 92024
Tel. (619) 745-0806
Hrs: See above.

No wonder The White Sale is noted as one of the five best places to shop for linen and bedding by *San Diego Home and Garden Magazine*. Proprietors, Lee and Jo Lynn Frodsham carry a total line of merchandise at up to 60% off regular prices.

You'll find brand name linens such as Martex, Fieldcrest and Wamsutta. There are bed spreads, sheets, bath towels, bathroom accessories and shower curtains. Looking for down pillows and comforters at great prices? Look no further. They are at the White Sale, along with waterbed sheets, flannel sheets and coordinated daybed accesories. Hard to fit beds such as California Kings and Eastern Kings can be easily fitted at the White Sale.

Other merchandise includes wall accessories, shelveing and iron and brass beds. The staff at the White Sale is exceptionally good at coordinating the color and style of fabrics and love to help put together just the right look. Special orders and shipping are available. When you want quality linen at prices you'll tell your friends about, visit The White Sale in San Marcos or Encinitas.

NEWSSTAND

ENCINITAS NEWS
566 1st Street
Encinitas, CA 92024
Tel.   (619) 942-9769
Hrs: Mon. - Fri.   8:00 a.m. - 6:00 p.m.
        Sunday   8:00 a.m. - 1:00 p.m.

There is something very special about Bonnie Jo Bechtold, owner of the Encinitas news store and the people of Encinitas know it. Bonnie opened this store in March of 1982. She realized the need for a quality news and magazine store. Originally, she carried farm fresh eggs, but since has replaced the "eggery" with a tremendous selection of unique greeting cards and over thirty major newspapers. She carries over 500 different current periodicals and newspapers form England, France, Italy and Germany. She also features an extensive tobacco product selection where a shopper can find the highest quality pipe, cigar and cigaretté items.

Some of the most important periodicals presented are business, politics, art, home design, architecture, health fitness, sailing, sports and literature. Also a good selection of food and wine and fashion periodicals. If she does not have what you need, she can try and order it. Bonnie Jo is a petite blonde with sparkling blue eyes and a huge smile. She welcomes everyone to come in, say hi, and enjoy the wide variety of periodicals and products at Encinitas News.

PET STORE

HOLIDAY PET HOTEL AND THE CATS PAJAMAS
551 Union Street
Encinitas, CA 92024
Tel.   (619) 753-6754
Hrs: Mon. - Fri.   9:00 a.m. - 5:00 p.m.
        Saturday   9:00 a.m. - 12:00 noon
        Sunday   2:00 p.m. - 4:00 p.m.
Visa and MasterCard are accepted.

The Holiday Pet Hotel is the next best place to home for your pet. This five star pet hotel has been designed to please animals and owners alike.

The Holiday Pet Hotel offers the concerned pet owner a "total concept" in pet hosteling.   Each pet at any stage of her/his life is provided with an environment that exceeds basic necessities. Accommodations are large and comfortable. There are both outdoor and indoor runs. Optional "playtime is available in outdoor exercise yards for dogs and indoor playrooms give cats opportunity for play. A special care ward is available for youngsters and geriatrics who require additinal care. Personnel who really care for animals are on the premises twenty-four hours a day. Veterinarians are on call. Soft music is piped in for the enjoyment of all the furry guests. A must for conscientious cat owners is The Cats Pajamas, probably the most luxuriously appointed, advanced cat boarding facility in the country. The Cats Pajamas has spacious, bright, sunlit rooms with custom designed, multi-level, expandable condos. Going on a vacation to Hawaii? You can have your precious pet checked into the Hawaiian suite replete with leis and tropical decor. Some of the rooms have their own attached playrooms and all feature soft beds and window views.

Exotics such as cockatoos and other parrots are acceptable guests too, however, they must come with their own cages and brown bag. The Holiday Pet Hotel's goal is to provide the responsible pet owner with a safe, spotless, comfortable boarding facility staffed by devoted animal loving professionals. This outstanding boarding facility has to be seen to be fully appreciated.

RESTAURANT

THE 101 DINER
552 1st Street
Encinitas, CA 92024
Tel. (619) 753-2123
Hrs: Wed. - Sun.   6:00 a.m. - 10:00 p.m.
           Monday   6:00 a.m. - 3:00 p.m.
Closed Tuesdays.

The 101 is an all day diner capturing the nostalgia of the 50s. There's mostly counter seating, one booth and one outside table. Decor is art deco, pink walls, plastic flamingos, a toy pink cadillac and a huge old Coca-Cola sign on the wall. Forget anything you ever heard about the "greasy spoon" reputations of some diners. The 101 Diner prides itself on everything served being super fresh, wholesome and homemade from scratch. Only fresh ground beef is used!

Owners, Steve Travis, Dennis Culton and Janice Hammack all used to work at an exclusive San Diego, French restaurant and have brought skills in gourmet cooking to a homey, relaxed restaurant. Folks drive up from San Diego just to enjoy the great breakfasts, lunches and dinners there. When did you last have an honest to goodness homemade malt or milk shake, or order of homemade fries from potatoes just sliced? The diner is also famous for its "Buffalo Style" chicken wings, seasoned mild, hot or red hot and served with celery sticks and blue cheese dressing.

Find the 101 Diner as you head North on First Street "old Highway 101." It's on the left, just beyond E Street. There's a big round neon sign in the window. One last warning: The sign over the grill inside announces that harassing the cook will result in smaller portions!

SHOE STORE

THE SECOND SOLE
437 Encinitas Boulevard
Encinitas, CA 92024
Tel. (619) 436-6222
Visa, MasterCard and AMEX are accepted.

In order to participate safely in any sport, you must have the right equipment, and this begins with the right footwear. Second Sole was started by Richard Hertz in 1976, with the idea of selling athletic shoes and offering the service of resoling them; hence, the name Second Sole. The idea took off, and, through franchising, there are now sixty-five Second Sole stores in thirteen states.

What sets Second Sole stores apart is they are truly "athletic shoe specialists." Many of the stores are owned by athletes. You will be amazed by the incredible selection of athletic shoes for every conceivable activity.

Though service seems to be a lost art at most stores today, when you visit The Second Sole you will find the sales staff is genuinely interested in helping you choose the right shoe; not just the one that best matches the color of your clothing, but the shoe that best matches your foot structure. That's because The Second Sole staff is taught about the bones of the foot, its stucture and alignment. They are familiar with injuries and what causes them. The next time you need athletic footwear, remember The Second Sole, the shoe store recommended by sports doctors.

ESCONDIDO

What was once a hidden valley, as the Spanish name implies, has become the cultural and commercial center of inland North County and is rapidly surpassing other county population centers. With a population of 75000, Escondido is now the fourth largest city in San Diego County.

The community, surrounded by lakes, is centrally located to provide quick access to attractions throughout North County, such as Wild Animal Park and Lawrence Welk Village, as well as major attractions in San Diego, just thirty miles to the South.

Escondido is more than a bedroom community. It includes the famous Golden Door Health Spa. The North County Fair shopping center serves a wide geographic area and the Via Rancho Parkway is a labyrinth of specialty stores. On hot days many cool off at nearby Dixon Reservoir and Lakes Hodges and Wohlford where there's a wealth of recreational opportunities.

Escondido started off as part of an old land grant called Ricon del Diablo, or "the devil's work place." During pioneer days it became the 13000 acre Wolfskill Ranch. At one point area farmers went deeply in debt to finance local irrigation projects. The big event in Escondido today is a celebration of the retiring of that debt. During the annual Grape Day Festival, held in early September, grapes from area vineyards are passed out to visitors in a carnival-like festival. The celebration began in 1905 with liquidation of the oppressive irrigation district bonds. During the original celebration, the bonds were burned before a crowd of 2000 cheering farmers.

For more information contact the Escondido Visitors and Information Bureau, 720 North Broadway, Escondido, CA 92025 Tel. (619) 745-4741.

ATTRACTION

In the North Inland region, head for Escondido's **North County Fair**, 272 East Via Rancho Parkway. This is a new shopping center with 179 shops and restaurants, in addition to five major department stores, including The Broadway, May Co., J.C. Penney, Nordstrom and Sears.

GIFT STORE

BASKET EXPRESS
200 East Via Rancho Parkway
North County Fair Mall
Escondido, CA 92025
Tel. (619) 747-GIFT
Hrs: Mon. - Fri.   10:00 a.m. - 9:00 p.m.
        Saturday   10:00 a.m. - 7:00 p.m.
        Sunday   11:00 a.m. - 6:00 p.m.
Visa, MasterCard and AMEX are accepted.

The products of this unique store are not simply baskets, but baskets filled with assortments of every possible gift idea you can imagine. And it is you who does the imagining. Just pick the things you'd like to give from a large and inventive selection of goods from crackers and cheese, soaps and sachets, to mugs, tea and coffee.

This great idea for a store, specializing in personalized gift baskets, is the brain child of owners, Mary Russel and Jerri Woods. They opened Basket Express in 1986 as one of the first stores in the new mall, so new the interior walls weren't up. Vitually anything can be celebrated by one of their great baskets. Behind the attractive display windows is everything needed to assemble your own idea for a gift, whether for a birthday, wedding , anniversary, baby shower, graduation, winning the big game or breaking 100 on the golf links. Perhaps you just want to tell someone you're thinking of them or say "thanks."

If you prefer not to pick out your own "ingredients," just tell one of the helpful staff and they'll put together a basket to mark your special occaision. It takes about thity minutes. Incidentally, Jerri and Mary have tried each of the products they carry, so you can count on quality. Try it. There's a basket for everyone.

WINE SHOP

DEER PARK

29013 Champagne Boulevard
Escondido, CA 92026
Tel. (619) 749-1666
Hrs: Mon. - Sun.   10:00 a.m. - 5:00 p.m.
Visa and MasterCard are accepted.

"Vintage wines and vintage cars" are what you get when you visit Deer Park Winery and Museum. An odd combination you say? Well, for vintners Kinta and David Clark and antique car collectors Lila and Bob Knapp, it's turned into a winning combination. The four have created a place where visitors can taste award winning wines and lunch on excellent deli fare while viewing one of the most outstanding car collections around.

The juxtaposition begins with the grape lined driveway that leads to a modern building filled with classic convertibles, gourmet food and displays of wine. At last count over seventy antique autos, all in mint condition, were on display. Knapp adds several more each year. A complete gourmet deli will build a perfect picnic to take on a stroll around the grounds.

Each year Deer Park sponsors a Harvest Festival, a Chile Cookoff and several car shows including two Concours events. And every month a calendar of special events is published and is available through a mailing list.

For those who find it hard to leave, rooms are available at Lawrence Welk Village. Deer Park makes a great place to hold convention meetings, birthday parties and weddings.

Unfortunately, if you're looking for deer you won't find them here. The name not withstanding, there's not a deer in sight. But you probably won't even miss them because there's always something cookin' at Deer Park. Come on out!

FALLBROOK

Five miles West of I-15 down country road S13 among hillsides checkered with groves of lemons, oranges and avocados is the quiet community of Fallbrook, a place known as "The Friendly Village." The area's farmers have been quick to capitalize on changing tastes, and in recent years some cashed in on the growing popularity of commodities such as kiwi fruit and Macadamia nuts. The area was first settled in 1880 because of its ideal soil and climate conditions. The area's mountains have long attracted deer hunters. Fallbrook is one of the few places in the county where you find few signs of the congestion that plagues so many areas in the county. But Fallbrook is not exclusively an off the beaten path farm town. Scattered among its shops are antique shops, quaint galleries and boutiques, and include an excellent Four Star restaurant known as the Grocery Store Cafe. The folks at the Fallbrook Chamber of Commerce can be reached at (619) 728 5848.

JULIAN

A jewel of a small town lies among pines and apple trees seventy-five miles northeast of San Diego. If any town could claim to be as American as "apple pie" it would be Julian, where a well-preserved gold mining town does a brisk business selling 4,000 apple pies a month to visiting tourists. Julian is, as its Chamber of Commerce says, "...a microcosm of the old West, the new West and the world. We can dig ditches or Einstein, brand cattle or critics."

At an altitude above 4,000 feet, the air is clean, the skies are blue, and at night, the Milky Way sweeps across the heavens. The higher elevation allows seasonal changes, not usually found in Southern California. Spring brings out the daffodils, in fall the trees offer a bountiful harvest of apples, and winter brings on snowball fights and hillside sledding.

Julian was an apple growing area before gold was discovered in 1870. But it was the rush for gold that brought enough people into the region to build the town. During the decade of the 1870s Julian's streets were to include a Main Street of a couple blocks, and four side streets to accommodate further growth. As it turns out 110 years later, the city's urban planners had figured just about right because the town is now about the size it was then.

For such a small town, population 500, it has an incredible number of attractions to lure visitors to this old fashioned world of 19th century buildings, gracious bed and breakfast inns, and friendly shopkeepers. You'll find a town full of people who are content with the life they have found away form the city, but still hospitable to its guests who come in large numbers for the fall apple harvest and a taste of the famous apple pie. The town has three bakeries that serve nothing but apple pie. A Julian "things to do" list would include taking a tour of an active gold mine, riding in a horse drawn carriage, tasting a little wine at a local winery, and dining in one of several fine restaurant.

For additional information, contact the Julian Chamber of Commerce, P. O. Box 413, Julian, CA 92036. Tel. (619) 765-1857.

ATTRACTIONS

The Julian Town Hall at the corner of Washington and Main, is a good first stop. The Julian Chamber of Commerce office is where you can pick up an historic map that will keep you pointed in the right direction.

The Julian Drugstore, built in 1886, dispenses some of the best sodas in the country from a vintage marble soda fountain that seems to make everything taste that much better. The drugstore is just across from the town hall.

One of the oldest operating hotels in California is the **Julian Hotel**, at the corner of Main Street. The hotel was built in 1897 by Albert Robinson, a freed slave. Unfortunately, you have to be a guest to poke around, but brochures describing the history of the hotel are available by the front door.

For a different sort of accommodation, there's the **Julian Jail** at the corner of 4th and C Street. The spartan facility was built in 1913 and served as the local cooler until 1954.

Witch Creek School on 4th Street serves as the local Public Library. The 1886 building is one of the finest specimens of Victorian architecture in town.

At the end of 4th Street, you'll find the **Julian Museum**, which is filled with memorabilia of the gold rush days.

The **Eagle and High Peak Mines**, at the east end of C Street, may look like relics of the past, but they are working gold producing mines and are open to the public. Tours are operated from 8:00 a.m. - 4:00 p.m.

The **Washington Mine**, just west of the Eagle Mine, was Julian's first mine. Little is left of what it once was, but it does offer a pleasant walk through the trees.

The intricately carved granite memorials to the town's founders stand within the Victorian ironwork enclosures of the **Haven of Rest Cemetery**, a quiet and peaceful place off A Street. The site offers a hilltop view of the town.

Menghini Winery, 1150 Julian Orchards Drive produces Sauvignons, Chardonnay, Reisling and a local Gamay called Julian Blossom. Visitors are welcome to picnic under the old apple trees behind the winery. Tel. (619) 765-2072.

If you relish classic, "who done its" of Agatha Christie or Sir Arthur Conan Doyle, you can try your own hand at catching the culprit at the **Pine Hills Lodge Mystery Theater**. A prime rib and seafood dinner is followed by an interactive mystery drama in which guests work to uncover the murderer. The mystery theater is produced on alternate Wednesdays. More conventional dinner theater productions are produced every Friday and Saturday night.

For information, contact the Pine Hills Lodge, 2960 La Posada, Julian, CA. Tel. (619) 765-1100.

ACCOMMODATIONS

JULIAN FARMS LODGING
2818 Washington Street
Julian, CA 92036
Tel. (619) 765-0250
Visa, MasterCard and AMEX are accepted.
Reservations are required.

Five years ago, Brenda Campbell bought a motel with three partners and together they remodeled the 1940s units into beautiful Victorian suites, surrounded by trees, lawns and a private garden with an ivy and rose gazebo. Each of the four rooms is decorated distinctively with its own individuality. Personal touches include Green Apple Soap in every private bathroom, as well as complimentary chocolates, cookies, coffee and tea in the rooms and wine from the local vineyard.

Perfect for a private getaway, guests treasure the location for its slow pace, the quiet and the delightfully friendly people of Julian.

The lodging is close to all the restaurants and shops of Julian. For fun browsing, a gift and antique shop is also located on the grounds. The shop features everything from Christmas ornaments to Victorian hutches and hats and specialty soaps. Open year-round except Thanksgiving and Christmas days, this is a popular and intimate Victorian style motel.

JULIAN LODGE
4th and C Streets
P.O. Box 1430
Julian, CA 92036
Tel. (619) 765-1420
Hrs: Year-round by reservation.
All major credit cards are accepted.

In the back country East of San Diego, Julian is nestled against the foothills. The air is pure and clear at 4,200 feet, and the climate is perfect for growing wonderful apples. In late fall tourists make the pilgrimage to Julian to bring back the crisp, crunchy apples and great homemade ciders. At other seasons, winter festivals, art shows, concerts and the Julian Weed Show attracts visitors who love the nostalgia of the town's by-gone gold rush days.

Julian Lodge, a twenty-three room bed and breakfast inn in the sleepy little town, is a favorite stopping place for travelers.

Designed after the Washington Hotel, built in 1885, the Julian Lodge is just steps away from rustic shops and historic points of interest. During good weather, and all summer long, guests can use the complimentary bicycles providied by the Lodge. Daily, a sumptuous Continental breakfast is served. The furnishings of each guest room combine the beauty of antique furnishings, the comfort of air conditioning, private baths and color TV. The Julian Lodge welcomes you to return time and time again.

(See special invitation in the Appendix.)

JULIAN VACATION CABINS
P.O. Box 1126
2725 Lilac Drive
Julian, CA 92036
Tel. (619) 765-0271
Open year-round
Cash or personal checks, sorry no credit cards or pets, please.

Julian is the ideal vacation spot, offering clean mountain air and an opportunity to leave urban living behind while you escape to the relaxed atmosphere of this historic mountain community.

Fishing, hiking, touring Julian's only operating gold mine, visiting the Julian Pioneer museum, sampling wines at a local winery, or enjoying a horse drawn buggy ride are just a few things one can do in Julian. And one of the best places to stay while enjoying any of these activities is Julian Vacation Cabins.

Each of the Julian Vacation Cabins is unique in design, vintage and size. There are one and two bedroom cabins in various locations, each offering privacy and seclusion among pine, cedar and oak trees. All cabins have complete kitchens with dishes, glassware and cooking utensils. There are fireplaces with some firewood provided. Fireplace burning is allowed October through May, but may vary due to weather and fire season. Even though you'll feel miles from it all, there's color cable television. Blankets and pillows are furnished, however guests are asked to provide their own sheets and pillowcases, bath towels, kitchen towels plus charcoal and lighter fluid for the individual barbecues.

During fall and winter months, guests are reminded to bring warm clothing and to inquire of the California Highway Patrol, (619) 293-3484, about advisability of tire chains. A brochure giving rates and individual cabin information is available.

BAKERIES

JULIAN PIE COMPANY
2225 Main Street
Julian, CA 92036
Tel. (619) 765-2449
Hrs: Mon. - Sun.   9:00 a.m. - 5:00 p.m.

This is just a short, sweet story about one small town baker who does just a few sweet things better than anyone else. Proprietor Elizabeth Smothers has built the reputation of the Julian Pie Company on apple pies. She starts her pies from scratch, using only choice fresh fruit for fillings. Cider, not sugar, is used for sweetener in a "natural" pie. Although apple pie is the specialty, you'll also find blackberry, cherry, strawberry, peach and rhubarb pie, when these fruits are in season. Anytime of the year, try the huge, delicious cinnamon rolls, the walnut apple muffins, or the chocolate chip cookies.

Monday through Friday, you can get specials such as half a sandwich and pie, soup and pie, or quiche. The Victorian decor of the pie shop is done in shades of blue. Patio tables are perfect for enjoying your pie treat outdoors in Julian's consistently agreeable weather.

MOM'S PIE HOUSE
2119 Main Street
Julian, CA 92036-1167
Tel. (619) 765-2472
Hrs: Mon. - Sun.   9:00 a.m. - 5:00 p.m.

There are usually folks waiting for the sinfuly delicious pies which come out of the ovens at Mom's Pie House. The little pie house seats only about thirty people. Don't be discouraged if you don't immediately get a table. These pies are worth waiting for.

Julian's Main Street looks right out of the "Old West," with adjoining buildings. Their appearance hasn't changed much since the turn of the century. Mom's Pie House is also as old fashioned as apple pie. Inside, you can warm yourself next to the wood stove and watch the pies being made in open work areas. The ovens are also in full view, so you can see and smell the pies baking. Choose seasonally from apple, cherry, peach, berry, apricot, rhubarb, strawberry, and holiday pies, such as pecan and pumpkin. Mom's uses Julian's own famous apples as long as they are in season, usually from September until December. Mom's also makes breads, cinnamon rolls and other bakery goods.

Pies can also be made to order, and Mom's is happy to box pies safely for traveling. If you're on vacation, or want to be, throw your diet journal out the window and visit Mom's Pie House in Julian.

MRS. GLAD'S APPLE PIE BAKERY
2122 Main Street
Julian, CA 92036
Tel. (619) 765-9930
Hrs: Mon. - Sun.   10:00 a.m. - 6:00 p.m.

Owner Richard Svehla grew up at his parent's side making pies, and in 1986 took over the family business. Best known for the apple pies made from famous Julian apples, the bakery also makes other pies, including strawberry, boysenberry and blueberry.

It's fun to eat at Mrs. Glad's. The bakery is a chalet style red building set off by trellised apple trees between outside tables. One of the secrets of pie making there is that the whole wheat flour they use creates a beautiful dark color, and a graham cracker like flavor in the crusts. Over 5,000 pies are sold here during the month of October alone.

The bakery will box its pies for traveling, so you can take several with you when you leave. For a "Best Choice" in homemade pies and bakery goodies, don't miss Mrs. Glad's Apple Pie Bakery.

BED AND BREAKFAST INNS

FAIR OAKS BED AND BREAKFAST
1390 Manzanita Drive
P. O. Box 902
Julian, CA 92036
Tel. (619) 765-0704
Hrs: Mon. - Sun.   Check in after 2:00 p.m.

A genuine ranch weekend, with horse corrals and horses as an actual part of the experience, yet city conveniences and accessibility, can be yours at the Fair Oaks B & B. Adam Belushi came West from Chicago and started his operation in August of 1986. He's a natural for it, with his warm personality and interest in sharing experiences with people, and is himself an interesting and gracious host who really cares about making your stay enjoyable.

The five bedroom red ranch house has a comfortable lived in atmosphere taht's compatible with the relaxed Western way of life in Julian. The rooms are all named, and the "Spit Fire" suite is particularly desireable, with a private bath, all the others are equally pleasant, well furnished, spacious and comfortable. Breakfast is a country affair in the large dining room with all the pancakes you can eat, eggs, sausages and coffee. The living room, with it's large brick fireplace, is spacious, inviting and comfortable, ideal for conversation, reading or watching television.

The ranch setting, with huge oak trees and horses, is a natural for a perfect weekend for anyone looking for a place to let down and relax, and at Fair Oaks it's so comfortable it will feel like home. There are all the pleasures and none of the chores.

PINE CONE INN BED AND BREAKFAST
3283 Salton Vista Drive
P.O. Box 1317
Julian, CA 92036
Tel. (619) 765-2191
Hrs: Check-in   2:00 p.m. - 4:00 p.m.
Credit cards are not accepted.

Encouraged by local residents to take advantage of the outstanding view of the Salton Seas and the Chocolate Mountains beyond, Forest and Beckey Burleson completely remodeled a large area below the main part of their home into private quarters to be used as a B & B. It has a private entry, living room, bedroom, fully equipped kitchen and a full bath. It's an attractive apartment that looks out on an area of the 600,000 acre Anza Borrego State Park. Views of the Salton Sea from the living room and bedroom are wonderful.

At 4,500 feet elevation, you can expect nights to be cool, so a large closet is stocked with quilts and warm jackets in case it becomes too chilly. A glass fronted wood stove is waiting in the living room for use in the winter months.

Nicely furnished in Victorian style, the bedroom boasts a four poster bed with a hand stitched quilt, and an antique writing desk and dressing table. A sleeper sofa in the living room provides comfortable sleeping for two, so the apartment can accommodate four. With a supply of games, cable television, outdoor table and barbecue, walkways and paths, and the incredible views, the Pine Cone Inn is a warm, relaxing and enjoyable place to stay. The little old mining town of Julian, with its working mine, winery and historic museum, offers dinner theater, restaurants and many small shops to make the time pass all too fast.

CARRIAGE RIDES

COUNTRY CARRIAGES
PO Box 66
Julian, CA 92036
Tel. (619) 765-1471
Hrs: Mon. - Thu.   11:00 a.m. - 5:00 p.m.
          Fri. - Sun.   10:00 a.m. - 9:00 p.m.
Seasonal adjustments.

A truly innovative and fun way to go out to dinner when you are in Julian is to ride in a horse drawn carriage. Yes, you can travel in style in this old mining town, where time seems to have stood still.

An elegant Victorian carriage may be ordered from Country Carriages to pick you up and take you to the restaurant of your choice, and at a pre-arranged time after dinner, it will be waiting to take you on a thirty minute drive, while you sink back on soft velvet seats while passing through the streets of Julian. Bearing the mark of its vigorous gold mining past, the town still boasts a working gold mine, as well as a winery and numerous antique shops that harbor the treasures of an earlier time. You'll find there are plenty of good restaurants to choose from, plus an enjoyable dinner theater.

Other arrangements can be made for you to engage a carriage for events such as weddings, anniversaries and birthdays. Why wait for an event? Take a carriage ride just to snuggle under a down filled comforter for a romantic drive under the stars, listening to the easy clop, clop of the horse's hooves as you return to another era.

GIFT SHOP

THE HIGHLAND HOUSE
2116 Main Street
Julian, CA 92036-1499
Tel. (619) 765-2255
Hrs: Mon. - Sun.   9:00 a.m. - 5:00 p.m.
Visa, MasterCard, AMEX, Diners Club, Carte Blanche and Discover are accepted.

Perhaps, if Dickens had visited The Highland House, he would have written about it instead of the Curiosity Shop. This is a very special place to visit. The store grew like Topsy. It started small selling coffee, teas and Jellie

Bellies then expanded to the top floor, which now houses country gifts, a folk art gallery, miniatures, hobby shop, tobacco shop and custom doll furniture.

Now the attic has been added and is full of rare custom furniture and antiques of every kind. The hobby shop has one of the most extensive model collections anywhere. Also included is a wood working shop filled with handmade clocks from all over the world. The collection of handcrafted quilts and dolls form Tennessee are worth a trip just to see for themselves. Fantastic saw paintings adorn the walls that are painted by a seventy year old San Diego artists. Here you will find special gifts made form burl, such as ornate burlwood clocks and everything is very reasonable, a shopper's dream.

The atmosphere is one of Christmas all year long. See the huge collection of unique German stained glass by Larry Trotter, a Julian resident, or the authentic toy tin soldiers and wooden nesting dolls form Holland. Beautiful handmade hickory brooms, and walking staffs from the Blue Ridge Mountains are also available. This store is incredible, a "must see" for any one who enjoys the best in antiques, hobbies, crafts, and special gifts. You'll find it here at The Highland House.

(See special invitation in the Appendix.)

KNIVES

QUINN KNIVES
P. O. Box 692
Julian, CA 92036
Tel. (619) 765-2230
Hrs: Mon. - Sun.   10:00 a.m. - 5:00 p.m.
Visa, MasterCard and AMEX are accepted.

It is said that good marriages are made in heaven, but even better is when husband and wife artisans team up to produce beautiful, unique works of art. This is certainly true of George and Nancy Quinn owners of the Quinn Knives shop in Julian. George is a highly skilled knife maker and Nancy is a professional Scrimshaw artist. She takes the top quality knives her husband makes and then turns the handles into works of art. George is self-taught and has passed all the demanding guild tests to be a full fledged member of the Knifemakers Guild. He is one of only two hundred and seventy-three people in the world to be a member of this prestigious group. He was formally Assistant Dean of Architectural studies and gave up teaching to devote his life to his craft.

The shop is located in the Coles Building on Main Street and is fashioned in an Old West style. The cabinets are filled with Nancy's Scrimshaw, custom knives, cutlery items, leather belts, gift items, accessories and much, much more. You will also find one of the largest collections of handmade duck decoys displayed anywhere. George and Nancy also feature American Art Gallery, Indian and Civil War themes as well as treasure of rare and unique steins.

All of George's knives are ground from flat bar stock 440 Carbon Stainless Steel and heat treated to hold a sharper edge. Selected woods are custom made to fit the blade and to fit your hand. The final touch is Nancy's artistic scrimshaw. These knives are increasing in value daily and the Quinn's reputation for excellence is spreading far and wide. He is the only knife maker south of San Francisco that owns and operates his own store. George and Nancy invite you to come in and have a chat. This truly a beautiful place that displays some of the finest craftmanship seen anywhere.

PHOTO STUDIO

BADBLOOD STUDIO SALOON
2608 B. Street
Julian, CA 92036
Tel. (619) 765-1899
Hrs: Thu. - Mon.   10:00 a.m. - 5:00 p.m.
Subject to seasonal change.
Visa and MasterCard are accepted.

Located in the bottom half of what used to be a three story water tower, this old style western saloon invites all comers, young and old, to come in for a shot. The kind of shot you can show your friends and keep as a souvenir of this great old mining town. Taken with an old style looking camera, the photo lab on the premises enables you to step out the door and return to the 20th Century in a few minutes with you "Old West" photograph in hand.

Your mood is set when you walk into the Badblood Saloon. You may sit at a table in this saloon, and look down to see you're holding an ace high straight flush. You look longingly at a bottle of Jack Daniels and the Derringer at your elbow which you know has overruled many a good hand. A saloon girl glances over your shoulder, and it happens that you know each other pretty well. She catches the mood and smiles coyly. The camera records the moment. You make quite a pair.

If you're inclined to think that a saloon shot doesn't exactly suit your style, you'll find owner Bethany Ballard has collect a variety of garb. If you're feeling more like a refined Southern Belle in Sunday finery, or a dapper gentleman of the Civil War, so be it. As they say, "Come in and get shot at the Badblood Studio Saloon."

RANCH

THE SHADOW MOUNTAIN RANCH
2771 Frisius Road
P.O. Box 791
Julian, CA 92036
Tel. (619)765-0323
Hrs: Thu - Sun. year-round.
By Reservation only.

Longing for a weekend getaway that takes you to another place and time? Try the Shadow Mountain Ranch, a pristine mountain retreat just off Highway 78, and a stone's throw from the Pacific Crest Trail.   Not just another Bed and Breakfast, the Shadow Mountain Ranch offers guests a real variety in accommodations. Loretta and James Ketcherside, your friendly hosts, have really put their imaginations to work.

Stay in one of three guest rooms in the main ranch house, where knotty pine is the rule. Go all out by choosing one of the separate guest cottages, each with its own theme. The most popular is the Enchanted Cottage, romantically furnished in Victorian style, with a cozy window seat large enough to sleep in. Adventurers can stay in the twenty-five foot high Tree House Cottage, perched in a giant oak tree. Grandmother's Attic will envelope you in hominess and security.

Whatever your choice for accommodations, everyone is treated to breakfasts even the locals rave about. Loretta puts out a real spread of eggs, sausage, pancakes, fruit, and cereal everyday. Tea time is at 4:30 and complimentary sherry before bed is a special treat.   The great outdoors and clean fresh air will draw you out for leisurely strolls by the lake. Other activities at Shadow Mountain include billiards, horseshoes, English darts, croquet, and archery. There is a large redwood hot tub, Jacuzzi and a two lane lap pool as well. At night the stars light up the sky. Shadow Mountain Ranch is so popular that reservations are suggested two or three months in advance.

RESTAURANT

ROMANOE'S DODGE HOUSE RESTAURANT
2718 B Street
Julian, CA 92036
Tel. (619) 765-1003
Hrs: Mon., Thu., Sun.   11:00 a.m. - 9:00 p.m.
           Fri. - Sat.   11:00 a.m. - 10:00 p.m.
Credit cards are not accepted.

This large yellow building was built in 1915 by the Dodge family, and though it's now Romanoe's, the early name of the place is in keeping with its rustic, warm interior. Tiffany style lamps, lace curtains, wooden tables and chairs with red and white checkered tablecloths, and family pictures on the walls combine to create a romantic and soothing atmosphere. It's a perfect setting for asking or answering the "Big Question"; marriage proposals, according to owner Carmel Romano, happen here more than occasionally.

An incredible antipasto can be described as the "best in the west," and the entire menu really depends on the customers, who choose the ingredients of their pizzas. The home prepared foods include breads, Ravioli, sausage, salads and dressings, and an especially tasty Sicilian Torte. Romanoe's has the only full bar in Julian, and features wine from the local winery, as well as Italian wine.

In addition to the restaurant, there is a quiet two room bed and breakfast cottage. Victorian furnishings and a blue color scheme make for a comfortable and romantic room, a haven for anyone arriving in town after the motels are full.

WINE SHOP

MEGHINI WINERY
1150 Julian Orchards Drive
Julian, CA 92036
Tel. (619) 765-2072
Hrs: Mon. - Thu.   By appointment
           Fri. - Sun.   10:00 a.m. - 4:00 p.m.

In order to produce wine, you must have a love affair with the grapes. Vineyard owner Michael Menghini qualifies, he's been involved with winemaking since he was very young. It wasn't until five years ago, however, that he made his dream come true and purchased land in Julian to start his own vineyard. "I began as a cellar rat, graduated to winemaker and finally became an owner," says Michael, happily.

The area's cool nights and short season will produce wines of great character. The ample winter rains means less seasonal irrigation and that results in grapes that are more intense. Two years after he bought the property, Michael began selling his first wines and they have been heralded as a very nice blend, made from selected regional and varietal grapes. The blends are unique with their own distinctive characters.

A fun afternoon will be to stop by the cozy tasting room, right in the winery itself, and sample some of the Napa Gamay or Sauvignon Blanc, and then adjourn to the nearby picnic area provided for you under the shade of a rolling apple orchard.

LEUCADIA

Leucadia has a reputation for blazing flower farms, memorable antiques and eye catching crafts. The community's biggest draw is the two mile beach which remains uncrowded by Southern California standards. Forty-eight car parking at the end of Leucadia Boulevard makes both the town's beach and shopping district a convenient stop on San Diego County's North Coast.

BOOK STORE

PHOENIX PHYRE BOOKS
704 North Highway 101
Leucadia, CA 92024
Tel. (619) 436-7740
Hrs: Mon. - Thu.   10:00 a.m.- 9:00 p.m.
           Fri. - Sun.   10:00 a.m. - 6:00 p.m.
Visa and MasterCard are accepted.

A crystal spider web glows in the window and a wafting fragrance of myrrh greets you as you walk into this esoteric shop where psychic phenomena are taken for granted as essential aspects of everyone's everyday reality. You'll be welcomed by owner Jo Anne Jordan, a former Marine Corps administrator who started the shop as an outlet for her own interest in metaphysics.

Jo Anne says her greatest satisfaction comes from "our rapport with the people. Our customers are important to us." Regular visitors and skeptics alike, come in droves to browse the excellent collection of books on metaphysics and explore a wide range of products associated with the psychic arts. You'll find tarot cards, runes, and crystal balls, as well as a dazzling assortment of uncut crystals from Arkansas. There are also self-help tapes, video rentals, incense and scented oils, greeting cards, posters, a rainbow of candles, gemstones, metaphysical jewelry, and a nice line of new age music.

For over five years the shop has offered psychic fairs on the last Saturday and Sunday of every month. On fair days, you can have various types of psychic readings done, either in a small group setting or in individual mini-sessions that last about fifteen minutes. During the week classes are available, as well as full length astrological and numerology readings and and biorhythm charts. Staff members are knowledgeable, ethical, and caring. If you've ever wanted to tune into the world of psychic understandings, this is a great place to begin.

RESTAURANT

WHEN IN ROME
828 North Highway 101
Leucadia, CA 92024
Tel. (619) 944-1771
Hrs: Tue. - Sun.   5:30 p.m. - 10:00 p.m.
Reservations are recommended.
Visa, MasterCard and AMEX are accepted.

If you can't be in Rome, you can still do as the Romans do. "When in Rome" is the name of a restaurant that lives up to its name. It's run by a traditional Italian family, and is a place where one couple who met on a blind date in Rome, held their wedding reception.

To start off a perfect meal, try the Antipasto all'Italiana, or the Prosccuitto e Melone. For entrees, you can't beat the Scaloppine alla Pizzaiolla, a mouth watering preparation of veal scaloppine sauteed in fresh tomato, garlic and oregano. Try the chicken breast sauteed in butter, and topped with mozzarella, marsla and cream. For dessert, there's genuine Italian ice cream call it "Gelati," but even better is "Tira Mi Su," which means "lift me up," a rich creamy cheese called Mascarpone whipped and served with a light cake soaked in espresso.

When you have had a memorable evening, you'll hate to say good bye. Just do as a Roman, say "ciao."

OCEANSIDE

Ocean Beach is located on the north side of Point Loma, right on Pacific Ocean. This small community is a cohesive, involved family neighborhood. Young families, retired people, and a surfing and fishing crowd live in harmony. They are a politically active and Ocean Beach's neighborhood atmosphere is important to the residents. The Ocean Beach Pier is a great place to meet local residents.

While the downtown area is small, many young entrepreneurs are starting innovative, quality businesses catering to the community. Several of these business people grew up in Ocean Beach and can tell you terrific stories based on the history of the community and its residents.

Ocean Beach celebrates Christmas the old fashioned way with a parade down Main Street, and old time street fair and the "planting" of a live Christmas tree on the beach.

For more information contact the **Oceanside Chamber of Commerce**, Tel. (619) 722-1534 or City Hall, Tel. (619) 225-1080.

EVENTS

Things really take off at the **Ocean Beach Kite Festival**, held during the first or second week of March. This is an annual kite decorating and flying contest for all ages. A parade down the beach follows judging. Tel. (619) 747-8702.

Mission San Luis Rey, east of Oceanside, holds its annual fiesta in July, which includes a western market, parachute divers and square dancing. Tel. (619) 757-3651.

As fall arrives, two of the County's cities host annual "rough water" swim races. Ocean Beach holds its race during the first week in September. Swimmers make a round trip to the end of the pier and back. For information about entering or watching call (619) 439-7325.

RESTAURANTS

LITTLE CHEF

4902 Newport Street
Ocean Beach, CA 92107
Tel. (619) 222-3255
Hrs: Mon. - Thu.   7:00 a.m. - 7:30 p.m.
     Fri. - Sat.   7:00 a.m. - 8:00 p.m.
     Sunday   7:00 a.m. - 7:30 p.m.
Credit cards are not accepted.

The Little Chef restaurant opened two years ago in the heart of Ocean Beach, and its excellent reputation is already spreading to other towns and counties in California. Little Chef offers excellent service and the best in quality foods.

Start the day with a choice of ten omelettes, including Greek, Spanish, Vegetarian or American, hot cakes made with a special homemade batter, French toast, or an inch high Belgian waffle with berries and real whipped cream. Include a side order from the bakery, and fresh squeezed orange juice and hot, rich coffee. Some of the breakfasts include fresh, home fried potatoes, made-from-scratch biscuits or a choice of fresh bread, baked that morning in their attached bakery.

Lunch and dinner offer homemade specials, such as the "Greek Special #2," Greek-style chicken, authentic Spanakopita, dolmades, rice pilaf, Greek salad and homebaked pita bread. Or try their barbecued ribs, steak and shrimp, or an authentic Mexican meal, such as Burritos Supreme, Enchiladas or a tostada. Friday and Saturday evenings offer a very special treat of succulent prime rib or fresh sword fish.

All the ingredients used in the preparation of Little Chef's menu are of the freshest, highest quality. Every recipe is prepared authentically, with a keen eye on food that is healthy and delicious.

Whatever you select from the menu, be sure to leave room for dessert. Considering the generous quantity of the servings, this may be a challenge. The homemade cheesecakes are exquisite and not to be missed. Any of the cakes, brownies or pies are also excellent choices.

Evans Johnson and his dad, affectionately known as "Pops," leave nothing to chance. They insist on the best quality, beautifully prepared and served food, and a warm and friendly ambiance. The value and quality of Little Chef restaurant definitely reflect the generous philosophy of the owners and make it one of San Diego's "Best Choices."

SOUP EXCHANGE
2665 Vista Way
Oceanside, CA 92054
Tel. (619) 433-7687
Hrs: Mon. - Sun.   11:00 a.m. - 9:30 p.m.
No credit cards are accepted.
Also,

7777 Fay Avenue
La Jolla, CA 92037
Tel. (619) 459-0212

7984 La Mesa Boulevard
La Mesa, CA 92041
Tel. (619) 697-8561

7305 Clairemont Mesa Blvd.
Kearny Mesa CA 92111
Tel. (619) 576-0622

1840 Garnet Avenue
Pacific Beach, CA 91745
Tel. (619) 272-7766

Soup Exchange restaurants offer convenient self-service soup, salad, bakery and fresh fruit dessert bars in a comfortable and casual atmosphere.

The Soup Exchange serves six freshly prepared homestyle soups daily. You may choose from over sixty garden fresh and prepared salad entrees with many dressings and condiments. Specialty muffins, breads, and pastries as well as fresh fruits and dessert are included with soup, salad or soup and salad main item purchases. A variety of beverages, including both domestic and imported beers and wines are also offered. Quantity and return privileges are unlimited. Senior and children are given discounts. Your heart as well as your appetite are considered at the Exchange. Soup Exchange is a participant in the American Heart Associations "Dine With Your Heart in Mind" program. The menu features items which are low in fat and cholesterol and moderate in salt. A special "express" service is offered for patrons in a hurry. The decor is light and airy with large skylights, mirrors, rich tile and designer tones to make a tasteful upscale atmosphere.

The Soup Exchange offers high standards for quality, fast and friendly service a comfortable atmosphere with attention to cleanliness. Also, offered is a customer newsletter called *Pot Pourri* which gives tips on nutrition, discusses the growth of the franchise and talks about current and future locations.

PALA

In the middle of a small Indian reservation of 519 Native Americans is the tiny town of Pala, about six miles up the San Luis Rey River from I-15. The settlement is dominated by an old Spanish chapel, La Asistencia De San Antonio De Pala, built 1816 as a branch of Mission San Luis Rey down river at Oceanside. It is only one of the original California missions that continues to serve a predominantly Indian congregation. An outstanding feature of the chapel is its detached campanile and the marvelous fresco murals painted by the area's Indians. At the time is was constructed the chapel served as one of the many ranchos that supplied the main mission, Mission San Luis Rey.

Another distinction of this region is that up a side road leading North is the site of a gemstone mine which is one of the only two places on earth where the gem kunzite is found. The transparent lilac colored crystal is found only in Pala and Madagascar.

POWAY

Poway is among the planned communities of the North County and retains a mixture of old and new. Horse trails wind through the town, including the central business district. The architecture is either Spanish or rustic providing some feel for the old West and plenty of rural charm. Just outside the new housing areas, families live on ranches and small farms.

The nightlife in Poway leans toward Country Western, but urban rock is not unknown. Although set among inland communities that place high premiums on high school athletics, Poway's residents point to the scholastic achievements of their students. And this emphasis does show in scholastic test scores that rank among the highest in the state. But don't get the impression that this is a "bookish" community. Poway's residents are quick to head out to nearby lakes and mountains where there are opportunities for fishing, boating and camping.

RANCHO BERNARDO

One of the first cities to spring up in San Diego County, Rancho Bernardo appears from the freeway as a series of red-tiled roofs. It started out in the 1970s as a relaxed retirement community, but later evolved into a residential community, carefully planned and controlled to provide housing, as well as employment, shopping, schools and cultural amenities.

It's worth getting off the freeway to visit the Mercado, one of the best of the new artsy shopping enclaves to be built in the county. On weekends you'll find most of the craftspeople at work. The streets and walkways are exciting with bold graphics and bright banners attached to the Spanish style buildings. Among these buildings, grouped around the courtyards, you'll find art and craft shops specializing in pottery, jewelry and other wares.

The community has created a traditional celebration: The annual Indian show, in May, is one of the largest community events of its type in Southern California. Another event is the four day display of art by the Mercado craftsmen held in August.

EVENT

The community of Rancho Bernardo turns out on the **Fourth of July** for a celebration featuring a carnival, parade and fireworks. Tel. (619) 487-9426.

RESORT

RANCHO BERNARDO INN
17550 Bernardo Oaks Drive
Rancho Bernardo, CA 92129
Tel.   (619) 487-1611
          (800) 542-6096 CA
          (800) 854-1065 US
Visa, MasterCard, AMEX and Diners Club are accepted.

This unique tennis and golf resort offers you both the ultimate in luxurious personal accommodations and tournament class athletic facilities. There are four golf courses, three nine-hole courses and a championship eighteen-hole course that must be played with rifle-like accuracy. Tennis facilities include twelve courts and a nationally known Tennis College. There are also two swimming pools and three jacuzzis.

Tucked into a tranquil, verdant valley, a group of seven Spanish style haciendas shelter 236 guest rooms and suites, each handsomely designed with custom furnishings and original works of art. The Inn's two restaurants are perennially found   on lists of San Diego favorites. El Bizcocho presents elegant French cuisine. Open for dinners and Sunday brunch, it is known for its Lamb Filets with lime sauce and Roasted Duckling with Calvados, sliced apples and green peppercorn sauce and also offers a masterful daily special that adds up to less than 800 calories. The mission-style Veranda Room offers American and continental cuisine. Open for breakfast, lunch and dinner, it specializes in fresh fish.

The extras are impressive at Rancho Bernardo Inn. Complimentary afternoon tea and sherry are served in the Music Room every day. There is live entertainment in both dining rooms: harp and piano music in El Bizcocho, a vocalist and band in the Veranda Room. A children's summer camp during August, Christmas and Easter vacations are free to hotel guests ages four to seventeen. Whether you want challenging golf and tennis with skilled instruction, a chance to just play and putter, or time to be coddled in California hacienda luxury, you'll find your dream vacation at Rancho Bernardo Inn. Call early to find out about special holiday programs.

RESTAURANT

JEREMIAH'S RESTAURANT
27051 West Bernardo Drive
Rancho Bernardo, CA 92127
Tel. (619) 487-7181
Hrs: Lunch   Mon. - Fri.   11:30 a.m. - 2:30 p.m.
         Dinner   Mon. - Sun.   5:00 p.m. - 10:00 p.m.
Visa, MasterCard and AMEX are accepted.

Jeremiah's opened in 1979 and rapidly became a popular dining spot for local residents.   The warm, comfortable restaurant has many booths, surrounded by plants, brass and stained glass. The multi-level design creates an intimate setting in which to enjoy terrific food. The menu will please you with its reasonable prices and extensive selection.

The lunch entrees offered include such delicacies as Lobster Quiche, Sizzling Chicken Luau, marinated strips of chicken breast with fresh vegetables and pineapple, and Prime Rib Stew, among others. A selection of delicious Prime Steak Burgers, sandwiches such as the Beefeater Grill and the Country Club Croissant as well as soups, salads and fresh Pastas round out the luncheon menu.

The dinner menu offers many wonderful choices, from appetizers to desserts. You might want to begin your meal with Mozzarella Marinara or Steamers, fresh clams steamed in Chardonnay, butter and garlic. Then choose from one of the many steak, prime rib, chicken or fresh seafood dishes. There is a selection of "Lite Entrees" for the less than hearty appetite or for those who want to be sure to have room for Mud Pie, New York Cheesecake or one of the other delicious desserts. The extensive selection and reasonable prices, combined with the comfortable atmosphere and excellent service make Jeremiah's a dining experience everyone will enjoy.

RANCHO PEÑASQUITOS

Residents of Rancho Peñasquitos will concede that their community is simply a fast growing collection of houses. The community of 35000 rests against Black Mountain and adjacent to the Carmel Mountain Ranch Country Club. Growth projections estimate the community will grow by another 25000 during the next ten years. In the summer of 1987 the community hosted a major music festival featuring jazz and bluegrass in the hope that it becomes an annual event that will put the community on the map. City planners have ideas about building a library, a meeting hall and an amphitheater. For further information call Rancho Peñasquitos hotline at (619) 484-KNOW.

RANCHO SANTA FE

Just a few miles inland from Del Mar among stands of eucalyptus, avocado and citrus groves, horse farms and luxurious estates is one of the most elite communities in the country, Rancho Santa Fe. The community offers its residents lakes, rolling hills and golf courses. The Rancho village town center has a small art and boutique shopping area as well as a good restaurant and tea room. Originally Rancho Santa Fe was a ranch occupied by the first Spanish mayor of San Diego. The mayor's original adobe, built in 1835, later became incorporated into the opulent country estate owned by Bing Crosby.

Before the region had been developed, the Santa Fe Railroad started a eucalyptus plantation with three million seedlings in the hope that the fast growing wood would become a cheap source of railroad ties. The eucalyptus timbers proved to be unsuitable. But all was not lost because in 1922 the railroad's investment succeeded in another way, as a planned development for the new community. Along with Crosby, Douglas Fairbanks Sr. bought a ranch here, calling it Rancho Zorro.

ACCOMMODATION

THE INN AT RANCHO SANTA FE
Linea del Cielo At Paseo Delicias
Rancho Santa Fe, CA 92067
Tel.   (619) 756-1131
        (800) 654-2928
Visa, MasterCard, AMEX and Diners Club are accepted.

Located twenty miles north of San Diego and seven miles inland from the Pacific Ocean, The Inn at Rancho Santa Fe is an elegant country hotel surrounded by rolling hills, citrus groves and towering eucalyptus. Blessed with the natural beauty of the area and year round sunshine, The Inn offers relaxation, warmth and tranquillity any season of the year.

The Inn is privately owned and a member of the elite Relais and Chateaux group. There are seventy-five individually air conditioned guest rooms. Almost all of the accomodations are located in cottages nestled throughout twenty acres of landscaped grounds. Each guest room is individually decorated, has a private bath and entrance and many have fireplaces, kitchenettes and secluded patios. Some bedroom cottages with complete housekeeping facilities are also available. Classic, California cuisine is offered in a variety of indoor and outdoor settings. Recreation can be found at the heated swimming pool, three tennis courts, English regulation croquet course, or at nearby Del Mar Beach or the two nearby golf courses. Meeting facilities for up to 100 people are fully equipped. Innkeeper is Daniel Royce, a third generation hotelier. The Inn has been operated by the Royce family since 1958. Daniel's daughters Betsy and Dede and nephew Duncan all are a part of the staff of The Inn.

The Inn at Rancho Santa Fe is a peaceful, quiet, sunny place nestled in a sylvan setting. It is secluded yet close to everything. Guests return year after year to enjoy the comfort, beauty, service and cuisine.

HOT AIR BALLOON RIDES

PACIFIC HORIZON BALLOON TOURS
16236 San Diequito
Rancho Santa Fe, CA 92067
Tel. (619)756-1790
Hrs: Mon. - Sun.   9:00 a.m. - 5:00 p.m.
Visa, MasterCard and AMEX are accepted.

As one of the first ballooning companies to fly in San Diego, Pacific Horizon Tours has time on its side when it comes to experience. Owners Hans Petermann, of Rancho Penasquitos, and Peter Gallagher, of San Diego, transformed their beloved hobby into a real life fantasy five years ago when they created Pacific Horizon Tours. Today it is their full time business, operating all year long. Twice daily flights offer a choice of either sunrise or sunset tours.

Balloon rides make unforgettable gifts for any special occasion such as birthdays, anniversaries, or weddings. Each tour is packed with memories of your breathtaking view of San Diego followed by dinner at the elegant Top O'The Cove restaurant in La Jolla.

The business presently has four modern balloons flown by a staff of five FAA licensed pilots, each with five or more years ballooning experience. Pacific Horizon Tours boasts a perfect safety record! A gift shop located at the tour headquarters has a wonderful potpourri of ballooning paraphernalia, including post cards, mugs, puzzles, books, crafts, mobiles, needlework and tee shirts. Experience one of mankind's most pleasurable experiences. Take a balloon tour with Pacific Horizon and see San Diego like you've never seen it before!

SAN MARCOS

People still call San Marcos an agricultural community. With an area of orchards and poultry ranches just beyond the community, it is in many ways still an agricultural center. But with a population of 20000 it has come a long ways since the mid- 1960s when there were just 3000 San Marcos residents. The community lies at the junction of the Twin Oaks, Richland and San Marcos Valleys on a former Spanish land grant.

The community almost completely surround the lake, bearing the same name, on the Southwest side of San Marcos. A special draw to the community is the annual Ye Olde English Fair, a depiction of an early-Renaissance English country market fair, which is held every November at 1755 La Cost Meadows Drive.

Vista is really two areas. One is the old downtown area which is now going through redevelopment and features Old California, an attractive area with a variety of restaurants.

San Marcos is also a college community. It's the home of Palomar Community College, locally known as East San Marcos State. San Diego State University has its North campus here and has plans for expanding that facility by as much as 400 acres in the near future.

EVENTS

In early June, 10,000 chili lovers head for the town of San Marcos for the **Annual Chili Cook Off**. It's the largest chili cooking contest and celebration in Southern California. Tel. (619) 744-1270.

RESORT

LAKE SAN MARCOS RESORT
1025 La Bonita Drive
Lake San Marcos, CA 92069
Tel. (619) 744-0120
Visa, MasterCard, AMEX and BancAmericard are accepted.

Lake San Marcos boasts an average of 340 marvelously clear, warm days a year, which makes it a perfect choice for a weekend get a way or a vacation retreat. The resort is tucked away in the northern San Diego County in a relaxing atmosphere of the lake and beautiful hillsides.

Regulation and paddle tennis courts provide the early riser a way to work up an appetite before breakfast. Don't forget your golf clubs when you visit the resort. The Lake San Marcos Country Club's golf course is available to all resort guests. You won't want to pass up the opportunity to try this excellent eighteen hole, par 72 championship course. The club's facilities are complete with driving range, practice trap and putting greens. Spend an afternoon taking advantage of a cooling excursion on the lake. A number of water bound conveyances are available including sailboats, canoes, rowboats or Kayot party boats. For something left behind or just an afternoon of browsing, the Lake of San Marcos Shopping Center is within easy reach.

Dine in elegance at the Quails Inn Dinnerhouse. While enjoying the spectacular view of sparkling lights on the lake, enjoy finely prepared American cuisine. Dancing and nightly entertainment are available at the Quails Inn Dinnerhouse.

RESTAURANT

OLD CALIFORNIA
1020 San Marcos Boulevard
San Marcos, CA 92069
Tel.   (619) 744-0550

You'll find no imitations here! From the natural bricks and Mexican tiles of its early Southwest architecture to its varied ethnic cuisines, everything at Old California is entirely authentic. Begun as a fruit stand over twenty years ago, this attractive complex now houses fourteen restaurants that can turn you into an instant world traveler.

Acapulco Mexican Food and Cantina offers traditional Mexican food, plus happy hours, disco dancing, and entertaining videos. Grecian Gardens specializes in whole lamb roasted on a spit, and also Greek pastries baked fresh in their exhibition kitchen. Rancho Vera Cruz is a time-trip back into the old west, with steak, fish and chicken broiled over mesquite. Fish House Vera Cruz features fresh seafood prepared in the style of Mexican cillage cookery, plus an oyster bar and seafood market. Bruno's Italian Restaurant & Pizzeria uses traditional family recipes for such specialties as veal, seafood, and handmade pizza. Old San Francisco China Wharf recreates the atmosphere and cuisine of the old San Francisco Chinatown. JK's Stage Shop offers down-home American cooking with roast beef, mashed potatoes and gravy, as well as gourmet hamburgers. Lydia's Mexican Kitchen features Mexican home cooking, "from her kitchen to your plate." Old California Soup And Salad offers a wide selection of homemade soups and fresh salads. Katsu Japanese Restaurant and Sushi Bar features a beautifully prepared, authentic Japanese cuisine. And finally, Gentleman's Choice specializes in prime rib and charbroiled steak dinners served in an English country inn setting.

In addition to the fine restaurants, you'll also find Sven's Danish Bakery, Salazar's Flower Shop, and Kawanso Farm Fresh Produce. Each of the Old California enterprises is individually owned and operated and most of the are family affairs. The Kawansos are typical; they grow their own produce on the family farm and pick early each morning for their shop. Your whole family will enjoy an around the world visit to this unique establishment.

SOLANA BEACH

Just north of Del Mar is Solana Beach, but if you don't keep a sharp look out, you might miss it, not realizing that you have passed through a separate and diverse community. It's not that there's nothing in this friendly community of 17,000, it's just that it does not seem to have a central core area.

You'll find most of the city's shops and businesses along Lomas Santa Fe Drive and Old Highway 101. A couple "claims to fame" for Solana Beach are that it is home of Kay Pro Computers and has a local tavern that features top flight blues and rock performers. The town takes its name from the Spanish meaning, "Sunny Place." It's hard to quibble with that designation when temperatures average close to seventy degrees all year round.

BOOK STORE

WORD JOURNEYS, A TRAVELER'S BOOKSTORE
971 C Lomas Santa Fe Drive
Solana Beach, CA 92075
Tel. (619) 481-4158
Hrs: Mon. - Thu.   10:00 a.m. - 6:00 p.m.
       Fri. - Sat.   10:00 a.m. - 8:00 p.m.
       Sunday   12:00 noon - 6:00 p.m.

If books can bring the world to you, Word Journeys works to bring you the world. This is the only book store in Southern California that specializes in travel related literature of all kinds. They have the largest selection of guidebooks, both domestic and international, of any store in Southern California.

Everything from tales of survival and exploration, to how to find a great beer or a sunny nude beach. Take for example, *Caught in the Crossfire*, a gripping story of an American woman's secret journey with the Afghan rebels. Even the cookbooks are in step with the store's theme, featuring international cuisine. Comfortable wing chairs make perusing more enjoyable. A children's play area makes it easy to skim a few pages without feeling an impatient little tug on your hand. Owners Tony and Susan Childs, a well traveled couple, like to personally advise and provide knowledge on just about any country or travel subject. Take a journey of words, and let your imagination fly at Word Journeys.

VISTA

From the freeway, Vista appears little different from many communities. But just one mile on either side of the State 78 are rolling hills, small ranches and farms, an environment with a truly rural feeling to it. Although it is a community of 42,000 people, in many ways it is small town in countenance. Like rural areas outside of metropolitan areas, high school football is a big draw, and for good reason: Vista High School is perennially one of the best in the state.

Just as every town likes to have some distinctive celebration it calls its own, Vista celebrates engines. In late October, the town puts on a parade and festival: Threshing Bee and Antique Engine Show. The city's Fourth of July celebration attracts crowds of outsiders who enjoy an old fashioned Independence Day celebration, and watch a 10K run.

Vista was first settled in 1890, but the town's growth was severely limited because of the unavailability of water. That changed in 1926 with irrigation water from the newly completed dam at Lake Henshaw, forty miles to the East. For more information contact the Vista Chamber of Commerce at (619) 726- 1122.

EVENT

The town of Vista puts on an **Independence Day Celebration**. It features a 10k run, music, food and fireworks at Bregle Terrace Park. Tel. (619) 724-6121.

SOUTH BAY

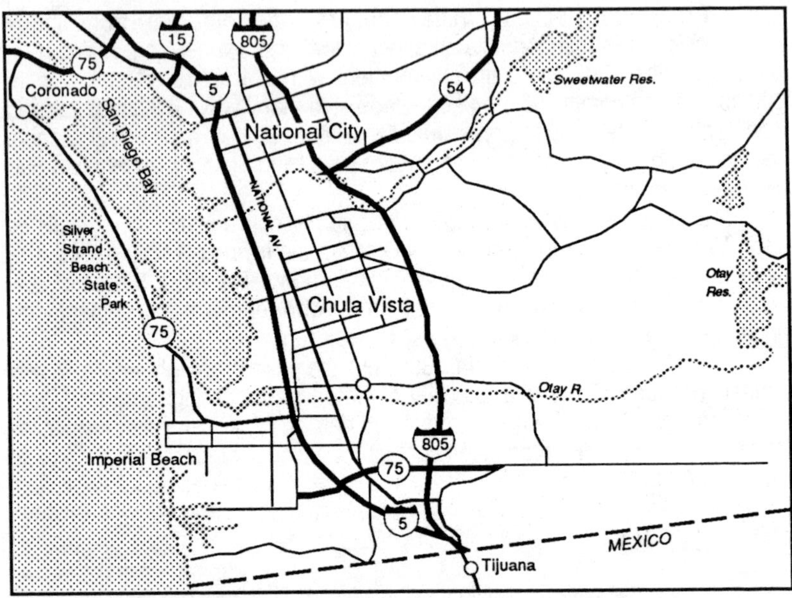

San Diego County's South Bay continues to grow rapidly as more and more young families look for what is probably one of the last affordable housing markets in the county. As a result, a lot of good things have taken place in South County. Businesses have been attracted to the lower land prices, and that in turn has prompted several of the communities to launch ambitious revitalization programs.

Carpenters' hammers have been creating massive new residential communities, such as Chula Vista's East Lake, as well as commercial centers like South Bay Plaza and Plaza Bonita. This building boom has given the area an economic vitality that many did not expect just a few short years ago (and many still look upon with disbelief).

Several decades ago, South Bay was known as the citrus capital of the world. The thousands of acres of orchards have long been cleared for housing tracts. There are still some of the old Victorian homes where the prosperous orchard owners once lived. Many of these buildings are being restored.

South Bay includes three waterfront cities: National City, Chula Vista and Imperial Beach. Each of these towns are in the process of revitalization. Commercial buildings have received face lifts, sidewalks have been covered with brick, and tacky commercial signs have been pulled down to make way for crisp graphics and colorful awnings. Hotels, restaurants and recreational facilities designed to lure tourists are beginning to pop up everywhere.

ATTRACTIONS

The **Tijuana River National Estuarine Reserve** includes both **Border Field State Park** and the **Tijuana Sloughs National Wildlife Refuge**. The four square mile section south of the city of Imperial Beach includes nearly two miles of ocean beach, as well as one of the last natural wildlife habitats of its kind in southern California. The region includes flora and fauna unique to it, rare cacti, sea dahlias and more than 240 species of birds. The area includes hiking and horse trails, picnic facilities, and a research laboratory. At this writing, a visitor center is scheduled for construction in 1988. From I-5, take Imperial Beach Boulevard. For more information, contact the **Southwest Wetlands Interpretive Association**, P.O. Box 575, Imperial Beach, CA 92032.

BEACHES

Silver Strand State Beach, just north of Imperial Beach, offers waters that are shallow and relatively calm.   Lifeguards patrol this area popular with young military families and residents of South Bay. Take Palm Avenue from I-5.

Imperial Beach is a favorite of teens and military personnel. Surfers enjoy the challenging waters, but the big event here is the annual **U.S. Open Sandcastle Competition** in July. (See under events). Take Interstate 5 to Palm Avenue.

Sewage problems from the Mexican side of the border make the beach at **Border Field State Park** unsuitable for wading, surfing or swimming. But the nearby estuary make it a good place for hiking and bird watching. Take I-5 to Dairy Mark Road, and then turn west at Monument Road.

During the week, **Bonita Cove** is filled with mothers and young children. The beach has a playground and lifeguard patrols are regular. The wind is warm, but the water can be deceptively treacherous. Sudden drop-off points appear in places just beyond water levels that seem just right for knee-deep wading, so it's important to keep a close eye on the little ones. The beach is along the 800 block of West Mission Bay Drive, near the Bahia Hotel.

GOLF COURSES

Chula Vista Municipal Golf Course, 4475 Bonita Road, Bonita, CA 92002; 6,559 yards, par 73. Tel. (619) 479-4141

Bonita Golf Club, 5540 Sweetwater Road, Bonita, CA 92002; 6,100 yards, par 71. Tel. (619) 267-1103.
Las Palmas Golf Course, 1439 Sweetwater Road, National City, CA 92050; 2,498 yards, par 57. Tel. (619) 474-3698.

SHOPPING

If you head south of the border, you'll find **Tijuana** full of shopping delights. The city contains many fine stores and small shops in a bazaar atmosphere. Shopping is at its best for leather goods, jewelry and crafts. Remember, bargaining is the name of the game. You may purchase up to $400 worth of merchandise duty free. For more information, see section under Tijuana.

WHALE WATCHING

Summer is the traditional time for vacations, but from mid-December to early March, you can still have a whale of a good time. That's because migrating gray whales come just about as close as they ever get to the coast on their annual 6,000 mile journey from arctic waters to the warm seas off the coast of Baja California.

You don't have to be a modern day Jonah to get a close look at one of these great mammals. The ease in which the whales can be spotted make whale watching the most popular natural attraction during the winter months. As many as 484 have been counted during a single ten hour period, but typically about 200 whales cruise the coastline during the peak season in January.

The whales begin their journey in October to escape the ice forming in Alaska's Bering Sea. Along the way, they mate, and swim the entire coast to give birth to the calves in the warm lagoons of Mexico. The long journey gives the gray whale the distinction of having the longest migration of any mammal. Almost everywhere you can spot the whales within a mile of land. A few enter the harbor, which offers an entertaining sight as they splash about for a few days before resuming their trip southward.

When these beautiful creatures measure thirty-five to fifty feet long, and weigh about a ton a foot, they are not difficult to spot, but binoculars make the show even more spectacular. They travel at a rate of about four knots. Some will pass by in groups of two and three called "pods." From some vantage points you can track a single whale for a mile or more.

Look for the whales' water spouts. Each whale will exhale clouds of steamy water ten to fifteen feet in the air. If you are watching more than one whale, you might notice that each whale's water spout is different. To track a whale, keep an eye on the spout. After every three to five minutes one of them exhales, then the whale usually makes a dive. It will surface in about three or more minutes after traveling about 1,000 feet ahead of where it began the dive. The more spouts you see between a dive, the longer the next dive is likely to be. You might even see a whale hurl his massive frame out of the water and splash back into the sea, a behavior called breaching.

Probably the best spot to view the whales from the shore is the tip of Point Loma at the **Cabrillo National Monument**. Frequently the whales pass by within a half-mile of this point. You can watch from the comfort of the enclosed whale watching station there and use a coin operated telescope. The lookout station includes a whale exhibit and a recorded presentation explaining the migration habits of the whales. In the Visitor Center, a film is usually shown several times a day.

Now if you want to get really close, there is no shortage of boat operators offering trips out to the whales. **Invader Cruises** (Tel. 619 234-tour) guarantees that you'll see a whale or you'll be given an opportunity to take another cruise free. You may be able to tell the different whales apart by their tail fins, or fluke. Each fluke has a slightly different configuration, most notably on the outside edge. The first sign of a whale might be his fluke print in the surface of the water. What appears to be a large slick or puddle will signal that a whale is just under the surface.

Among the cruises available is one offered by the **San Diego Natural History Museum**. The museum's cruise is a two hour excursion off the coast narrated by a marine naturalist. The cruises begin in Late December and continue through January. Tickets must be purchased in advanced. For further information, contact the San Diego Natural History Museum, P.O. Box 1390, San Diego, CA 92112. Tel. (619) 232-3821.

BONITA

The unincorporated community of Bonita, just east of Chula Vista is sometimes called Rancho Santa Fe South. The reference to the exclusive North County community alludes to Bonita's gentle country charm. It's set among rolling hills, valleys, two golf courses, a private tennis club and horse pastures. Its 5,000 residents are mostly professional and college educated. Their children grow up riding horses along the rustic eucalyptus shaded roads. Homes here range from cottages under restoration to meticulously maintained country estates. Shopping in Bonita is something of a social event in the attractive rural shopping villages full of friendly businesses and pleasant restaurants.

GOLF COURSE

**CHULA VISTA MUNICIPAL GOLF COURSE
AND SOUTH BAY GOLF CLUB RESTAURANT**
4475 Bonita Road
Bonita, CA 92002
Tel. (619) 267-7700
Hrs: Lunch   Mon. - Sat.   11:30 a.m. - 2:00 p.m.
      Dinner   Mon. - Sun.   5:00 p.m. - 9:00 p.m.
      Brunch   Sunday   9:30 a.m. - 2:30 p.m.
Visa and MasterCard are accepted.

Quality is the prerequisite for entry into this publication and quality is what you'll find when you first see the Chula Vista Golf Course and it's lovely garden like restaurant. Here, largely due to major financial commitments from the American Golf Corporation, significant changes have occured, making this one of the South Bay's most sought after golf and dining establishments.

In the past two years, six greens have been completely rebuilt, as well as several of the tees. This has produced a par seventy-three course which is perfectly manicured, creating consistency for all players. Two full-time teaching professionals are available for your instructional needs. The course is also able to handle anything involving tournaments and has a fully trained staff to assist with such projects. For those who would like to get their golfing in a little later in the day, there are special discount rates at 3:30 p.m. and again at 5:00 p.m.

Michael Carey, the general manager of the property, has not only achieved this much in such a short time with the golf course, he has also worked wonders with the South Bay Golf Club Restaurant. Here, you will find a relaxing and elegant dining experience second to none. So, if you like to golf and dine in a style that can't be found elsewhere, visit Chula Vista Municipal Golf Course and the South Bay Golf Club restaurant. They are both "Best Choices" in their respective specialities.

CHULA VISTA

The second largest city in San Diego County, Chula Vista grew out of a small agricultural village prior to World War II, became a quiet retirement community during the 1950s, and matured into what is now a 90,000 population, urban and commercial center of South San Diego County.

The community's promoters like to point out that the city has maintained its comfortable residential qualities while allowing its economic base to thrive. Downtown redevelopment has revitalized its commercial district. The downtown streets are wide and lined with newly planted trees growing from tiled planters.

The city's success in attracting industry is apparent. Rhor Industries, a major aerospace firm, maintains its corporate headquarters near Chula Vista's bay front. In addition, Hughes Aircraft, Ratner Corporation and Amex Systems have made Chula Vista their home.

Chula Vista's eastern foothills are the scene of major residential construction. More than 2,200 new homes were built in a recent year. The East Lake planned development along a man made lake will eventually house 30,000 residents. For information about Chula Vista, contact the Chula Vista Information Center, 99 Bonita Road, Chula Vista, CA 92010. Tel. (619) 239-9628.

EVENT

The Starlight Yule Parade welcomes the Christmas season in Chula Vista on the first Monday following Thanksgiving. Tel. (619) 420-6602.

MARKET

GLENN'S FINE FOODS
262 3d Avenue
Chula Vista, CA 92010
Tel. (619) 422-6125
Hrs: Mon. - Sun.   10:00 a.m. - 6:00 p.m.
Visa and MasterCard are accepted.

Glenn's Fine Foods, in business since 1942, has a slogan that you should hear, "The best or nothing." Now that says a lot, and while some could say that slogans are nothing more than empty words, at Glenn's Fine Foods they back it up one hundred percent.

Most food magazines suggest that you find a good gourmet store before planning to cook or entertain. Glenn's, following the Golden Rule of satisfaction and quality, is a fine example of the type of gourmet shop that will provide whatever you may need in regards to cooking and entertaining. Some of the many products they carry include English bisquits, baked speciality breads, pastas from Italy, olive oil from Spain, mushrooms from all over the world, all types of produce, twenty-five varieties of fresh coffee beans, wild game, such as quail, pheasant capon and squab, and wines from small vineyards in California.

Their meat department specializes in the very best quality meats, including Wisconsin veal, homemade sausage and corn-fed Kansas beef. Are you looking for catering service? Glenn's does everything from party trays to gourmet dinners for 5 to 5,000 people! No one in this country does it better. Stop by Glenn's Fine Foods and see how "The best or nothing." comes true.

DULZURA

Dulzura was named for the Spanish word meaning "sweetness." In the 1870s the creek near Dulzura was so named because honey production was started there. Placer gold was discovered there later in the decade. Some mining was attempted but without great success.

RESTAURANT

THE BARRETT CAFE
1029 Barrett Lake Road
Dulzura, CA 92107
Tel. (619) 468-3416
Hrs: Tue. - Thu. 11:00 a.m. - 8:00 p.m.
     Fri. - Sun. 11:00 a.m. - 9:00 p.m.
Visa and MasterCard are accepted.

Thirty-four miles out on highway 94 from downtown San Diego, and maybe a few decades beyond that, sits a war surplus quonset hut. You're in downtown Barrett, population 200 and home of the world-famous fish fry.

Ninety-five percent of the people who come out here are not looking for the scenery, nor are they interested in the great frog legs, or the fried chicken. It's the fish, which is known in more places on this planet than you can shake a frogsticker at. Everything is made right there, right down to the tartar sauce. The fish is never fried in anything but pure vegetable oil and is served up family style, all you can eat, on oilcloth tablecloths. Remember, mind your manners. (Pass the salt, please.)

This all started back in the late Forties when cafe owners Bill and Vi Avril began catching more fish than they could eat down by Ensenada. They began frying it up on weekends for their friends in the area, but after awhile the friends were a little embarrassed about eating all that free food, so the Avrils began charging fifty cents a head. The local fish fry then grew into the business it is today. Now, no one is embarrassed to come in, including personalities such as Barbra Streisand and Lee Majors (a regular who has his own special table.) Long a favorite in Barrett, the Barrett Cafe keeps on cooking and becoming more famous for fried fish.

It's now operated by daughter and son-in-law Cathy and "Steve" Stephens, and still serves the great fish, plus a complete array of foods and sandwiches.

IMPERIAL BEACH

Imperial beach can boast that it has some of the finest beaches in San Diego County. It's enviable position of being bounded by the ocean, the bay and the Mexican border makes it a promising area for future development.

Until recently, sewage from Mexico has polluted much of the shoreline, but the smart money continues to filter into the city sometimes called "the sleeping giant," betting that the best is yet to come. Long time residents and retired Navy personnel will extol Imperial Beach as one of the few places where one can find affordable waterfront and oceanside housing. It is also an area of very affluent families. Some homes are up to $1 million or more.

Several new major economic ventures have sprung up in recent years. The city has three large neighborhood shopping centers and a variety of smaller retail shopping areas. Lately, growth in the retail and residential sectors has been unprecedented in the city. Crown Isle, an $80,000,000 hotel and resort marina is scheduled for completion in 1988. (Southern California's largest boat show was in September of 1987.)

For visitors, Imperial Beach is best known for its Sandcastle Days, which has been touted as America's largest family oriented beach event. The July event draws more than 100,000 visitors each year to watch or compete in the sandcastle contest.

for additional information on the community, contact the Imperial Beach Chamber of Commerce, (619) 424-3151.

EVENT

The world's largest and longest running sand castle contest is held in mid-July in Imperial Beach, for **Sand Castle Days**. The imaginative works of art and sculpture are formed on the beach by the pier. The event also includes a parade and fireworks. Tel. (619) 424-3151.

NATIONAL CITY

Just South of San Diego is National City, home to about 56,000 residents. Incorporated in 1887, National City is the second oldest city in the county. Some its history is retained in many of the turn of the century homes being restored. Several are on the National Register of Historic Sites.

National City is probably the most commercially oriented of the South Bay communities. Many retail outlets have found a comfortable home at Plaza Bonita, one of the few indoor shopping centers in the county. And many know National City as the place to buy a car. Its "Mile of Cars" section is a long strip of competitive auto dealers. National City's Marine Terminal has attracted scores of new businesses to the community. If National City has been good for business, so has business been good to National City. The business revenues helped the city to finance two high rise senior citizen residential complexes. National City's Chamber of Commerce can be reached at (619) 477-9339.

EVENT

Among the popular **Fourth of July Celebrations** is one held in National City featuring a carnival with booths, children's rides, games and fireworks. Tel. (619) 479-1550.

TIJUANA

Some of the fun of San Diego is that is lies on an International border. One can be eating a hotdog in San Diego's Balboa Park, and within an hour enjoy a taco in downtown Tijuana. Unlike crossing into Canada, upon entering Tijuana one immediately sees a whole new cultural world. As a border town it does show some rather obvious signs of commercialism that, but no one can really deny that Tijuana is "authentic" Mexico.

You can shop in the colorful bazaars, attend a bullfight, horserace, dog race or become a spectator in the world's fastest game, jai alai. Shoppers will be pleased that the Miguel Hidalgo Market on Avenida Negrete has changed little. Here, one can barter over fresh produce, cheese and crafts. Nearby, you can pick up genuine Indian handicrafts, leatherwork, pottery, jewelry, or a piñata for your next party. Remember, you are not expected to pay the first asking price. To get the "real" price, you need to "haggle" a little, but that's part of the fun!

The city has several fine hotels, good restaurants for every taste, and lively night clubs. The nightlife continues to be vibrant in Tijuana.

To visit Mexican border areas, there is none of the red tape associated with international travel. United States citizens do not need passports or visas for visits within seventy-five miles of the border. The coastal community of Ensenada in an easy drive. If you do drive into Mexico, don't risk not having Mexican insurance, the only kind Mexican authorities recognize. If you're in an accident, you'll have two choices for proving financial responsibility: cash or Mexican insurance. A simple way to arrange for short-term auto insurance is to call the Mexican Tourist Committee and order it with your credit card. From the San Diego area, the number is (619)-299-8518. Your policy will be sent to you, or you can pick it up at the Visitors Center just on the other side of the crossing. Mnay Us auto rental companies also offer it at better prices.

Many people avoid the hassle of driving into Tijuana. San Diego's Red Trolley will take you right up to the border, where many cross by foot, and take an inexpensive cab ride downtown. Believe it or not, this often saves time on your return, as US Customs inspections frequently cause delays.

ATTRACTIONS

Dog and horses races are held through out the year at the **Agua Caliente Racetrack** in Tijuana. For information contact Agua Caliente Racetrack, Boulevard Agua Caliente, Tijuana, BC, Mexico 01152. Tel. (706) 668-62001.

Jai alai is a fast paced game in which two-man teams use long curved scoops to hurl a speeding ball at each other. Betting is as popular here as at the race track. For information contact the San Diego office for the Fronton Palacio, 445 Twain Avenue, Suite B, San Diego, CA 92120. Tel. (619) 282-3636.

If you enjoyed the special effects of San Diego's Space Theatre, and the art museums of Balboa Park, you'll also enjoy the ultra modern **Tijauna Cultural Center**. The complex includes a shopping arcade, a restaurant, exhibits and **Omimax Theatre**. For information contact the **Tijuana Cultural Center**, Paseo de los Heroes y Mino Zona Rio Tijauna, Tijuana, BC, Mexico 01152. Tel. (706) 668-41132

APPENDIX

You are cordially invited to the Grosvenor Inn, 3145 Sports Arena Boulevard, San Diego, CA to receive a 10% discount on your lodging. Offer valid through 1988.

You are cordially invited to Chic Accessories at 333 Fashion Valley, San Diego, CA to receive a 10% discount on any item.

You are cordiall invited to Londontowne, University Towne Centre, 4417 La Jolla, Village Drive, Suite Q3, San Diego, CA, or 200 E Via Rancho Parkway, Suite 217, North County Fair, Escondido, CA to receive a 10% discount on any regularly priced item. Offer valid through 1988.

You are cordially invited to Price Breakers Apparel Mart at any of their locations to receive a 10% discount on any purchase. This offer valid through 1989.

You are cordially invited to Southwest Car Rental at 1111 Fashion Valley Road, San Diego, CA to receive a 10% discount on a car rental.

You are cordially invited to Ensenada Express, B Street Pier, Cruise Ship Terminal, San Diego, CA to receive a 10% discount on the regular fare of an Ensenada cruise. Reservations are requested.

You are cordially invited to board the Red Witch, 1380 Harbor Island Drive, San Diego, CA and receive a ten percent discount on any cruise. Not valid with any other offer. Good through 1988.

You are cordially invited to San Diego Yacht Charters, 1880 Harbor Island Drive, San Diego, CA to receive a 5% discount on any charter. Not valid with any other offer. Good thru 1988.

You are cordially invited to Midway Books, 3944 West Point Loma Boulevard Suite E, San Diego, CA to receive a 10% discount on any purchase over $5. Not valid with any other offer.

You are cordially invited to Campland On The Bay, 2211 Pacific Beach Drive, San Diego, CA to receive 20% off on daily rates. Not valid with any other offer or in overflow.

You are cordially invited to the Same Old Grind at 3007 Clairemont Drive, San Diego, CA to receive $1 off any one pound purchase of fresh roasted coffee. Offer is good through 1988.

You are cordially invited to Hook Line and Sinker, 1224 Scott Street, San Diego, CA to receive a 10% discount off of any purchase. Not valid with any other offer. Offer good through 1988.

You are cordially invited to the Sharp Cabrillo Gift Corner 3475 Kenyon Street, San Diego, CA to receive a 10% discount on any purchase of gifts or jewelry.

You are cordially invited to Carter's Diamonds, 861 6th Avenue, Suite 329, San Diego, CA to receive a free polishing, cleaning and inspection. A qualified appraiser is available.

You are cordially invited to Diamond Designs, Mission Valley Center, San Diego, CA, or Grossmont Center, La Mesa, CA or La Jolla Village Drive at Regents Road, La Jolla, CA or Clairemont Mesa Boulevard/corner of Convoy, San Diego, CA or Highway 78 at Nordahl Road, San Marcos, CA or Terra Nova Plaza, I-805 at H Street, Chula Vista, CA to receive a 10% additional discount on any diamond or gold purchase. This invitation can be combined with any special offer. Offer valid through 1988.

You are cordially invited to Cook's Corner, 6404 Nancy Ridge Drive, San Diego, CA, or Plaza Camino Real, 2525 El Camino Real #231, Carlsbad, CA, or Fashion Valley, 290 Fashion Valley #535, San Diego, CA, or North County Fair, 200 E Via Rancho Parkway, Escondido, CA to receive $1 off a pound of coffee. Offer valid through December 1988.

You are cordially invited to SongMasters, 4150 Mission Boulevard, San Diego, CA to receive a free microphone with the purchase of any Karaoke recording equipment.

You are cordially invited to Nelson Photo Supplies, 1909 India Street, San Diego, CA to receive a free camera inspection.

You are cordially invited to De Anza Harbor Resort, 2727 De Anza Road, San Diego, CA to receive a 10% discount on daily rates. Valid from September 15 to May 15 with this offer only. Offer good thru 1988.

You are cordially invited to Baci's Restaurant, 1955 Morena Blvd., San Diego, CA to receive 10% off any full dinner purchase. Not valid with any other promotion. Offer valid through 1988.

You are cordially invited to the Mission Bay Sportcenter, 1010 Santa Clara Place, San Diego, CA to receive 1/2 hour free sailing with each hour of sailboat rental. Offer valid through 1988.

You are cordially invited to Offshoot Botanical Tours, 1640 Monroe Avenue, San Diego, CA to recieve a free guided tour. Explore intimately the impressive gardens, unique architecture and fascinating history of Balboa Park. For details call (619) 297-0289.

You are invited to Old Town Walking Tours, 3977 Twiggs Street, San Diego, CA to stroll through 200 years of history. Offer good two years from November 1987.

You are cordially invited to Traveler's Depot, 1539 Garnet Avenue, San Diego, CA to receive a 20% discount on any purchase of $20 or more.

You are cordially invited to Up Your Alley, 7717 Fay Avenue, La Jolla, CA to receive a 20% discount on any one item one time only. Not valid with any other discount. This offer is valid through 1988.

You are cordially invited to Gallery of Two Sisters, 1298 Prospect Street, La Jolla, CA to receive an 11" x 17" pen and ink print with your purchase of $25 or more. Offer good through 1988.

You are cordially invited to Fitness Is Fun, 7614 Fay Avenue, La Jolla, CA to receive a 50% discount on your first workout. This offer is valid through 1989.

You are cordially invited to La Jolla Spice Company, 7556 Fay Avenue, La Jolla, CA to receive a free muffin with the purchase of your lunch. Offer good thru 1988.

You are cordially invited to the Nectar Juice Bar, 6830 La Jolla Boulevard, La Jolla, CA to receive one free smoothie with the purchase of a smoothie. This offer is valid through 1989.

You are cordially invited to Windansea Beachan'surf, 6830 La Jolla Boulevard, suite 102, La Jolla, CA for a free tide book or shop sticker. This offer is valid through October 1989

You are cordially invited to Lacrosse Plus, 618 Faith Avenue, Cardiff-By-The-Sea, CA to receive a 5% discount on all equipment and a 10% discount on all t-shirts not on sale. This offer is valid through 1989.

You are cordially invited to Sharon Wilson Shoes and Accessories at 2810 Roosevelt Street, Carlsbad, CA to receive a 10% discount on all non-sale items.

You are cordially invited to Country Rooms, 585 Grand Avenue, Carlsbad, CA to receive a 10% discount on any purchase at regular price. Offer valid through 1988 with this coupon.

You are cordially invited to A Skysurfer Balloon Co., 14072 Rue d'Azur, Del Mar, CA to receive 10% off on a flight for four or more adults if you mention this offer.

You are cordially invited to C'est Soule´, 897 First Street, Encinitas, CA to receive distinctive clothing for the contemporary woman at a 10% discount off any purchase.

You are cordially invited to Julian Lodge, 4th and C Streets, Julian, CA to receive a 15% discount Sunday to Thursday, except on holidays. Not valid with other offers. Valid through 1988.

You are cordially to The Highland House, 2116 Main Street, Julian, CA to receive a 10% discount on selected items Monday through Thursday. Not valid with any other offers.

INDEX

A LETTER TO THE READER

The staff of Gable & Gray want to take this time to thank you for purchasing this book. We hope it contributed substantially to your enjoyment of the area.

In our never ending quest to better these books, we ask you, the visitor, to help us; if in your travels you encounter a service or business establishment you feel should be a "Best Choice," then please take the time to let us know about them.

If your "Best Choice" is interviewed and selected for our next edition, we will ship you one of our books as our way of saying "Thank You." Simply choose the book from the list at the front of this book and denote it in your letter.

If you would like to order other books, please call us at (800) 522-7753 USA.

NOTES: